Motivation and Foreign Language Learning

Language Learning & Language Teaching (LL&LT)

The LL&LT monograph series publishes monographs, edited volumes and text books on applied and methodological issues in the field of language pedagogy. The focus of the series is on subjects such as classroom discourse and interaction; language diversity in educational settings; bilingual education; language testing and language assessment; teaching methods and teaching performance; learning trajectories in second language acquisition; and written language learning in educational settings.

For an overview of all books published in this series, please see
http://benjamins.com/catalog/lllt

Editors

Nina Spada
Ontario Institute for Studies in Education
University of Toronto

Nelleke Van Deusen-Scholl
Center for Language Study
Yale University

Volume 40

Motivation and Foreign Language Learning. From theory to practice
Edited by David Lasagabaster, Aintzane Doiz and Juan Manuel Sierra

Motivation and Foreign Language Learning

From theory to practice

Edited by

David Lasagabaster
Aintzane Doiz
Juan Manuel Sierra
University of the Basque Country UPV/EHU

John Benjamins Publishing Company

Amsterdam / Philadelphia

The paper used in this publication meets the minimum requirements of the American National Standard for Information Sciences – Permanence of Paper for Printed Library Materials, ANSI z39.48-1984.

Library of Congress Cataloging-in-Publication Data

Motivation and Foreign Language Learning : From theory to practice / Edited by David
      Lasagabaster, Aintzane Doiz and Juan Manuel Sierra.
p. cm. (Language Learning & Language Teaching, ISSN 1569-9471 ; v. 40)
Includes bibliographical references and index.
1. Language and languages--Study and teaching. 2. Second language acquisition.
      3. Motivation in education. I. Lasagabaster, David, 1967- editor. II. Doiz,
      Aintzane, editor. III. Sierra, Juan Manuel, editor.
P118.2.M6755   2014
418.0071--dc23   2014019015
ISBN 978 90 272 1322 8   (Hb ; alk. paper)
ISBN 978 90 272 1323 5   (Pb ; alk. paper)
ISBN 978 90 272 6975 1   (Eb)

John Benjamins Publishing Co. · P.O. Box 36224 · 1020 ME Amsterdam · The Netherlands
John Benjamins North America · P.O. Box 27519 · Philadelphia PA 19118-0519 · USA

Table of contents

Contributors

Vera Busse
Carl von Ossietzky Universität
Fakultät I Bildungs-
und Sozialwissenschaften
Institut für Pädagogik
26111 Oldenburg
Germany
Email: vera.busse@uni-oldenburg.de

Do Coyle
University of Aberdeen
MacRobert Building
King's College
Aberdeen
AB24 5UA
United Kingdom
Email: do.coyle@abdn.ac.uk

Zoltan Dörnyei
University of Nottingham
School of English
University Park
Nottingham NG7 2RD
United Kingdom
Email: zoltan.dornyei@nottingham.ac.uk

Aintzane Doiz
University of the Basque Country
Faculty of Arts
English Studies
Paseo de la Universidad 5
01006 Vitoria-Gasteiz
Spain
Email: aintzane.doiz@ehu.es

Alastair Henry
Department of Social & Behavioural Studies
University West
461 32 Trollhättan
Sweden
Email: alastair.henry@hv.se

Zana Ibrahim
University of Nottingham
School of English
University Park
Nottingham NG7 2RD
United Kingdom
Email: zana.ibrahim@outlook.com

Maggie Kubanyiova
University of Birmingham
School of Education
Birmingham B15 2TT
UK
Email: m.kubanyiova@bham.ac.uk

David Lasagabaster
University of the Basque Country
Faculty of Arts
English Studies
Paseo de la Universidad 5
01006 Vitoria-Gasteiz
Spain
Email: david.lasagabaster@ehu.es

Francisco Lorenzo
Dpto. Filología y Traducción
Universidad Pablo de Olavide
Ctra de Utrera km. 1 41013
Sevilla
Spain
Email: fjlorber@upo.es

Christine Muir
University of Nottingham
School of English
University Park
Nottingham NG7 2RD
United Kingdom
Email: christine.muir@nottingham.ac.uk

Juan Manuel Sierra
University of the Basque Country
Faculty of Arts
English Studies
Paseo de la Universidad 5
01006 Vitoria-Gasteiz
Spain
Email: juanmanuel.sierra@ehu.es

Ema Ushioda
University of Warwick
Centre for Applied Linguistics
Social Sciences Building
University of Warwick
Coventry CV4 7AL
UK
Email: e.ushioda@warwick.ac.uk

Introduction

David Lasagabaster, Aintzane Doiz and Juan Manuel Sierra

Motivation is a key aspect of second language learning. There is no doubt that abstract models are basic to gain theoretical insights into motivation; however, teachers and researchers demand comprehensible explanations for motivation that can help them to improve their everyday teaching and research. The driving force of this endeavour was an international symposium held in May 2013 at the University of the Basque Country in Vitoria-Gasteiz (Spain) which was organized by the *Language and Speech Laboratory* research group (www.laslab.org) to cater for both researchers and teachers. This successful event led us to gather the contributions of the presenters (Do Coyle, Zoltan Dörnyei, Maggie Kubanyiova, Francisco Lorenzo, Ema Ushioda), two invited collaborators (Vera Busse, Alastair Henry), as well as our own in an attempt to respond to the keen interest in producing a book based on the issues discussed at the symposium.

The aim is to provide both theoretical insights and practical suggestions to improve motivation in the classroom. With this in mind, the book is divided into two sections: the first part includes some innovative ideas regarding language learning motivation, whereas the second is focused on the relationship between different approaches to foreign language learning – such as EFL (English as a foreign language), CLIL (Content and Language Integrated Learning) or immersion – and motivation. Both sections have an emphasis on pedagogical implications that are rooted in both theoretical and empirical work.

The predominant tradition in motivation research has delved into this complex construct mainly from a quantitative (positivist) perspective. A review of the literature reveals that many studies are quantitative in design and hinge on instruments such as questionnaires and language tests (Dörnyei & Ushioda 2009; Ushioda 2011). Consequently, most motivation theories have been concerned more with the general concept, supported by statistical averages and relations, rather than with providing practical paths that teachers might follow to improve their students' foreign language learning and their own teaching practice. However, some authors and many teachers argue that such an approach to EFL/ESL motivation research may have its limitations regarding practical implications, that it does not help to bridge the gap between research and everyday teaching in the classroom. Although teachers need to know about theoretical models of motivation, they are undoubtedly more willing to learn about particular strategies and activities that boost students' and their own motivation, as well as those that have a negative effect.

This compilation may help satisfy both these needs. The book embraces three different dimensions: the teachers, the learners and the learning context, and analyses how these different dimensions interact with motivation.

The first section (Theoretical and practical insights into motivation) is made up of four chapters. In the first chapter Dörnyei, Muir and Ibrahim introduce the concept *Directed Motivational Current* (DMC), which can be described as an intense motivational drive which is capable of stimulating and supporting long-term behaviour, such as learning a second language. This concept brings together many of the current strands of motivational thinking – such as the L2 Motivational Self System, Dynamic Systems Theory and Future Time Perspective – into a comprehensive construct with compelling motivational power. Its authors state that it has great potential as a tool to motivate learners in the classroom and outline three levels of application: lesson level, term level and course level.

The second chapter by Ushioda focuses on the motivational processes involved in learning a second or foreign language. From the point of view of sustaining long-term engagement in L2 learning, Ushioda highlights that personal goals and targets (long-term and short-term) are important in providing a motivational rationale for such engagement. However, goals and targets may be insufficient in themselves to regulate motivation to engage with the day-to-day demands of language learning, particularly as these challenges increase in cognitive and linguistic complexity beyond the early basic stages of learning a new language. Specifically, she considers how processes of motivation may interact with the metacognitive dimension of language learner autonomy to enable learners to regulate their motivation and strategic thinking skills.

In the third chapter, Coyle shares the findings of two studies where language learners in primary and secondary schools became researchers of their own learning. The first study was undertaken in secondary schools across the UK where young people were learning French, German and Spanish. The second involved a composite class of primary pupils in a Gaelic-medium classroom. Learners became co-researchers with their teacher, investigating and identifying successful learning in classrooms where a language other than the learners' first is used. Motivation became both the object and the outcome of the studies. This led to the objectification of the learning process which encouraged teachers and their learners to work together to create a learning environment tailored to successful learning. The findings provide pupil evidence of what motivates learners and suggest that when learners engage in an analysis of their own learning, it can lead to greater ownership of their language learning.

In the fourth chapter Kubanyiova builds on her recent research on language teachers' conceptual change which has shown that in order to help students discover and pursue their L2 visions, teachers need to start with a deeper reflection about who they are, who they want to become and, ultimately, what kind of language learning environments they envisage for their students. Rather than focusing on techniques for 'motivating' teachers in the traditional sense, she seeks to inspire language teachers' vision. The chapter focuses on explaining and illustrating three important processes, including the teachers' reflection on the who (i.e. the person doing the teaching), the why (i.e. the bigger purposes guiding language teachers' work) and the image (i.e. a construction of a visual representation of desired teaching selves).

The second part of the volume (Studies on motivation in foreign language classrooms) revolves around the relationship between different foreign language teaching approaches and motivation. The globalizing process is forcing education systems to pay more and more attention to the learning of foreign languages. Consequently, schools and universities are offering courses taught in foreign languages, overwhelmingly in English (Doiz, Lasagabaster & Sierra 2013). CLIL is included in the motivational equation due to the increasing and rapid spread of this approach not only throughout Europe, but also in countries in many other parts of the world, such as Brasil, Brunei, China, Colombia, Indonesia and Saudi Arabia, to name but a few. However, it is important to note that the ideas and evidence put forward in the chapters centered on CLIL can be applied to EFL, the teaching of other foreign languages, and immersion settings. Although there is no doubt that English plays a paramount role in the complex European multilingual landscape at all educational levels (De Houwer & Wilton 2011), German, Gaelic and French are also considered in this compilation.

Henry (Chapter 5) underscores that learners may develop a 'mindset' in which naturalistic settings are seen as providing the optimum environment for effortlessly learning a language. Possessing this type of 'mindset' can be problematic in that, over time, beliefs in the efficacy of hard work may diminish, thus leading to declining classroom motivation. In settings such as Sweden where young people spend substantial amounts of time in English-language digitally-mediated environments, the type of 'naturalness mindset' provides a useful theoretical take on the emerging trend of a lack of motivation to learn English in school. Drawing on the results of a questionnaire focusing on students' perceptions about where they learn most of their English, he considers the value of a 'mindset' approach to understanding and addressing declining classroom motivation. In particular, given that substantial differences were found in girls' and boys' beliefs about the relative efficacy of learning arenas, he examines the ways in which gender is implicated in students' English learning mindsets and how it affects motivation.

In Chapter 6, Doiz, Lasagabaster, and Sierra focus on what makes students feel (de)motivated in secondary education CLIL classes. They gave students the chance to freely express their opinions about what they liked most and least in their CLIL classes, and the advantages and disadvantages they associated with this groundbreaking approach. Despite the fact that students clearly stated that learning subjects in English was difficult, required an additional effort to understand the content, and involved more work, they were still highly motivated by the CLIL approach. In fact, they thought they learned more English, they found it extremely useful for their future and they believed it enabled them to communicate with foreign people. The chapter ends with some thoughts regarding how to implement CLIL programs more successfully.

In Chapter 7, Lorenzo explores ways to make the L2 classroom a more engaging place by adjusting teaching to learning paths, while he focuses on the role to be played by classroom materials. The chapter analyses how a better matching of L2 teaching and learning can enhance motivation. Examples come from bilingual (Spanish and English) classrooms and CLIL settings, and a selection of CLIL materials is presented to show how they can help with new language programs, new forms of assessment and how CLIL triggers goal-oriented behaviour.

Busse's article (Chapter 8) is aimed at lecturers in higher education and disseminating the knowledge derived from research motivation that can be of use in the classroom. In particular, she discusses ways of improving student motivation against the backdrop of a longitudinal mixed-methods study involving first year students enrolled on German degree courses at two major UK universities. She focuses on the importance of perceived progress for sustaining student motivation in higher education. The chapter outlines how the learning environment can foster students' sense of progress by increasing their exposure to the target language on the one hand and by optimising the potential of teacher feedback on the other. A major role is also ascribed to nourishing short-term and long-term goals, and the pedagogical potential of ideal self visions are discussed.

In the epilogue the five dimensions of the Directed Motivational Current proposed in the opening chapter are used as a framework to make connections between different theoretical aspects of motivation and the practical data gathered in language classrooms. Theory and practice, diverse educational contexts and different teaching approaches are brought together with the aim of arriving at a better understanding and a more integrated view of motivation in second foreign language learning.

Acknowledgements

We would like to thank all the contributors for their willingness to participate in this book. Their expertise has made our editing job an exciting and enriching venture which has significantly contributed to our better understanding of such a complex construct as motivation. We are also very grateful to the editors of the Language Teaching & Language Learning series, Nina Spada and Nelleke Van Deusen-Scholl, for their work and support throughout the process.

This work has received the support of the following research projects: FFI2012-34214 (Spanish Ministry of Economy and Competitiveness) and IT311-10 (Department of Education, University and Research of the Basque Government).

References

De Houwer, A. & Wilton, A. (2011). *English in Europe Today: Sociocultural and educational perspectives*. Amsterdam: John Benjamins. DOI: 10.1075/aals.8

Doiz, A., Lasagabaster, D. & Sierra, J. M. (eds.) (2013). *English-Medium Instruction at Universities: Global Challenges*. Bristol: Multilingual Matters.

Dörnyei, Z. & Ushioda, E. (eds.) (2009). *The L2 Motivational Self System. Motivation, language identity and the L2 self*. Bristol: Multilingual Matters.

Ushioda, E. (2011). Motivating learners to speak as themselves. *Identity, Motivation and Autonomy in Language Learning* (pp. 11–24). Bristol: Multilingual Matters.

PART I

Theoretical and practical insights into motivation

CHAPTER 1

Directed Motivational Currents

Energising language learning by creating intense motivational pathways

Zoltán Dörnyei, Christine Muir and Zana Ibrahim

In this chapter, we introduce a novel psychological construct whose key aspects are well-established in major motivation theories. A Directed Motivational Current (DMC) is a conceptual framework which depicts unique periods of intensive motivational involvement both in pursuit of and fuelled by a highly valued goal/vision. The heightened motivational state of individuals or groups involved in a DMC is maintained through the deployment of a salient facilitative structure that includes reinforcing feedback loops, positive emotionality and the prospect of reaching a new level of operation. When applied in second language contexts, DMCs can energise language learners to perform beyond expectations and across several levels and timescales, including long-term engagements.

Keywords: language learning motivation, Directed Motivational Current, vision, goal-setting, eudemonic well-being

A Directed Motivational Current (DMC) can be described as an intense motivational drive which is capable of both stimulating and supporting long-term behaviour, such as learning a foreign/second language (L2). Drawing on several aspects from mainstream motivation theories in psychology as well as current strands of motivational thinking in Applied Linguistics, such as the L2 Motivational Self System, language learning vision and Dynamic Systems Theory, DMCs form a multipurpose construct with compelling motivational capabilities: they are capable of acting as a fundamental organiser of motivational impetus in general and, as such, have considerable potential as a specific tool to motivate learners in the language classroom. In this chapter we first provide an introduction to the concept and then discuss its main dimensions and features. We go on to outline links to established motivation theories and conclude by describing several relevant practical areas where DMCs can offer benefits.

What is a Directed Motivational Current?

The best way of giving an idea about what DMCs are is by offering a few examples, all of which follow the same pattern: a clearly visualised goal combined with a concrete pathway of motivated action brings a new lease of life and burst of passion to an otherwise dormant situation. Imagine, for example, an overweight university professor who would like to have a healthy lifestyle but whose job involves too much sitting in front of computer screens and too many lavish meals at motivation conferences. One day, something changes: he enrols at the local gym, arranges regular gym dates with friends and surprises colleagues with decisive shifts in his eating habits, swapping from a chocolate biscuit to an apple mid-morning and to salads at lunch. Imagine how this initiative gains momentum when his bathroom scales start showing decreasing figures and his efforts begin to be recognised by family and friends, immeasurably focusing his resolve. As a result, he loses over 20 lbs. in four months.

Alternatively, imagine a pensioner whose life literally takes a turn when she hires a plot in an allotment and starts growing a range of vegetables, with the village show's coveted first prize at the forefront of her mind. We might also imagine someone joining a photography club and getting involved in a socio-photo project leading to a special feature at an exhibition, or someone else starting to attend an evening course in order to finally learn the skills necessary to realise a long-standing dream; in all these activities a great deal of energy is released and the achievement of clear goals ultimately comes to fruition through a powerful surge of highly focused motivation.

Examples of DMCs in educational contexts are equally recognisable. Imagine, for instance, a school which is average both in academic terms and in terms of pupil engagement: students are not particularly absorbed in their lessons and nor do they arrive to class with a great deal of enthusiasm, and perhaps less often still with their homework. Imagine a project which, for some reason, sparks their attention and acts as a catalyst and starting point for a few weeks, or perhaps even months, of motivated activity. Picture these students taking control of the scheme and managing its direction and content, whether they are interested in the autonomy suddenly offered to them or the subject matter of the goal itself. As a result, students are suddenly, if only for this period of time, able to work together at a heightened level of intensity, even surpassing the targets originally set for them and becoming carried away with the achievement they are now imagining possible for themselves. This could happen, for example, in a state school which struggles to generate interest in modern languages when a new and dynamic L2 teacher arrives and manages to turn things around through a few well-selected initiatives, making the L2 a desirable subject choice.

A similar phenomenon is also identifiable over a shorter time scale, with, for example, an invigorating language task set over the course of a single lesson, possibly turning into a project spanning a mini-series of lessons. Imagine the students captured in some way by the topic, the task or the medium at hand and driven to best themselves, pushing to exceed all expectations. Imagine hearing the affirming whines of 'but Miiiiss' or 'but Siiiiir', vocalisations of the frustration at the lack of time remaining at the end of a lesson and a signal that students have become truly invested in achieving their goal. Likewise within academia, picture a motivation symposium bringing together a large group of language teachers and researchers in order to present and exchange ideas about their profession in spite of their extremely busy lives, with this goal of furthering understanding overriding a sparkling May day passing by seemingly unnoticed on the other side of the conference room door.

Each of the above scenarios depicts a powerful motivational drive which unfolds over time and impacts its participants in a significant way. The people featuring in these scenarios achieve something more than they expected they could, and successfully work towards a personal/personalised goal that may not have otherwise been achievable. We hope that at this point these highly charged motivational pathways – or currents – are intimately recognisable; however, to further illustrate them let us take an analogy from nature, the mighty Gulf Stream.

DMCs and the Gulf Stream

The Gulf Stream is one of the strongest currents in our oceans; it runs from Florida northwards up the Eastern coast of the United States before heading east out around Newfoundland, and forms one section of the North Atlantic's endless circular system of currents. It is typically 62 miles wide, anything from 800 to 1200 metres deep and at points is capable of transporting water at a rate of 150 cubic metres per second. It also transports enough heat to satisfy around 100 times the world energy demand (hence it has recently been considered how this immense power can be harvested). The foremost connection between the Gulf Stream and DMCs concerns the formidable flow of energy, which, crucially, the Gulf Stream maintains without at any point requiring any external replenishment. We believe that a similar motivational stream is evident in the various examples of DMCs offered above: if the correct conditions can be engineered to allow these motivational pathways to be created, a motivational jetstream will emerge that is capable of transporting individuals forward, even in situations where any hope of progress had been fading. Once a DMC is in place, through its self-propelling nature learners become caught up in this powerful flow of motivation and are relayed forwards towards to achieve their goals.

What a DMC is not

Not all motivated behaviour can be described as a DMC. A DMC is a unique and temporary boost to motivation, although in some unique cases real motivational Gulf Streams may emerge which last for decades. The important point to note is that any superstar learner in a given class is not necessarily operating within a DMC; a DMC is a unique drive which is so identifiable that those around the person in the flow are able to recognise a significant change in him/her to the point where, for a short period of time, it becomes a prominent feature of the individual's identity. "Jo won't be coming out tonight; she has her final Japanese exam next week and is completely in the zone with her revision – I don't think I've seen her with her head outside of a textbook for the last two weeks!' 'Harry won't be joining us for pizza tomorrow, he says he feels so much better after all that training, and not just that, he looks great - there's no way he's going to do anything to jeopardise his chances in the marathon next Saturday!"

A DMC is qualitatively different from the ongoing motivation of a good student, due to the fact that it is a relatively short-term, highly intense burst of motivational energy along a specific pathway towards a clearly defined goal: it is *over and on top of* the steady motivation any student will exhibit throughout the year. We do not see it manifest itself in people who are working methodically towards a general life goal five years down the line, but rather in those who set a specific goal in the present, and whose motivation to achieve it takes on such an influence as to disrupt the daily routine of their lives and temporarily alter their identity and priorities. A DMC proper brings a far greater sense of urgency and, perhaps, just a little more drama than regular motivated behaviour; not unlike an injection of motivation into the system. After the accomplishment of the goal, life resumes its normal balance – although perhaps at a modified level – and long-term goals and visions once again assume control of directing thought and action, until the day the conditions may once again fall into place to allow another DMC to emerge.

The main dimensions of DMCs

If we consider the various motivational surges and streams which might qualify to come under the DMC rubric, we find a number of dimensions – characteristic features, typical components and necessary conditions – which these phenomena share in common. It is crucial that all of these conditions are present and are correctly balanced, the specific formula of which being defined by the nature of the DMC itself. It may be the case that there are occasions when several of the required factors are in place, yet they will not be sufficient to fire up the motivational engine of a DMC. Below we offer a list of what we currently believe to be the main constituents of the DMC make up.

Goal/vision-orientedness

Similar to the streams and currents in nature, a DMC is always directional, taking individuals forwards towards a specific goal. In other words, action is neither random nor spread across different trajectories. Such a powerful motivational drive will not emerge in the absence of a salient goal which provides both cohesion to one's efforts and which allows people to focus their energies towards a clear finish line. This criterion distinguishes a DMC from some other practices where motivation is relatively high – such as pursuing an interest or hobby – as these are not associated with any specific end goal but rather are practiced merely for the sake of enjoyment. In contrast, a DMC has a clearly defined goal: the target weight of a dieter, the performance or presentation students are preparing for, the culmination of an extra-curricular project or the home-grown vegetables our green fingered gardener wants to see win at the village show next spring.

Thus, goal-orientedness is a prerequisite for the generation of a DMC. This characteristic explains why *vision* also becomes a key factor in this respect. Technically speaking, goals and vision both represent similar directional intentions to reach future states, but there is one fundamental difference between the two concepts: as Dörnyei and Kubanyiova (2014) explain, unlike an abstract, cognitive goal, a vision includes a strong *sensory element*: it involves tangible images related to achieving the goal. Thus, for example, the vision of becoming a doctor exceeds the abstract goal of earning a medical degree in that it involves the individual actually seeing him/herself receiving the degree certificate and practising as a qualified doctor. That is, the vision to become a doctor also involves the sensory experience of *being* a doctor. In this sense, a vision can be understood as a goal that the learner has made his/her own by adding to it the imagined reality of the actual goal experience. We believe that the intensity of a DMC cannot be achieved without adding this visionary quality to guiding goals, and therefore view DMCs as motivational currents heading towards a potent personalised vision (the concept of imagery and vision will be further discussed in a separate section below).

Salient and facilitative structure

While surging forwards, the Gulf Stream moves unwaveringly along a clear pathway and does not falter: a quality not coincidental but rather characteristic of the phenomenon in question. Similarly, a DMC always has a salient, recognisable structure which does not merely frame the process, but which also plays a vital role in facilitating the unfolding action.

At the genesis of each occurrence of a DMC there must be a clear *starting point* which can unmistakably be identified as the beginning of the process; that is, a DMC never simply drifts into being but rather is triggered by something specific. Consider how important the launch of a spacecraft is: the moment of take-off is a crucial phase of the overall journey as it determines the trajectory, movement, sustainability and of course the final destination. For a successful DMC journey, an elaborate launch system is equally necessary, where all prerequisite conditions are precisely calibrated, since the launch will determine the longevity and strength of the resulting current.

One advantage of a powerful launch is that the system can quickly achieve 'motivational autopilot', that is, a state where the initial momentum rules out the necessity for a motivational intervention each and every time a new step within the sequence is to be carried out. In this respect, the process of undertaking the various steps becomes a *routine* that is directly linked to the initial set-up. This could be compared to domino pieces that, when properly lined up, will all fall one after another from a single push because they are all part of the same chain. Therefore, a key feature of a DMC is the existence of motivated behavioural routines which do not need ongoing motivational processing or volitional control: they will be executed simply because they are part of the structure. The overweight professor does not need to make a principled decision every time he goes to the gym, and in language learning contexts such routines might, in the run up to what might be an important exam or test for example, involve the decision to spend 30 minutes each afternoon watching L2 television or to memorise 10 new L2 phrases every day. In a DMC, sticking to such set routines becomes a smooth and self-evident part of the process, such as with the same semi-automatic process of brushing one's teeth before going to bed.

The exact nature of this start may take different forms, ranging from a tornado-like beginning whereby flow progressively gathers momentum before building to a formidable intensity, to a deluge of motivation as when flood gates are opened and energised movement begins in a manner both powerful and immediate. Likewise, the emerging DMC may take different shapes and forms, depending on how the constituent components relate to one another. In an *upward spiral* the energy level associated with the behavioural sequence grows incrementally as one builds up momentum or expertise, or as the outcome becomes increasingly more within arm's reach; the common observation that success breeds further success falls under this category. Another common type – which we might describe as a *plateauing spiral* – is characterised by an initial rush of energy which leads to the formation of effective behavioural routines which, although they are sustained, are carried out with a gradually waning enthusiasm. The common appreciation that when losing weight it is hardest to lose the last 2 lbs. than the first 18 lbs. is reflective of this structure.

To conclude, a DMC is always associated with a prominent structure, which not only provides an accommodating framework for the process, but which also takes an active role in keeping the current flowing. Further research will be highly instrumental in mapping out the main structural archetypes of DMCs, and in furthering understanding of how the manipulation of certain conditions may alter their functional properties. For example, it is reasonable to assume that adding regular feedback points to the structure will intensify the current (as is the case with the dieter who steps on the scales every week in the hope of receiving energising feedback), and in a similar vein, making the pathway rich in meaningful subgoals and useful subroutines to be done on an "autopilot" might conceivably increase the robustness of the forward-surging motivational current.

Participant ownership and 'perceived behavioural control'

A person may be caught up in a DMC only if he/she fully internalises the vision driving the current forwards. Although a DMC can be initiated by others, joining it must be a fully autonomous decision and, in order for a DMC to begin, complete ownership of the process and its outcome must be felt. This sense of ownership can only exist if the individual believes that he/she has sufficient capabilities to perform the required actions and thus to participate in the project effectively. This perception has been termed in psychology 'perceived behavioural control' (see the description of Ajzen's theory of planned behaviour below). Thus, a fundamental condition for DMCs is that participants come to believe in the necessity and significance of the project and be fully confident of the possibility of achieving their goal.

Clear perception of progress

People may only continue in a DMC if they have a clear and ongoing perception that they are on track towards reaching their vision. The satisfaction and sense of wellbeing one gains from this sense of progress is one of the main forward drives in a DMC, and in order to feel this satisfaction one needs to receive some sort of tangible feedback while moving forward: some aspects of continuous progress need to be visible. Individuals in a DMC are aware of the fact that they are experiencing something unique, a drive which is not commonly experienced in everyday situations, not even during those times when individuals might feel highly motivated. This unique experience is fed by the unmistakable signs of achieving the goal: the decreasing waist size in a dietary programme, the coming together of a performance, the growing bibliography marking the progress in an MA dissertation or the visibly growing cucumbers in an allotment plot.

Positive emotional loading

Individuals in a DMC usually experience highly positive and supportive emotionality towards the process. This stems from the emotional loading of the vision which is at the heart of the DMC: anything which helps to approach the goal feels rewarding and takes on some of the positive affect associated with the outcome. It is as if each step along the way reproduces – or becomes permeated with – some of the overall passion linked to the whole journey. This is goal-oriented behaviour with a difference: the positive emotional loading of each step generates further energy, and evident in each phase of the motivational journey is the promise of a new experience, a new opportunity, a new identity, or perhaps, as for our esteemed professor, a new level of fitness. This element of exploring something new is highly valuable to DMCs; it offers something beyond the banalities of everyday life. The emotional loading of a DMC is therefore different from the intrinsic pleasure of engaging in a joyful activity, the enjoyment is related not so much to the pleasantness of the activity itself but to the pleasure of goal attainment. This means that even if the specific DMC-related task is not particularly pleasurable – for example memorising the Highway Code during the process of learning to drive – the feeling that one is doing something useful and meaningful that takes one towards their goal endows it with a unique sense of excitement and fulfilment.

Motivation theories related to DMCs

Although the concept of Directed Motivational Currents is a novel idea, this is not to say that aspects of the phenomenon have not been discussed in motivation literature in the past. In fact, given that DMCs are such a potent organising force in several notable aspects of our behaviour, it would be somewhat alarming if we were not to find any references to it in the literature. Before discussing several of the most significant theoretical links however, let us ask an obvious question: why have motivation scholars not come across this concept before?

The most likely answer is that they were simply not looking for it. Motivation theory has traditionally been concerned with identifying generalisable components of an overall motivation construct, which was seen as a static entity. When trying to explain why, say, Rupert was motivated, scholars offered varied contributing factors, but did not seem to be concerned with the fact that Rupert's motivation might not be constant, and that he could be motivated one day and demotivated the next: that is, the issue of temporal processes characterising motivational change was not on the radar of researchers. The powerful motivational states which accompany a DMC were largely explained in terms of the nature of the goals involved and other generalisable factors related to the individuals, such as their expectations of success, their perception of the value of succeeding or their intrinsic interest in the task. An insufficient focus on the time aspect in this regard is able to explain the fact that it is not possible for a single mainstream motivation theory to subsume this new construct, whereby the channelling of such dispositions into a specific process with a specific structure is able to hugely amplify the motivational energy released. Even one of the closest parallels of a DMC, Csikszentmihalyi's (1988, 1990) concept of 'flow' (see below), is only concerned with engagement in *single* tasks without taking into account any prolonged, sustained time element.

Over the past decade there has been a broad yet notable change within the social sciences. Situated, temporally sensitive theories have become more prominent, and in response to this an increasing number of scholars have started to look at the world in a more holistic manner, adopting a form of complex dynamic systems perspective. Taking a dynamic systems approach means that we attempt to consider the combined impact of multiple factors which influence every human decision and every social phenomenon; this perspective therefore foregrounds the *complexity* of everyday existence (for further explanation, see below). However, while this approach might have increased ecological validity, it has a significant downside in researchability: because everything is related to everything else, it is an immensely challenging task to assess and interpret specific events. It is against this backdrop that DMCs carry a special significance: the intense motivational drive involved can override the distractions and complications an individual faces, and can thus align diverse factors to energise action. DMCs are able to act as a precious organising force which is able to regulate events in a complicated world and thus help to maintain predictability (and therefore researchability).

Although we do not find any past theory of motivation that has explicitly identified or highlighted the DMC phenomenon in its totality, virtually all mainstream theories have something valuable to say about an aspect of DMCs. In the following, we list some of the most relevant theoretical paradigms, indicating as we go what we may learn from them.

Goal setting theory

A prerequisite for a DMC to emerge is the existence of a clearly defined goal at the finish line and clearly marked signposts along the way to provide continuous feedback about one's progress. This aspect of DMCs makes Locke and Latham's (1990) *goal-setting theory* highly relevant, as this theory seeks to explain performance in terms of differences in goal attributes. Locke (1996) summarises the main findings of past research under five points:

1. The more difficult the goal, the greater the achievement.
2. The more specific or explicit the goal, the more precisely performance is regulated.
3. Goals that are both specific and difficult lead to the highest performance.
4. Commitment to goals is most critical when goals are specific and difficult (i.e. when goals are easy or vague it is not hard to feign commitment: it does not require much dedication to reach easy goals, and vague goals can be easily redefined to accommodate low performance).
5. High commitment to goals is attained when (a) the individual is convinced that the goal is important; and (b) the individual is convinced that the goal is attainable (or that, at least, progress can be made towards it).

These goal characteristics can undoubtedly help us to clarify what kind of directional pathways may work best when trying to initiate a DMC, but it is a further aspect of goal-setting theory which offers the most obvious benefits: the issue of *proximal* versus *distal goals*. Because goals are not only outcomes to shoot for but also standards by which to evaluate one's performance and provide a definition of success, distal goals may be less effective in this respect than a series of *proximal subgoals* the overall process can be broken down into (e.g. taking tests, passing exams, satisfying learning contracts). These subgoals have a powerful motivating function in that they mark progress and provide immediate incentive and feedback – they are therefore an indispensable part of any DMC.

Self-determination theory

Deci and Ryan's (1985) *self-determination theory* offers a detailed discussion of autonomous – or self-determined – engagement with tasks. The theory introduced the renowned concept of *intrinsic motivation*, referring to behaviour performed for its own sake, and its counterpart, *extrinsic motivation*, which involves regulation coming from outside of the learner through the incentive of external rewards. Of particular interest for us are two sub-theories complementing the intrinsic/extrinsic dichotomy; first, it has been consistently found that people will be more self-determined in performing a particular behaviour if the task engagement supports three fundamental human needs: (a) *autonomy* (i.e. experiencing oneself as the origin of one's behaviour), (b) *competence* (i.e. feeling efficacious and having a sense of accomplishment) and (c) *relatedness* (i.e. feeling close to and connected to other individuals). Second, Vallerand (1997) further distinguishes between three subtypes of intrinsic motivation: (a) *to learn* (engaging in an activity for the pleasure and satisfaction of understanding something new, satisfying one's curiosity and exploring the world), (b) *towards achievement* (engaging in an activity for the satisfaction of surpassing oneself, coping with challenges and accomplishing or creating something) and (c) *to experience stimulation* (engaging in an activity to experience pleasant sensations). These categories all have bearings on a more nuanced understanding of DMCs.

Theory of planned behaviour

Broadly speaking, Ajzen's (1988) well-known *theory of planned behaviour* states that someone's intention to perform an action is a function of two basic factors: a person's 'attitude towards the behaviour' and the 'subjective norm', the latter referring to the social pressures put on a person to perform the behaviour in question. What is particularly relevant for our purpose is a third component introduced into the model, *perceived behavioural control*. This refers to the perceived ease or difficulty of performing the behaviour (e.g. perceptions of required resources and potential impediments or obstacles). Behavioural performance is thus seen to be determined not only by people's intentions to perform the behaviour in question but also by their perceptions of control over the behaviour. To be fully motivated, an individual must believe that they have the ability to do the job and that there are no impeding factors beyond their control. This is in full accordance with our earlier argument that people can only enter a DMC if they believe that they are in full ownership and control of how things progress.

Theories of self-imagery and vision

Over the past decade the concepts of imagery and vision have become important components of motivational understanding, and because this approach has been highly influential in shaping recent L2 motivation theory, let us consider it in more detail. Ever since Allan Paivio's (1985) seminal paper introduced imagery as a method of positively inspiring athletes to improved performance, imagery training has taken a central place in the psychological toolkit of the sporting world.

Visualisation-based approaches also stand prominent in other areas of research, such as within the field of medicine, and continue to exert a growing influence on all areas of psychology (see Taylor, Pham, Rivkin & Armor 1998).

How can we best understand the motivational dimension of vision? Or to turn the question around, which theoretical approach to motivation can best accommodate this visionary aspect? And what bearing does any of this have on our understanding of DMCs? The answer is provided through a seminal paper in 1986 by Markus and Nurius, which introduced the concept of 'possible selves'. These represent an individual's ideas of what they *might* become, what they *would like to* become and what they are *afraid of* becoming. Imagery is a central element of possible selves theory: possible selves are more than mere long-term goals, they involve tangible images and a sensual experience of the goal. They are a *reality* for the individual: people can 'see' and 'hear' their future possible self. Thus, in many ways, possible selves are similar to dreams and visions about oneself.

The two types of possible selves most relevant to the motivation to learn are (a) the *ideal self*, which refers to the future self-image that represents the attributes that someone would ideally like to possess (i.e. representation of hopes, aspirations or wishes) and (b) the *ought-to self*, which refers to the future self-image that represents attributes that one believes one ought to possess (i.e. representation of someone's sense of personal or social duties, obligations or responsibilities) (Higgins 1987). Drawing on possible selves theory, Dörnyei (2005, 2009) introduced the *L2 Motivational Self System,* which offers a framework for vision in second language education. It involves a tripartite construct of the learners' motivational experience. The key aspect, from the point of view of our present discussion into the dimensions of DMCs, is that the first two components involve future self-states the learner envisages in a vision-like manner, and experiences as if reality:

- *Ideal L2 Self.* This concerns the L2-specific facet of one's *ideal self*: if the person we would like to become speaks an L2 (e.g. the person we would like to become is associated with travelling or doing business internationally), the ideal L2 self is a powerful motivator to learn the L2 as we work to reduce the discrepancy between our actual and ideal selves.
- *Ought-to L2 Self.* This concerns the attributes that one believes one *ought* to possess to avoid possible negative outcomes, and which therefore may bear little resemblance to a person's own desires or wishes.
- *L2 Learning Experience.* This concerns situation-specific motives related to the immediate learning environment and experience (e.g. the positive impact of success or the enjoyable quality of a language course).

Recently, Dörnyei and Kubanyiova (2014) have summarised in a book-length overview the various methods for generating vision in both language learners and teachers. They understand vision as 'one of the highest-order motivational forces' (2014: 9), thus, through vision, it becomes possible to consider motivation as a long-term, ongoing endeavour: when students are able to create a long term vision of the version of themselves they are working towards, this is ever present regardless of the day to day levels of motivation which we know will wax and wane. Vision also seems to be one of the most reliable predictors of students' long-term intended effort (ibid.), which explains its relevance to the understanding of DMCs: in order to create the environment in which a DMC may emerge, students' visions need to be actively nurtured. Dörnyei and Kubanyiova describe six key components of a framework for developing a vision-inspired teaching practice:

1. *Creating the vision:* The logical first step in a visionary motivational programme is to help learners to create desired future selves, that is, construct visions of who they could become as L2 users and what knowing an L2 could add to their lives.

2. *Strengthening the vision:* The more intensive the imagery accompanying the vision, the more powerful the vision; therefore, we need to help students to see their desired language selves with more clarity and, consequently, with more urgency for action.

3. *Substantiating the vision:* Possible selves are only effective insomuch as learners perceive them as plausible (hence the term, 'possible' self); therefore, students need to anchor their ideal L2 self images in a sense of realistic expectations.

4. *Transforming the vision into action:* Vision without action is merely a daydream: future self-guides are only productive if they are accompanied by a set of concrete action plans, that is, the blueprint of a tangible pathway which leads to them.

5. *Keeping the vision alive:* Everybody has several distinct possible selves which are stored in their memory and which compete for attention in a person's limited 'working self-concept'; therefore, in order to keep our vision alive we need to activate it regularly so that it does not get squeezed out by other life concerns.

6. *Counterbalancing the vision:* A classic principle in possible selves theory is that for maximum effectiveness as a motivational resource, a desired future self should be offset by a corresponding feared self.

Flow theory

We all understand what it means when someone tells us they are 'in the zone'; indeed, any given individual is likely to have experienced this feeling at some point throughout their lives. At those times when we are 'in the zone', we are aware of it and others can also see it in us: we lose track of time and become completely engaged in the task at hand. This sense of abandonment and focus is at the heart of the concept of *flow* as outlined by Csikszentmihalyi (1990) where people become completely lost in the moment, and time and outside influences fall away. Thus, flow is a highly focused motivational state – some would say that it is the ultimate task engagement – when motivation, cognition and emotion are fully aligned with the task under completion. The powerful drive evident in flow is in some respects akin to the drive visible in DMCs: in both cases people are highly engrossed in what they are doing, leading to the concerns of the outside world becoming secondary to the powerful motivational current consuming their attention.

The significant difference between Csikszentmihalyi's concept and that of DMCs lies primarily in the time scale upon which they occur. Csikszentmihalyi is concerned with short-term, one-off tasks such as painting, reading and playing music, while the focus of DMCs is on ongoing behavioural sequences spanning longer-term periods. Furthermore, in discussing the flow experience, Csikszentmihalyi observed that 'it was quite typical for an artist to lose all interest in the painting he had spent so much time and effort working on as soon as it was finished' (1988: 3). This focus on the intrinsic satisfaction with the subjective experience without much concern for the final outcome is in stark contrast to the goal-oriented conceptualisation of DMCs, in which the constituent learning episodes are seen as expressly paving the way for an end goal. Another stark contrast is the emphasis in Csikszentmihalyi's theory on optimal task engagement – or total absorption – without any concern for the structural aspects of the process as it unfolds over time: in other words, DMCs add a salient temporal, structural dimension and directionality to Csikszentmihalyi's original concept.

What can we learn from flow theory? One particularly relevant aspect is the set of conditions which are required for the flow state to occur. As Egbert (2003) summarises, the relevant task conditions can be organized along four dimensions: (1) there is a perceived balance of task challenge and participant's skills during the task; (2) the task offers opportunities for intense concentration and the participants' attention is focused on the pursuit of clear task goals; (3) the participants find the task intrinsically interesting or authentic; and (4) the participants perceive a sense of control over the task process and outcomes. These conditions appear to apply equally to DMCs.

Future time perspective

Time perspective (e.g. Zimbardo & Boyd 1999) is a recent theoretical domain that has not, as yet, exerted significant influence in changing the course of motivational research. It has, however, been gathering momentum, the impact of which is likely to be felt soon. Simply stated, time perspective refers to an individual's disposition towards looking always to the past, thinking only of the present or being highly aware of the future. In particular, research into time perspective is interested in what effect one's time-related bias has on an individual's decision making process both on a day-to-day basis and also over longer periods of time.

The time perspective of most relevance to our discussion of DMCs is Future Time Perspective, which can be defined as 'the present anticipation of future goals' (Simons, Dewitte, & Lens 2004: 122) and is primarily concerned with 'an individual's beliefs or orientation toward the future concerning temporarily distant goals' (Bembenutty & Karabenick 2004: 36). The foundation of much of today's research stems from a 1982 study by De Volder and Lens which demonstrated that students who ascribe higher valence to goals in the distant future will be more persistent and obtain better academic results in the present: in short, one's temporal relation to the future matters. Since then, many studies have confirmed the existence of strong links between a future time perspective and academic achievement, and this critical link is also present in DMCs: looking ahead and being able to set distant goals helps learners to ignore the confusing complexities of the learning environment and thus helps retain focus on what they want to achieve.

Process-oriented approaches to motivation

Current research on time perspectives is closely related to past efforts to conceptualise motivation as a process. There have been some attempts to adopt a process-oriented perspective on motivation in psychology when discussing career motivation and motivation across the life span. Regarding the former, Raynor (1974) introduced the concept of a *contingent path*, referring to a series of tasks where successful achievement is necessary to be guaranteed the opportunity to perform the next task, that is, to continue along the path. An example of this sequence would be someone taking an exam to be able to carry on studying towards a further exam and eventually a degree, resulting thus in a form of chain reaction. In discussing vocational and career contexts, Raynor argues that it is difficult to imagine any sustained motivational disposition without some sort of a contingent path structure. Other scholars have also been interested in the long-term developmental and strategic implications of trying to achieve major goals that span across one's life (e.g. Heckhausen & Schulz 1995), but such efforts have not gained mainstream status (see Ryan & Dörnyei 2013, for an overview).

Within L2 research, the most elaborate attempt to model the process dimension of motivation was developed by Dörnyei and Ottó (1998). Their model organises the motivational influences of L2 learning along a sequence of discrete actional events within a chain of initiating and enacting motivated behaviour, describing a 'goal → intention → action → accomplishment of goal → evaluation' progression. Drawing on Heckhausen and Kuhl's (1985) Action Control Theory, Dörnyei and Ottó divide this chain up into three main phases: (a) the *preactional phase,* which corresponds to 'choice motivation' leading to the selection of the goal or task to be pursued; (b) the *actional phase,* which corresponds to 'executive motivation' which energises action while it is being carried out; and (c) the *post-actional phase,* which involves critical retrospection either after action has been completed, or interrupted for a short period of time (e.g. for a holiday).

The main lesson of the model is that the three phases are characterised by different sets of motives, and once an individual has actually embarked on the task (e.g. enrolled in a language course), the motivational emphasis shifts from deliberation and decision-making to implementation. The implementation-related motives are of obvious importance from a DMC perspective, as it involves an extended action sequence; the Dörnyei and Ottó model describes it in relation to three basic processes: (a) *subtask generation and implementation* to break down action plans into manageable units and short-term goals; (b) a complex ongoing *appraisal* process to evaluate the multitude of stimuli from the learning environment and to monitor progress towards the goal; and (c) the application of various *action control* mechanisms or self-regulatory strategies to enhance, protect and sustain motivation and learning progress.

Dynamic systems approaches

As already discussed, the most recent theoretical approaches to describing the nature of human motivation have adopted a complex dynamic systems perspective, bringing the social sciences more in line with the description of many world phenomena studied by the natural sciences. A key tenet of this perspective is that the behaviour of a system emerges out of the dynamic interaction of its multiple components, which are themselves also constantly changing. The occurring interferences typically cause highly complicated, sometimes chaotic and generally nonlinear patterns, often making the exact outcome of system behaviour unpredictable, with the weather system being a good example (for reviews, see Dörnyei 2009; Dörnyei, MacIntyre & Henry 2014; Larsen-Freeman & Cameron 2008; van

Geert 2008; Verspoor, de Bot & Lowie 2011). As a result of this, cause-effect re-lationships between single variables can no longer be taken for granted; we are no longer safe in relying on answers which might, for example, suggest that con-scientious students who love travelling are likely to be good at languages, or that girls might be better language learners than boys. Indeed, even if an observation is replicated as many as ten times, we cannot say with confidence that the particular event is certain to occur on the eleventh occasion.

It is against the backdrop of this always-changing, unstable and busy nature of our dynamic world that the significance of DMCs is apparent: it is a powerful regulatory process whose course and end-state are, to a large extent, predictable (and thus researchable). DMCs are uniquely able to function in the midst of the confusion of the surrounding world thanks to the fact that their very essence includes the alignment of diverse factors along a goal-oriented pathway, accom-panied by a release of energy capable of overriding these distracting influences. It may be of use to picture it in this way: imagine a long haired swimmer's hair billow around her while she floats, unmoving, under the surface of a vast body of water. Under these conditions each strand of hair moves independently, respond-ing to the currents in the water, reacting to meetings with other strands of hair and other bodies in the water, along with a host of other influences. Imagine now that the swimmer starts to swim forwards towards a fixed point in the distance. As she moves down this path, however slowly, her hair will begin to align behind her and all strands, or variables, in the case of DMCs, will start to line up with one another; as long as this attractor is in place we will, to a considerable extent, be able to predict the movement of each strand.

Practical implications

DMCs do not stand as a replacement for everyday classroom motivational prac-tices and nor do they seek to replace any of the tried and tested techniques and activities all teachers have safely stored away in desk drawers. Instead, a DMC is able to offer something supplementary to these. It can be imagined of as a potent boost of motivation which may be utilised to transport individuals towards a cho-sen destination of special personal significance. At this stage, the details of how exactly to apply this motivational intervention in the classroom are yet to be fully developed – we foresee substantial creative methodological work in this respect over the next five years. We can, however, already at this early stage delineate several broad levels of application, among them: *lesson level, term level* and *course level*. Although each of these applications functions on a different time scale, each follows the same core principles of the DMC framework as described.

Lesson level

Within the time scale of a single language class, we may conceptualise a DMC as occurring within the context of a *task*. An effective language task already includes several elements of the DMC framework: it will be well structured, subsuming multiple smaller elements each of which functioning as proximal sub-goals, and there will be a clear starting point and a well-defined pathway which frames progression towards a specific outcome. To activate the full potential of a DMC however, the task's goal needs to be aligned with the students' broader language visions – that is, they need to see the task as meaningful and effective with regards to their L2 goals – and be given full control over execution. The final ingredient which needs to be ensured is a clear perception of progress – this condition favours tasks where attainment is incrementally perceptible, that is, where students have an ongoing perception of how the final product is taking shape (e.g. producing a visual display or preparing for a role-play performance).

Term-level

Moving beyond this, perhaps the most typical instructional example which may facilitate a DMC is *project work*. Inherently it is often very well set up to allow for maximum autonomy as the project progresses, and it usually has clearly visible and understandable starting and end points. The duration of a project may span anything from a few lessons to a whole semester, yet, regardless of its length it will need to include a generous number of proximal subgoals to act as markers of progress and to allow for continual feedback. It is important that the teacher be clear regarding what is expected from students and through what criteria the resultant product will be judged, so that students will likewise be clear about how they may interpret this brief and how exactly their work will meet the standards expected of them. While project work may have the ability to launch a DMC, it must be emphasised, as with a DMC over any time scale, that it is not assumed this will happen as a matter of course: the connection with a personal L2 vision is a critical component of DMCs and there must be sufficient emotional resonance in each student towards the task, which is where creative content-specifications are of crucial significance.

Course-level

The third level of DMCs spans beyond a single term and concerns a language course as a whole. We have witnessed in the past again and again how effective some longer-term pathways can be in invigorating learning and generating focus, for example in the run-up to a school trip which has been promised after the successful completion of a language course, or through participation in a competition in which students are able to show off their skills. For some students, the prospect of taking the L2 as a university subject may also initiate a DMC. These extended versions of DMCs are undoubtedly harder to create and need substantially more powerful visions to energise them; although the rewards are far greater, there is also a far greater change and commitment needed in individuals in order to achieve success.

Conclusion

A DMC is an intense motivational pathway which occurs when a variety of time and context-related factors come together in an individual to prompt a firm decision to pursue a goal/vision which is considered personally significant, highly relevant to one's desired identity and emotionally satisfying. A DMC emerges within the framework of a salient structure of behavioural acts – many of them being routines performed on 'motivational autopilot' – which are permeated by the sense of elevated emotionality associated with approaching a coveted prize. After a powerful launch, a DMC is motivationally self-supporting as the initial momentum takes the individual through a set of sub-goals which generate positive feedback and further momentum towards the final goal. In this way, the energy level of the current is sustained throughout the whole pathway and this current carries the individual beyond his/her everyday boundaries towards a personalised goal which may not have otherwise been achievable.

Although in its present conceptualisation a DMC is a novel theoretical concept, several established motivation theories have touched upon key aspects of it. Its current timeliness is explained by the fact that within a dynamic systems perspective of the social world, it offers a template which outlines a powerful drive that has the capability to cut through the complexity of the interrelated factors characterising any learning situation. It can thus allow for directed, goal-oriented action and can serve as a motivation boost in contexts where a system – whether a single learner or a larger learner grouping – drifts somewhat aimlessly and without focus. In such situations we believe DMCs may be consciously generated to align diverse factors along a directional pathway, and therefore they can be seen as an intense motivational strategy to combat apathy and demotivation. Thus, DMCs have considerable theoretical and practical potential, both of which we look forward to being developed further through future research.

References

Ajzen, I. (1988). *Attitudes, personality and behaviour*. Chicago, IL: Dorsey Press.

Bembenutty, H., & Karabenick, S.A. (2004). Inherent association between academic delay of gratification, future time perspective, and self-regulated learning. *Educational Psychology Review*, 16(1), 35–57. DOI: 10.1023/B:EDPR.0000012344.34008.5c

Csikszentmihalyi, M. (1988). Introduction. In M. Csikszentmihalyi & I.S. Csikszentmihalyi (Eds.), *Optimal experience: Psychological studies of flow in consciousness* (pp. 3–14). Cambridge: Cambridge University Press. DOI: 10.1017/CBO9780511621956.001

Csikszentmihalyi, M. (1990). *Flow: The psychology of optimal experience*. New York, NY: Harper & Row.

De Volder, M.L., & Lens, W. (1982). Academic achievement and future time perspective as a cognitive-motivational concept. *Journal of Personality and Social Psychology*, 42(3), 566–571. DOI: 10.1037/0022-3514.42.3.566

Deci, E. L., & Ryan, R.M. (1985). *Intrinsic motivation and self-determination in human behaviour*. New York, NY: Plenum. DOI: 10.1007/978-1-4899-2271-7

Dörnyei, Z. (2005). *The psychology of the language learner: Individual differences in second language acquisition*. Mahwah, NJ: Lawrence Erlbaum Associates.

Dörnyei, Z. (2009). The L2 Motivational Self System. In Z. Dörnyei, & E. Ushioda (Eds.), *Motivation, language identity and the L2 self* (pp. 9–42). Bristol: Multilingual Matters.

Dörnyei, Z., MacIntyre P.D., & Henry, A. (Eds.). (2014). *Motivational dynamics in language learning*. Bristol: Multilingual Matters.

Dörnyei, Z., & Kubanyiova, M. (2014). *Motivating learners, motivating teachers: Building vision in the language classroom*. Cambridge: Cambridge University Press.

Dörnyei, Z., & Ottó, I. (1998). Motivation in action: A process model of L2 motivation. *Working Papers in Applied Linguistics (Thames Valley University, London)*, 4, 43–69.

Egbert, J. (2003). A study of flow theory in the foreign language classroom. *Modern Language Journal*, 87(4), 499-518. DOI: 10.1111/1540-4781.00204

Heckhausen, J., & Schulz, R. (1995). A life span theory of control. *Psychological Review*, 102, 284–304. DOI: 10.1037/0033-295X.102.2.284

Heckhausen, H., & Kuhl, J. (1985). From wishes to action: The dead ends and short cuts on the long way to action. In M. Frese & J. Sabini (Eds.). *Goal-directed behaviour: The concept of action in psychology* (pp. 134–160). Hillsdale, NJ: Lawrence Erlbaum Associates.

Higgins, E. T. (1987). Self-discrepancy: A theory relating self and affect. *Psychological Review*, 94, 319–340. DOI: 10.1037/0033-295X.94.3.319

Larsen-Freeman, D., & Cameron, L. (2008). *Complex systems and applied linguistics*. Oxford: Oxford University Press.

Locke, E.A. (1996). Motivation through conscious goal setting. *Applied & Preventive Psychology*, 5, 117-124. DOI: 10.1016/S0962-1849(96)80005-9

Locke, E.A., & Latham, G.P. (1990). *A theory of goal setting and task performance*. Englewood Cliffs, NJ: Prentice Hall.

Markus, H., & Nurius, P. (1986). Possible selves. *American Psychologist*, 41, 954–969. DOI: 10.1037/0003-066X.41.9.954

Paivio, A. (1985). Cognitive and motivational functions on imagery in human performance. *Canadian Journal of Applied Sport Sciences*, 10, 22S–28S.

Raynor, J.O. (1974). Motivation and career striving. In J.W. Atkinson, & J.O. Raynor (Eds.), *Motivation and achievement* (pp. 369–387). Washington, DC: Winston & Sons.

Ryan, S. & Dörnyei, Z. (2013). The long-term evolution of language motivation and the L2 self. In A. Berndt (Ed.), *Fremdsprachen in der perspektive lebenslangen lernens* (pp. 89–100). Frankfurt: Peter Lang.

Simons, J., Dewitte, S., & Lens, W. (2004). The role of different types of instrumentality in motivation, study strategies, and performance: Know why you learn, so you'll know what you learn! *British Journal of Educational Psychology*, 74(1), 343–360. DOI: 10.1348/0007099041552314

Taylor, S.E., Pham, L.B., Rivkin, I.D., & Armor, D.A. (1998). Harnessing the imagination: Mental simulation, self-regulation, and coping. *American Psychologist*, 53(4), 429–439. DOI: 10.1037/0003-066X.53.4.429

Vallerand, R.J. (1997). Toward a hierarchical model of intrinsic and extrinsic motivation. *Advances in Experimental Social Psychology*, 29, 271–360. DOI: 10.1016/S0065-2601(08)60019-2

van Geert, P. (2008). The Dynamic Systems approach in the study of L1 and L2 acquisition: An introduction. *Modern Language Journal*, 92, 179–199. DOI: 10.1111/j.1540-4781.2008. 00713.x

Verspoor, M.H., de Bot, K., & Lowie, W. (Eds.). (2011). *A dynamic approach to second language development: Methods and techniques*. Amsterdam: John Benjamins. DOI: 10.1075/lllt.29

Zimbardo, P.G., & Boyd, J.N. (1999). Putting time in perspective: A valid, reliable, individual-differences metric. *Journal of Personality and Social Psychology*, 77(6), 1271–1288. DOI: 10.1037/0022-3514.77.6.1271

CHAPTER 2

Motivation, autonomy and metacognition

Exploring their interactions

Ema Ushioda

From the perspective of sustaining long-term engagement in L2 learning, personal goals and targets are important in providing a motivational rationale. However, purposeful effortful striving may not be sufficient in itself to regulate motivation when the challenges derive from not knowing how to deal with problems and difficulties in one's learning – that is, from lack of metacognitive know-how. In this chapter, I problematize this aspect of motivation in L2 learning and examine how processes of motivation may interact with the metacognitive dimension of language learning. Drawing on insights from the literature on autonomy and self-regulated learning, I consider how teachers may mediate the interaction between motivation and metacognition to help learners sustain their engagement in L2 learning.

Keywords: motivational self-regulation, metacognition, autonomy, will and skill, sociocultural theory

Introduction

Motivation is widely recognised as a variable of importance in human learning, reflected in goals and directions pursued, levels of effort invested, depth of engagement, and degree of persistence in learning. In the field of L2 learning research, these conative features of purposeful and effortful striving have been core to the analysis of motivation. While conceptual frameworks for theorising L2 motivation have changed and evolved over the past fifty years, they commonly seek to describe and analyse the reasons why people learn (or do not want to learn) a language, and how far they persist and succeed in this endeavour. A concerted focus on these areas is not surprising since it is clear that reasons or goals are important in providing a motivational rationale for initial engagement in L2 learning, while short-term targets, effort, persistence and motivational control (self-regulation) are important in sustaining motivated engagement in learning and ensuring long-term success.

However, as I will discuss in this chapter, purposeful, controlled and effortful striving may not be sufficient in itself to regulate motivation to engage with the day-to-day demands of language learning, particularly as the learning challenges increase exponentially in cognitive and linguistic complexity as one moves beyond the early basic stages of proficiency. Simply applying more effort or focusing on goals and targets may have little effect when the challenges to motivation derive from not knowing how to deal with the problems and difficulties in one's learning – that is, from lack of metacognitive knowledge and skills. In this chapter, I will problematize this aspect of motivation in L2 learning and examine how processes of motivation may interact with the metacognitive dimension of language learning. Drawing on insights from the literature on learner autonomy and self-regulated learning, I will consider what role teachers may play in mediating the interaction between motivation and metacognition to help learners sustain their engagement in L2 learning.

To begin with, in order to understand better the relationship between processes of motivation and processes of long-term engagement in L2 learning, I think it is useful to map these motivation and L2 learning processes onto a directional timeline and consider them from a range of macro and micro temporal perspectives.

Motivation and L2 learning timeline

Figure 1 is a simple representation of this motivation and L2 learning timeline. It is adapted from a schematic framework I developed previously to represent motivation from a temporal perspective (Ushioda 1998: 82; for additional discussion, see also Ushioda 2001; and Ushioda 2014).

In Figure 1, the L2 learning process is mapped onto a directional timeline represented by the long diagonal arrow. This arrow is merely a simplified metaphorical representation of a person's L2 learning trajectory and is not intended to imply that L2 learning is a straightforward linear and additive process. The metaphorical representation does not try to take account of the internal complexities of interlanguage development, such as variability, backsliding and restructuring; or of the circumstantial complexities of an individual's L2 learning career, such as transferring or repeating courses of study or retaking a test. Along this L2 learning trajectory within a particular sociocultural environment, we can imagine different learners A and B at different stages of learning or L2 development, or the same learner at different points in time, represented as A or B.

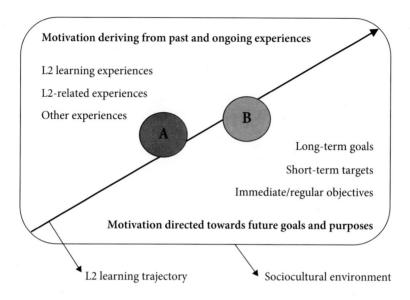

Figure 1. Motivation and L2 learning timeline (adapted from Ushioda 1998: 82)

In terms of motivation, learners' progression along this L2 learning trajectory will have a forward-looking dimension, shaped by particular goals or targets. These may be long-term goals, such as career plans, or more short-term goals such as passing an upcoming language test or finishing a project. These goals or targets may be largely internally regulated and self-determined, or they may be externally imposed and regulated by others, such as teachers, parents, the education system or university entrance requirements.

The motivation of learners progressing along the L2 learning trajectory will also have a historical dimension, shaped by past experiences of learning this particular language or other languages, communicating in a foreign language or having relevant cultural encounters of some kind. The historical dimension may also include experiences not directly related to L2 learning which are nevertheless significant for L2 motivation, such as poor academic performance in science and mathematics motivating a student to specialise in language studies instead.

Sandwiched between and interacting with these forward-looking and historical dimensions of motivation are learners' ongoing motivational experiences in the here and now – for example, as they participate in a lesson, engage in a learning activity, struggle to express an idea, or receive corrective feedback from the teacher. Of course, these evolving day-to-day experiences and micro-level moment-to-moment experiences cumulatively become part of the historical dimension of motivation. These cumulative experiences may be positive or negative or more likely a mixture, and will affect motivation for L2 learning in different ways.

The overall balance between cumulative experiential perspectives and future-oriented perspectives in shaping motivation will vary from learner to learner and at different stages of L2 learning. Such differences are represented schematically by the relative positions of circles A and B in Figure 1 in relation to motivation deriving from past and ongoing experiences, and motivation directed towards future goals and purposes. Thus, the motivation of learner B is more strongly goal-focused than that of learner A, for whom motivation is predominantly influenced by cumulative experiential factors. As I have suggested in a previous commentary (Ushioda 2001: 119), this schematic representation is useful in decoupling the forward-bound trajectory of the L2 learning process from the evolving multidirectional configuration of past experiences, current experiences and future temporal perspectives shaping an individual's motivational process.

So, how do these different temporal perspectives and macro- and micro-levels of motivation affect learners' progression along the L2 learning timeline? How do they contribute to sustaining or hampering engagement in the L2 learning process, and in what ways do they interact with the metacognitive dimension of L2 learning? I will begin by focusing on the future temporal perspective of motivation directed towards goals and purposes.

Long-term goals, reasons, orientations, future self-representations

Traditionally, reasons why people learn particular languages have been classified as instrumental or integrative orientations, reflecting either pragmatic goals (such as enhancing one's employment prospects) or more cultural and social goals (such as seeking contact and friendship with target language speakers). This longstanding dual classification stems from Gardner and Lambert's (1972) pioneering programme of social-psychological research on L2 motivation in the 1960s and 1970s, and has strongly influenced the way we analyse people's motivational purposes in learning a second or foreign language. Nevertheless, we should note that Gardner (1985: 51) did speculate on other more sinister orientations for learning a language (e.g. manipulative or machiavellian orientations). Moreover, research has pointed to some context-specific motivational orientations, such as a national security orientation among Israeli Jews learning Arabic (Kraemer 1993); a required motivational orientation among learners of English in Chinese cultural settings such as Taiwan (Warden & Lin 2000); or a religio-ethnic orientation among learners of Hebrew at a Jewish school in a diaspora community (Spolsky 1989: 202–220; on religious orientations to L2 learning, see also the collection of studies in Wong, Kristjánsson & Dörnyei 2013).

While conceptual frameworks for analysing L2 motivation have now diversified considerably beyond their social-psychological theoretical base, it is worth reflecting that the bulk of research on L2 motivation over the past fifty years has effectively focused on this future-oriented dimension of motivation – that is, on the largely extrinsic goals and purposes shaping people's engagement in L2 learning. In recent years, these motivational goals or purposes have become framed in relation to a person's desired or imagined future self-representations, as theorised in particular in Dörnyei's (2005, 2009, and this volume) influential L2 Motivational Self System. Here the theoretical focus is not so much on what one might do in the future but on who one might become, and how L2 skills might fit into this future self-image. These future self-representations or "possible selves" (Markus & Nurius 1986) may be personally desired and valued (ideal L2 self), or desired for us by significant others (ought-to L2 self).

In short, the future temporal dimension of L2 motivation is now increasingly theorised in terms of the pursuit of particular social, professional, cultural or global identities that are defined in part by proficiency in a certain language (see for example the studies in Dörnyei & Ushioda 2009; also in Murray, Gao & Lamb 2011). This shift towards identity-related frameworks of analysis reflects a wider critical concern with issues of identity across the field of research on L2 learning and use since the turn of the millennium (e.g. Block 2007; also Norton & Toohey 2011), as well as a growing focus on theories of identity in mainstream motivational psychology (see Kaplan & Flum 2009).

Returning to our timeline in Figure 1, whether we speak of orientations, goals, imagined identities or future possible selves, these long-term objectives provide a motivational rationale for initiating and sustaining engagement in L2 learning from a macro temporal perspective. Without a personal long-term objective of this kind, it may be difficult to sustain motivated engagement in L2 learning (unless of course one's motivation for L2 learning derives principally from intrinsic factors such as enjoyment, interest or sense of challenge). Thus, students who have no interest in and cannot see the point of learning foreign languages will most likely opt out at the first opportunity, as suggested for example by the declining numbers of UK secondary school pupils continuing with foreign languages beyond their compulsory phase in the curriculum (Coleman 2009). In this regard, the strength of this future temporal perspective in sustaining motivation will depend very much on the personal value ascribed to long-term goals and objectives by the learner. Goals and objectives that are fully internalised or self-determined (e.g. an ideal L2 self) are likely to sustain motivation better than those that are less internalised (e.g. an ought-to L2 self) or those that are externally imposed and regulated by others (e.g. obligatory language tests).

Interim short-term goals and targets: Towards metacognition

However, even for L2 learners who have clearly defined L2-related aspirations, this long-term rationale will not be sufficient in itself to sustain motivation and progression along the L2 learning timeline. Another important forward-looking dimension of motivation is the setting of interim short-term goals and targets, such as what might be achieved over the following days, weeks and months. These short-term targets help to regulate motivation by marking successful and structured progression along the L2 learning timeline. The motivational value of realistic short-term targets is well recognised in the popular literature on, for example, life coaching, dieting or personal fitness training, while the psychology of "optimal challenge" (Deci & Ryan 1985:123) is fundamental to the design of many kinds of computer games where players are constantly motivated to improve their score or advance to the next skill level.

Moreover, if learners themselves are involved in the process of setting meaningful short-term targets or what Bandura and Schunk (1981:595) have called "proximal self-motivators", this necessarily engages them in self-evaluation of their current abilities and needs, and thus helps develop and consolidate their metacognitive awareness of their developing language skills and knowledge. The process of setting interim targets also engages learners in planning their learning and understanding how to break it down into manageable steps leading to their long-term goals, or what Dörnyei and Kubanyiova (2014) describe as the construction of realistic action plans or roadmaps leading to the achievement of desired future selves. This planning and goal-setting process thus helps learners in developing and exercising metacognitive skills through which they come to manage and regulate their learning.

In addition, as learners strive towards achieving their own targets, they will cultivate feelings of competence and skill development as well as a sense of agency or personal control in the learning process. In turn, these feelings can contribute to fostering and strengthening intrinsic motivation for learning (i.e. motivation deriving from affective rewards such as enjoyment and satisfaction), since intrinsic motivation is theorised to be underpinned by perceptions of competence and autonomy (in the sense of personal agency) in one's engagement in a particular activity (Ryan & Deci 2002). These intrinsic motivational processes can thus help further sustain day-to-day engagement in L2 learning, in interaction with the long-term goals and objectives that provide the underlying motivational rationale. For as van Lier (1996:112–113) has emphasised, in complex and extended human activities such as language learning, intrinsic and extrinsic motivational factors "must work in concert" to stimulate and sustain learning.

To summarise thus far, long-term goals and objectives provide an underlying rationale for motivated engagement in L2 learning, while interim targets help to regulate and sustain motivation by marking incremental progression along the L2 learning timeline. As we have seen, by becoming involved in setting and working towards their own short-term targets, learners can also develop metacognitive awareness of their language skills and abilities, and metacognitive skills in planning and regulating their learning. Furthermore, setting and accomplishing optimal challenges can help nurture feelings of competence and autonomy, thus strengthening intrinsic motivation for learning. In other words, we have identified interactions between the future temporal perspectives shaping motivation and its ongoing experiential dimension of skill development and growth in competence. We have also already identified some interactions between processes of motivation and processes of metacognition. These combined interactions contribute to regulating and sustaining learners' motivated engagement in learning and their progression forward along the L2 learning timeline.

Experiential dimension of motivation: Responding to challenge

However, the process of regulating and sustaining motivation entails not just a focus on progressing forward and developing one's skills and competence. Crucially, it also entails an ability to respond effectively to the demands, challenges and setbacks that often punctuate progression along the L2 learning timeline – in other words, a capacity to deal with the unmotivating or demotivating aspects of L2 learning and L2-related experience, such as disappointing test performance, boring and repetitive tasks, difficulty understanding a text, or communicative failure and frustration. Here the focus is on the cumulative experiential dimension of motivation in Figure 1, whereby L2 motivation evolves through and is influenced by past and ongoing experiences. While good experiences will most probably have positive influences on motivation, the impact of negative experiences may largely depend on how individual learners perceive and respond to these experiences.

For example, poor performance on a language test for some students may prove disheartening and weaken their motivation to try further, while for others it may prove the motivational stimulus they need to work more diligently and strive harder. Such differences in motivational response to negative outcomes may partly reflect differences in personal value ascribed to L2 learning (i.e. the long-term goals and objectives shaping motivation), and may also partly reflect differences in beliefs about the reasons for negative outcomes (i.e. differences in causal attributions – see Weiner 2007). For example, learners who believe that lack of effort or insufficient study may have negatively affected their test performance are more likely to feel motivated to try harder than learners who believe that they lack the ability to do well on the test.

Similarly, in the case of boring and repetitive tasks, the impact on motivation will again depend on the nature of learners' response, as well as of course their strength of commitment to long-term goals and objectives. Learners who can respond strategically to regulate their motivation are likely to be able to deal better with the tedious drudgery of the L2 learning process. For example, learners may exercise self-discipline to get through the tasks that need to be accomplished, or engage in self-regulatory strategies such as removing distractions from their study environment, or motivate themselves with self-administered incentives to boost their flagging spirits (on L2 learners' self-motivational strategies, see for example Ushioda 1996).

In short, strength of personal commitment to L2 learning, coupled with quality of strategic response to learning setbacks and demands, may help determine the degree of learners' resilience to unmotivating or demotivating experiences during the L2 learning process. Clearly, such determination and strategic resilience are important factors in enabling learners to stay on track and progress along the L2 learning timeline. However, determination and resilience may not be sufficient in themselves when the challenges to motivation lie in *not knowing how* to deal with problems and barriers in learning or using the L2, such as the struggle to understand a text or communicate an idea effectively.

Such problems and difficulties are likely to increase as learners advance beyond the early basic stages of studying a new language when simple cognitive learning strategies (e.g. memorisation, repetition, rehearsal) may work well. As language proficiency develops, the cognitive and linguistic demands of L2 learning and use increase exponentially in difficulty and complexity, requiring higher level (i.e. metacognitive) coordination of various learning strategies, language skills and resources. At the same time, learners' sense of progress and skill development may become much slower and less transparent, compared with the initial phase of moving from zero competence to learning basic words and phrases and developing simple communication skills. Motivation is thus likely to be increasingly challenged when learning requires not simply more time and effort but also more complex thinking skills, while the actual learning and linguistic gains seem less tangible. Under these circumstances, it is perhaps hardly surprising that common experience and research point to a characteristic decline in levels of motivation in post-beginner stages of L2 learning (e.g. Williams, Burden & Lanvers 2002).

To deal successfully with these challenges to motivation, it is clear that learners need to develop their metacognitive capacity to think through the learning or linguistic difficulties they face and marshal the necessary strategies, skills and resources to address them. In other words, they need to be able to combine their motivation to learn with the necessary metacognitive know-how – or to adopt a catchphrase from the literature on self-regulated learning, they need to have both "will and skill" (McCombs & Marzano 1990). In this respect, we have already identified some interactions between "will and skill" in relation to the setting of short-term goals or "proximal self-motivators" (Bandura & Schunk 1981:595), and its interactions with the development of metacognitive awareness through self-evaluation of abilities and needs, and the exercise of metacognitive skills of planning and regulating learning. In the next part of this chapter I will explore in more detail the interface between motivation and metacognition.

Motivation, autonomy and metacognition: Analysing the interface

The interface between L2 motivation and metacognition has attracted some theoretical attention over the years, particularly among researchers interested in examining relationships between students' motivation and their use of language learning strategies. On the whole, however, this line of research has tended to adopt a quantitative analysis of associations between range or frequency of strategy use and degree or type of motivation (e.g. MacIntyre & Noels 1996; Schmidt, Boraie & Kassagby 1996; Schmidt & Watanabe 2001; Vandergrift 2005). While such studies can usefully uncover general patterns in motivation and strategy use, this kind of research inquiry offers a limited analysis of how motivation may interact with metacognition in the L2 learning process, since it can shed little light on how motivation shapes the development of metacognitive thinking processes, or on what teachers can do to help learners in this regard.

To analyse the interface between motivation and metacognition, I will begin by discussing two notions of autonomy, building on a useful conceptual distinction succinctly highlighted by Lamb (2007). In my earlier discussion of proximal self-motivators, I made the point that the process of setting and working towards optimal challenges not only promotes the development of metacognitive awareness and skills but can also cultivate feelings of competence and autonomy, thereby nurturing intrinsic motivation. This is because perceived competence and autonomy are theorised to be fundamental "nutriments" (Ryan & Deci 2002:7) or psychological needs underpinning the healthy growth and internalisation of motivation, particularly intrinsic motivation to engage in a skill-based activity where enjoyment and satisfaction derive from feeling effective and in control. Autonomy here is the sense that we are exercising personal control and agency in what we do, so that our actions and behaviours are freely chosen and *self*-determined rather than controlled by others – hence the motivational theory of self-determination (Ryan & Deci 2002) in which this concept of autonomy is grounded.

Yet, this psychological sense of autonomy shaping self-determined motivation and action does not necessarily lead to effective forms of learning. For example, learners might be freely and autonomously engaged in off-task behaviours during a language practice activity when unmonitored by the teacher. Or a learner may spend a great deal of time autonomously doing L2 activities she enjoys but pay scant attention to the less enjoyable aspects of learning or language use she needs to work on. In short, autonomy in the sense of personal agency may underpin self-determined forms of motivation, but this may not necessarily be the motivation needed to engage with the increasing cognitive and linguistic challenges of learning.

However, as Lamb (2007) points out, there is also another concept of autonomy in the sense of taking responsibility for, managing and regulating one's learning – or what is more appropriately called *learner autonomy*, or even more specifically, as Little (2007) emphasises, *language learner autonomy*. Autonomy in this sense implies both a willingness to take charge of one's language learning and a capacity for "detachment, critical reflection, decision-making, and independent action" (Little 1991:4). This capacity entails applying metacognitive skills and strategic thinking processes to overcome problems and difficulties in language learning and use, and to manage and regulate one's learning.

In other words, this concept of learner autonomy integrates what Littlewood (1996) describes as "willingness and (metacognitive) ability", akin to the earlier cited notion of "will and skill" deriving from the literature on self-regulated learning. More specifically, the exercise of this metacognitive ability or skill presupposes willingness or motivation to apply and control higher order thinking processes, address problems in one's learning, and regulate one's learning process. Autonomy in this sense of exercising self-regulation and metacognition clearly depends on the motivation to do so since, as Bronson (2000:55) notes, "self-directed learning, problem solving, and action can occur only when the ability to control thinking or behaviour is accompanied by the wish to do so".

Taking both concepts of autonomy into consideration then, we can argue that autonomy in the psychological sense of personal agency underpins self-determined forms of motivation, while autonomy in the metacognitive sense of self-regulated learning is underpinned by personal motivation or willingness. In other words, in order to develop and apply metacognitive know-how, learners need to feel motivated to do so, and to be motivated they need to experience a sense of personal agency in this process. However, as I hinted earlier, this psychological sense of agency shaping self-determined motivation needs to be channelled in quite specific ways if it is to lead to willing engagement with the cognitive and linguistic challenges of learning, rather than to indulgence in its more pleasurable aspects or in off-task behaviours. In this regard, it would seem that a critical issue is whether learners come to develop awareness of their agency not only for their chosen actions and behaviours but also for constructing and managing the thinking processes that shape their motivation to act and behave in certain ways. Here I am drawing on arguments I have previously summarised elsewhere (Ushioda 2003, 2007), deriving from the work of McCombs (1994) on motivation and self-regulated learning.

McCombs suggests that an essential precondition for the exercise of will and skill is learners' awareness of their own agency in constructing the thoughts, beliefs, goals, attributions and expectations that shape their motivation. Unless learners understand their own cognitive agency in this regard, they cannot realise their potential to exercise control over their thinking and thus control over their motivation and learning. As she argues:

> How aware individuals are that they have voluntary control over their thinking, including being able to step outside the boundaries of their own constructed thoughts, is what fundamentally fuels or motivates self-regulated behaviors.
>
> (McCombs 1994: 49–50)

Integrating will and skill to regulate motivation and learning depends on this higher order metacognitive self:

> who steps outside the boundaries of thoughts or beliefs and exercises control at a higher level of awareness, perspective taking, and choosing to redirect the thinking processes in healthier ways.   (McCombs 1994: 57)

By the same token, learners who fail to recognise the "self-as-agent" in controlling cognition and motivation and who are unable to step outside the boundaries of their thoughts may become trapped in negative patterns of thinking, motivation and behaviour. These negative patterns may lead to, for example, persistent teacher dependency, task avoidance or defeatist attitudes in the face of learning problems and challenges.

In short, as Bruner (1996: 49) has commented, once learners come to realise that they act not directly "on the world" but on beliefs they hold about the world, they can begin to "think about their thinking" and so take control of their learning. In the next part of my chapter I will examine the pedagogical implications of this analysis.

Developing motivation and metacognitive know-how: The role of dialogue

As I have discussed elsewhere (e.g. Ushioda 2003, 2007, 2010), from a pedagogical point of view, the key to helping learners step outside negative patterns of thinking and take control of their learning may lie in problem-focused dialogue or talk. This is because the process of talking and externalising thought can help to make explicit the underlying cognitions that shape motivation and learning, and turn these cognitions into objects for analysis so that they can be manipulated and re-structured in various ways, thereby leading to metacognition. This argument is of course strongly influenced by Vygotskian sociocultural theory, which emphasises the role of talk or social interaction in mediating learning, and which has become increasingly influential in the analysis of L2 learning and teaching (see for exam-ple the collection of studies in Lantolf & Poehner 2008). Drawing on sociocul-tural theory, let us examine in more detail how teacher-guided social-interactive processes can mediate learners' motivation and metacognitive abilities to engage constructively with problems in their learning.

Within the framework of sociocultural theory, the goal of all learning is what Vygotsky (1978: 86) refers to as "independent problem solving". This goal is achieved through the social-interactive process of joint problem solving with oth-ers such as parents, teachers or more capable peers. For example, the young child learns how to solve jigsaw puzzles on her own through the social experience of doing jigsaw puzzles together with parents or older brothers and sisters. Accord-ing to sociocultural theory, language plays a crucial role in this gradual transition from joint problem solving to independent problem solving or self-regulation, where self-regulation implies strategic (i.e. metacognitive) control of the thinking processes needed to solve the problem. A central principle of the theory is that the interior language of thought developed by the child (or learner) to achieve this metacognitive control is internalised from the social-interactive discourse of joint problem solving with more capable others, during which various strategies and solutions are discussed and talked through. By actively participating in the *social speech* (Vygotsky 1986) of problem-focused interaction, the child (or learn-er) gradually internalises these vocalised strategic processes as the *inner speech* of metacognition, which may also occasionally surface as audible *private speech* – i.e. talking aloud to oneself to regulate one's thinking and concentration during a complex task.

However, this process of internalising strategic control and progressing to independent problem solving does not happen automatically. To facilitate and *motivate* the process of internalisation, particularly in formal learning settings, the problem-focused interactions need to be carefully shaped and structured by the teacher so that they provide the necessary *scaffolding* (Wood, Bruner & Ross

1976). This is more than just a question of providing support to learners, since the purpose of scaffolding is not simply to help learners solve a problem but rather to develop their willingness and metacognitive ability to think through the problem for themselves. In this way, going back to McCombs' (1994) arguments about cognitive agency, learners may be helped to step outside the boundaries of negative or defeatist patterns of thinking and take control of their learning.

One approach to scaffolding thinking may be for the teacher to model specific self-verbalisations that highlight and structure the strategic processes needed when approaching a problem or task. For example, the teacher might think aloud with the learner in the following way:

(1) a. Okay, the first thing we need to ask ourselves is …
     b. Next, we need to work out a plan …
     c. Then we can focus on …

The idea here is that learners may pick up and reproduce these self-verbalisations in their private speech to regulate their thinking when working through a problem. However, as Diaz, Neal and Amaya-Williams (1990) report in a review of studies aiming to train private speech in this manner, research findings are rather inconclusive. In particular, it is not clear whether this approach to modelling self-verbalisations will lead learners spontaneously (i.e. motivate them) to transfer and build on these metacognitive processes when faced with other problems and tasks. In other words, the *will* dimension of *will and skill* may not necessarily be developed through this modelling approach.

Rather, research evidence (e.g. Diaz, Neal, & Amaya-Williams 1990; Hadwin, Wozney, & Pontin 2005) suggests that a pivotal element in the problem-focused dialogue between teacher and learner is the explicit transfer of the regulatory role to the learner during this dialogue. Instead of simply modelling self-verbalisations or guiding with instructions and directives, the teacher needs to engage in what Diaz, Neal, and Amaya-Williams (1990: 151) describe as "relinquishing strategies" which encourage and motivate learners to do the thinking and troubleshooting rather than just sitting back and listening.

Relinquishing strategies include *conceptual questions* which "cannot be answered by simply attending to the immediate perceptual field but rather require a mental representation of the rules or goals of the task" (Diaz, Neal, & Amaya-Williams 1990: 148). In helping learners to address a problem in reading comprehension or vocabulary understanding, for example, the teacher might pose conceptual questions such as the following:

(2) a. What do you understand to be the key message in this paragraph?
     b. How do you think these two words differ in meaning?

Similarly, in the context of difficulties relating to productive skills in speaking or writing, one could imagine conceptual questions such as the following:

(3) a. Can you think how you might express this message in a more polite way?
     b. What could you say or do here to hold the floor and give yourself more planning time for formulating what you want to say?

Examples of conceptual questions focusing on sentence grammar or text grammar might be:

(4) a. How would you go about correcting this sentence?
     b. Do you think it would be better to change the verb tense here? Why?
     c. What would be a good way of combining these short sentences into a single sentence to make the text more concise?

Conceptual questions such as those illustrated above function as relinquishing strategies because they hand over the initiative to learners themselves, encouraging them to think aloud about the problem and talk things through. Conceptual questions are thus preferable to simple perceptual questions where the answer is obvious from the context (e.g. "Is this word singular or plural?" "What verb tense is this?"), or directive questions (e.g. "Can you write that down?" "Can you say that again?").

Relinquishing strategies also include *verbal encouragement and praise* (e.g. "Good, you're nearly there!"), and most importantly the *direct relinquishing of the regulatory role* to the learner whereby control is handed over to the learner for the whole task or large parts of it. For example:

(5) a. So now go ahead and talk me through the next bit.
     b. So you've corrected two paragraphs with a little help – now tackle the last paragraph on your own and I'll just listen and watch.

In short, relinquishing strategies stimulate learners to undertake much of the thinking and do much of the talking in the problem-focused dialogue, and eventually to take full regulatory control as the teacher fades the interactive support provided. In this way, the dialogue is shaped to motivate and enhance learners' own sense of cognitive agency (cf. McCombs 1994, cited earlier) in constructing and regulating their thinking so that they become more confident, willing and able to engage with the cognitive and linguistic challenges of learning.

Conclusion and research agenda

To summarise my arguments in this chapter, I have suggested that personally val-ued long-term goals and objectives are important in providing an underlying mo-tivational rationale for L2 learning, while interim short-term targets are import-ant in regulating and sustaining motivation by marking incremental progression along the L2 learning timeline. By being involved in setting their own short-term goals or proximal self-motivators, learners engage in processes of self-evalua-tion, planning and monitoring and thus develop their metacognitive awareness and metacognitive skills through which they come to manage and regulate their learning. Setting and working towards optimal challenges will also cultivate feel-ings of competence and autonomy (in the sense of personal agency) in the learn-ing process, thereby fostering intrinsic motivation.

However, as the cognitive and linguistic challenges of L2 learning increase in difficulty and complexity, these goal-focused motivational processes are unlikely to be enough to sustain engagement in learning. While a degree of resilience, self-discipline and self-motivation may be effective in dealing with some learning setbacks and demands, these inner resources may prove insufficient when the challenges to motivation lie in not knowing how to address particular cognitive and linguistic difficulties – that is, in lack of metacognitive know-how. As I have suggested, it is at this micro-level of motivational and metacognitive engagement where significant challenges to sustaining L2 learning lie.

In the rest of my chapter, I examined the nature of this interface between motivation and metacognition or *will and skill*. Drawing on two concepts of au-tonomy, I discussed how the exercise of learner autonomy (in the sense of meta-cognition and self-regulation) is dependent on the motivation or willingness to do so, and how this motivation is based in learners' sense of personal agency and control (i.e. autonomy) in the learning process. I then unpacked what this concept of agency means in terms of learners' awareness of their own role in constructing the thinking processes that shape their motivation to act and behave in certain ways, and thus by extension, in strategically managing and regulating these think-ing processes to productive ends. Finally, I explored how the teacher can help me-diate the development of these strategic thinking skills through problem-focused dialogue with learners. In this dialogue, her role is not so much to show them how to think but to motivate them to do the thinking for themselves.

Within the field of L2 learning research, this intersection between motiva-tional and metacognitive engagement remains a largely under-theorised and under-explored area (though for a different and interesting perspective focusing on the interface between the imaginative dimension of motivation and metacognition, see Murray 2011). As I indicated earlier, much of the research on motivation in L2 learning to date has focused on the broader macro perspectives of long-term future goals and objectives or interim short-term targets along the L2 learning timeline. In recent years, there is also growing interest in the macro perspective of the past experiential dimension of L2 motivation, as reflected in typically qualitative research on language learning histories, life stories and trajectories (e.g. Chik & Breidbach 2011; Shoaib & Dörnyei 2005). Comparatively speaking, however, there is far less research that narrows the focus on the more micro-level of learners' ongoing motivational experience during the day-to-day process of L2 learning, or in relation to a specific task, learning problem or critical event. There is clearly scope for developing a research programme that focuses the lens more sharply on how motivational and metacognitive processes develop through dialogic interactions around particular cognitive or linguistic problems in the L2 learning process. In this regard, teachers are well placed to conduct this kind of research on their own practice and, through forms of exploratory practice (Allwright 2003; Allwright & Hanks 2009), to work with their students to develop their will and skill to engage with cognitive and linguistic challenges in their learning.

References

Allwright, D. (2003). Exploratory Practice: Rethinking practitioner research in language teaching. *Language Teaching Research*, 7(2), 113–141. DOI: 10.1191/1362168803lr118oa

Allwright, D., & Hanks, J. (2009). *The developing language learner: An introduction to Exploratory Practice*. Basingstoke: Palgrave Macmillan.

Bandura, A., & Schunk, D. (1981). Cultivating competence, self-efficacy, and intrinsic interest through proximal self-motivation. *Journal of Personality and Social Psychology*, 41, 586–598. DOI: 10.1037/0022-3514.41.3.586

Block, D. (2007). The rise of identity in SLA research, post Firth and Wagner (1997). *The Modern Language Journal*, 91(5), 863–876. DOI: 10.1111/j.1540-4781.2007.00674.x

Bronson, M. (2000). *Self-regulation in early childhood: Nature and nurture*. New York, NY: Guilford Press.

Bruner, J. (1996). *The culture of education*. Cambridge, MA: Harvard University Press.

Chik, A., & Breidbach, S. (2011). Identity, motivation and autonomy: A tale of two cities. In G. Murray, X. Gao, & T. Lamb (Eds.), *Identity, motivation and autonomy in language learning* (pp. 145–159). Bristol: Multilingual Matters.

Coleman, J.A. (2009). Why the British do not learn languages: Myths and motivation in the United Kingdom. *Language Learning Journal*, 37, 111–127. DOI: 10.1080/09571730902749003

Deci, E.L., & Ryan, R.M. (1985). *Intrinsic motivation and self-determination in human behavior*. New York, NY: Plenum Press. DOI: 10.1007/978-1-4899-2271-7

Diaz, R.M., Neal, C.J., & Amaya-Williams, M. (1990). The social origins of self-regulation. In L.C. Moll (Ed.), *Vygotsky and education: Instructional implications and applications of sociohistorical psychology* (pp. 127–154). Cambridge: Cambridge University Press. DOI: 10.1017/CBO9781139173674.007

Dörnyei, Z. (2005). *The psychology of the language learner: Individual differences in second language acquisition.* Mahwah, NJ: Lawrence Erlbaum Associates.

Dörnyei, Z. (2009). The L2 Motivational Self System. In Z. Dörnyei, & E. Ushioda (Eds.), *Motivation, language identity and the L2 self* (pp. 9–42). Bristol: Multilingual Matters.

Dörnyei, Z., & Kubanyiova, M. (2014). *Motivating learners, motivating teachers: Building vision in the language classroom.* Cambridge: Cambridge University Press.

Dörnyei, Z., & Ushioda, E. (Eds.). (2009). *Motivation, language identity and the L2 self.* Bristol: Multilingual Matters.

Gardner, R.C. (1985). *Social psychology and second language learning: The role of attitudes and motivation.* London: Edward Arnold.

Gardner, R.C., & Lambert, W.E. (1972). *Attitudes and motivation in second language learning.* Rowley, MA: Newbury House.

Hadwin, A.F., Wozney, L., & Pontin, O. (2005). Scaffolding the appropriation of self-regulatory activity: A socio-cultural analysis of changes in teacher–student discourse about a graduate research portfolio. *Instructional Science*, 33(5–6), 413–450. DOI: 10.1007/s11251-005-1274-7

Kaplan, A., & Flum, H. (2009). Motivation and identity: The relations of action and development in educational contexts. An introduction to the special issue. *Educational Psychologist*, 44(2), 73–77. DOI: 10.1080/00461520902832418

Kraemer, R. (1993). Social psychological factors related to the study of Arabic among Israeli high school students. *Studies in Second Language Acquisition*, 15, 83–105. DOI: 10.1017/S0272263100011670

Lamb, M. (2007). Which came first – the worm or the cocoon? *Independence*, 49, 28–9.

Lantolf, J.P., & Poehner, M.E. (Eds.). (2008). *Sociocultural theory and the teaching of second languages.* London: Equinox.

Little, D. (1991). *Learner autonomy, 1: Definitions, issues and problems.* Dublin: Authentik.

Little, D. (2007). Language learner autonomy: Some fundamental considerations revisited. *Innovation in Language Learning and Teaching*, 1(1), 14–29. DOI: 10.2167/illt040.0

Littlewood, W.T. (1996). Autonomy: An anatomy and a framework. *System*, 24(4), 427–435. DOI: 10.1016/S0346-251X(96)00039-5

MacIntyre, P., & Noels, K.A. (1996). Using social-psychological variables to predict the use of language learning strategies. *Foreign Language Annals*, 29, 373–386. DOI: 10.1111/j.1944-9720.1996.tb01249.x

Markus, H., & Nurius, P. (1986). Possible selves. *American Psychologist*, 41, 954–969. DOI: 10.1037/0003-066X.41.9.954

McCombs, B. (1994). Strategies for assessing and enhancing motivation: Keys to promoting self-regulated learning and performance. In H.F. O'Neil, & M. Drillings (Eds.), *Motivation: Theory and research* (pp. 49–69). Hillsdale, NJ: Lawrence Erlbaum Associates.

McCombs, B., & Marzano, R.J. (1990). Putting the self in self-regulated learning: The self as agent in integrating will and skill. *Educational Psychologist*, 25(1), 51–69. DOI: 10.1207/s15326985ep2501_5

Murray, G. (2011). Imagination, metacognition and the L2 self in a self-access learning environment. In G. Murray, X. Gao, & T. Lamb (Eds.), *Identity, motivation and autonomy in language learning* (pp. 75–90). Bristol: Multilingual Matters.

Murray, G., Gao, X., & Lamb, T. (Eds.). (2011). *Identity, motivation and autonomy in language learning*. Bristol: Multilingual Matters.

Norton, B., & Toohey, K. (2011). Identity, language learning, and social change. *Language Teaching*, 44, 412–446. DOI: 10.1017/S0261444811000309

Ryan, R.M., & Deci, E.L. (2002). Overview of self-determination theory: An organismic dialectical perspective. In E.L. Deci, & R.M. Ryan (Eds.), *Handbook of self-determination research* (pp. 3–33). Rochester, NY: University of Rochester Press.

Schmidt, R., Boraie, D., & Kassagby, O. (1996). Foreign language motivation: Internal structure and external connections. In R. Oxford (Ed.), *Language learning motivation: Pathways to the new century* (pp. 9–70). Honolulu, HI: University of Hawaii Press.

Schmidt, R., & Watanabe, Y. (2001). Motivation, strategy use, and pedagogical preferences in foreign language learning. In Z. Dörnyei & R. Schmidt (Eds.), *Motivation and second language acquisition* (pp. 313–359). Honolulu, HI: University of Hawaii Press.

Shoaib, A., & Dörnyei, Z. (2005). Affect in lifelong learning: Exploring L2 motivation as a dynamic process. In P. Benson & D. Nunan (Eds.), *Learners' stories: Difference and diversity in language learning* (pp. 22–41). Cambridge: Cambridge University Press.

Spolsky, B. (1989). *Conditions for second language learning*. Oxford: Oxford University Press.

Ushioda, E. (1996). *Learner autonomy, 5: The role of motivation*. Dublin: Authentik.

Ushioda, E. (1998). Effective motivational thinking: A cognitive theoretical approach to the study of language learning motivation. In E.A. Soler & V.C. Espurz (Eds.), *Current issues in English language methodology* (pp. 77–89). Castelló de la Plana: Universitat Jaume I.

Ushioda, E. (2001). Language learning at university: Exploring the role of motivational thinking. In Z. Dörnyei & R. Schmidt (Eds.), *Motivation and second language acquisition* (pp. 93–125). Honolulu, HI: University of Hawaii Press.

Ushioda, E. (2003). Motivation as a socially mediated process. In D. Little, J. Ridley, & E. Ushioda (Eds.), *Learner autonomy in the foreign language classroom: Teacher, learner, curriculum and assessment* (pp. 90–102). Dublin: Authentik.

Ushioda, E. (2007). Motivation, autonomy and sociocultural theory. In P. Benson (Ed.), *Learner autonomy 8: Teacher and learner perspectives* (pp. 5–24). Dublin: Authentik.

Ushioda, E. (2010). Motivation and SLA: Bridging the gap. *EUROSLA Yearbook*, 10, 5–20. DOI: 10.1075/eurosla.10.03ush

Ushioda, E. (2014). Motivational perspectives on the self in SLA: A developmental view. In S. Mercer & M. Williams (Eds.), *Multiple perspectives on the self in SLA* (pp. 127–141). Bristol: Multilingual Matters.

van Lier, L. (1996). *Interaction in the language curriculum: Awareness, autonomy and authenticity*. Harlow: Longman.

Vandergrift, L. (2005). Relationships among motivation orientations, metacognitive awareness and proficiency in L2 listening. *Applied Linguistics*, 26, 70–89. DOI: 10.1093/applin/amh039

Vygotsky, L.S. (1978). *Mind in society: The development of higher psychological processes*. Cambridge, MA: Harvard University Press.

Vygotsky, L.S. (1986). *Thought and language*. Cambridge, MA: The MIT Press.

Warden, C.A., & Lin, H.J. (2000). Existence of integrative motivation in an Asian EFL setting. *Foreign Language Annals*, 33, 535–547. DOI: 10.1111/j.1944-9720.2000.tb01997.x

Weiner, B. (2007). Motivation from an attribution perspective and the social psychology of perceived competence. In A.J. Elliot & C.S. Dweck (Eds.), *Handbook of competence and motivation* (pp. 73–104). New York, NY: Guilford Press.

Williams, M., Burden, R.L., & Lanvers, U. (2002). 'French is the language of love and stuff': Student perceptions of issues related to motivation in learning a foreign language. *British Educational Research Journal*, 28, 503–528. DOI: 10.1080/0141192022000005805

Wong, M.S., Kristjánsson, C., & Dörnyei, Z. (Eds.). (2013). *Christian faith and English language teaching and learning: Research on the interrelationship of religion and ELT*. New York NY: Routledge.

Wood, D., Bruner, J.S., & Ross, G. (1976). The role of tutoring in problem-solving. *Journal of Child Psychology and Psychiatry*, 17(2), 89–100. DOI: 10.1111/j.1469-7610.1976.tb00381.x

CHAPTER 3

Motivating teachers and learners as researchers

Do Coyle

This chapter explores how when learners as well as teachers are engaged in analysing their own classroom practices, the potential to sustain motivation is enhanced. Using an inclusive approach to creating shared understandings of 'successful' learning (the LOCIT process), learners and teachers research and reflect on their own teaching and learning in practical, co-constructed ways. This approach is built on the premise that classroom conditions are dynamic and that learning has to be 'owned' and understood by learners if progression and challenge are to impact on motivation. The chapter draws on studies in CLIL classrooms, where languages other than English are used as the medium for learning. However, the ideas and evidence presented could also be applied to language learning classrooms.

Keywords: CLIL, dialogic practices, successful learning, strategic engagement, learner-teacher research

Introduction

This chapter explores how an inclusive approach to investigating classroom practices by teachers and learners has the potential to sustain motivation and lead to 'successful' learning. It is built on the premise that classroom conditions are dynamic and that for learning to be 'owned' by learners in terms of progression and challenge in the 'here and now' (McCombs & Marzano 1990), learners and teachers will have to share responsibility for researching and reflecting on their own teaching and learning in practical, co-constructed ways.

The contexts for experimenting this approach are those where language learning and subject learning are integrated, i.e. CLIL – Content and Language Integrated Learning. CLIL is broadly a "developing, flexible concept where thematic or subject content and foreign languages are integrated in some mutually beneficial way to ensure more learners are motivated to learn and use other languages in the future" (Coyle 2013: 23). It should be pointed out, however, that the ideas and evidence expressed throughout this chapter could also be applied to language learning classrooms.

There is growing evidence linking increased learner motivation to CLIL settings. Studies for example by Lasagabaster (2011), Sierra (2011), Dooly and Eastment (2008), Lorenzo, Casal and Moore (2010) and Seikkula-Leino (2007) all report positively on learner motivation in CLIL contexts. However, given the multiple factors involved in any learning contexts such as learner characteristics, teaching styles, composition of the class and pedagogic approaches, there is a need for caution when generalising from these studies. Taking account of the specificities of language experiences in CLIL/language classrooms, the need to provide a basis for developing collaborative tools with teachers and their learners which lead towards a shared understanding of 'what works and why' became increasingly apparent. Whilst these tools were developed during research undertaken in England and Scotland (Coyle 2011a, 2011b), I should emphasise that this approach can be adapted and applied to any classroom context where conditions conducive for successful learning can be nurtured and developed. More recent work tries to gain a deeper understanding of what teachers and learners believe motivates their individual and collective learning in CLIL/language classrooms (Coyle 2013). Given that any learning is non-linear and that motivation is not a constant (see also Ushioda in this volume), then monitoring its effects on different approaches to learning in the confines of the school curriculum is challenging.

Motivation and achievement

Over recent years, two factors which are fundamental to high quality and successful language learning and using in schools have emerged. The first, motivation, is the driver for any learners to engage in the learning process. In the UK context, it is clear that for many learners current language experiences neither sustain interest nor provide the challenges needed to lead to success (Evans & Fisher 2009). The second, learner achievement, is closely related to the first. Measurable achievement in terms of examination entries is in decline with the result that fewer young people are leaving school with appropriate linguistic skills to equip them for the future (The Nuffield Languages Report, Department for Education and Science 2002). Learners are often required to invest heavily in learning languages which provide little immediate reward in terms of content and interesting challenge until the more advanced stages. It is now seven years ago since the Guardian Weekly reported "We have passed the point of no return for languages in secondary schools. Fewer youngsters taking languages also reduce the pool of graduates and potential teachers… schools need to find more imaginative ways of teaching languages" (Guardian Weekly 25.08.2006).

Whilst it is accepted that motivating learners is a key condition for learning in formal education settings, despite its fundamental role in the learning process, there remain differences of opinion about the nature of motivation and the necessary conditions for it to impact learning. It is often stated that teachers can easily recognise motivation, yet it is difficult to define. The term is open to wide interpretation and crosses boundaries of different theoretical fields including the pedagogic, social, cognitive and psychological. Moreover, motivation becomes inextricably linked to achievement often described by a simplistic cause-effect formula such as 'low motivation leads to low achievement' and vice versa. Yet it is clear that linking motivation and achievement is much more complex and dynamic than can be explained through attitudes to work and ensuing test results.

Dörnyei and Otto (1998: 5) define motivation as

> The dynamically changing cumulative arousal in a person that initiates, directs, coordinates, amplifies, terminates and evaluates the cognitive and motor processes whereby initial wishes and desires are selected, prioritised, operationalised and (successfully or unsuccessfully) acted out.

Whilst the above describes the processes of motivation, what is more challenging is to understand the conditions or socio-dynamic influences which will activate those processes and lead to successful language learning for individual learners. Gardner's (1985) early work into integrative motivation, (involving a learner's wish to communicate and integrate within the target language community), and instrumental motivation (where the learner focuses on pragmatic outcomes of language learning such as passing an examination) seems in the current climate of global events and technological advancement to provide only part of the picture.

More recently, theorists have underlined the importance of goal-setting (e.g. Locke & Latham 2002), whilst others emphasise the role of the specific learning context – including the teachers' role, the classroom climate, learning opportunities, materials and the quality of the learning tasks, as well as the relationships between language learners (Ushioda 2013). The impact that the interrelationships of these variables have on language learning confirms the intricate and dynamic nature of motivation.

Ryan and Deci (2002), Vandergrift (2005) and Dörnyei and Ushioda (2011) draw attention to the changing landscape of motivation research which transfers the focus from individual intrinsic and extrinsic drivers to more socially situated contexts. Ushioda (2010) highlights the need to take a *relational* view rather than a linear view of learning. From this perspective, multiple contextual elements such as the classroom, social relations within, activities undertaken, personal goals set and learner-teacher self-reflection, all interact and interrelate with learners who find themselves located in cultural and historical contexts. In other words, as would be expected, social and affective influences are fundamental to and impact on individual motivation and identities. Yet these influences are dynamic and can change over time. Williams and Burden (1997) usefully separate out what triggers initial motivation to learn and the conditions needed to sustain that motivation. Further evidence points to the importance of the pedagogic approaches for language learning which impact on sustaining learner attitudes and motivation (Pae 2008; Bradford 2007). Thus, given the increasing attention to the importance of the classroom context for learner engagement, a priority is to gain a deeper understanding of the 'explanatory power of why learners behave as they do in specific learning situations' (Dörnyei 2002: 138) i.e. what learners find interesting and enjoyable about their language learning in particular contexts. As Dörnyei (2007: 719) usefully states:

> Long-term, sustained learning – such as the acquisition of an L2 – cannot take place unless the educational context provides, in addition to cognitively adequate instructional practice, sufficient *inspiration* and *enjoyment* to build up continuing motivation in the learners. Boring but systematic teaching can be effective in producing, for example, good test results but rarely does it inspire life-long commitment to the subject matter.

During the last twenty years or so, building on earlier work of educationalists such as Gardner, several theories have been used to try to understand motivation better in terms of the learners and their perceived sense of 'self' in the learning process, e.g. goal-related theory very much associated with self-efficacy and self-worth, values-related theory linked to learner investment and self-determination theory relating to learner autonomy and the classroom environment. Here the emphasis is less on what a learner might do in the future but rather on who the learners will become in the future. It is likely that all of these impact in different ways on different learners at different times during their (language) learning experiences. Noels et al. (2000: 75) suggest that to foster sustained learning "it may not be sufficient to convince students that language learning is interesting and enjoyable; they may need to be persuaded that it is also personally important for them."

An increasingly strong case begins to emerge that in language learning/using contexts, due to their very nature, motivation and learner identity are closely connected. According to Norton (2000: 4), identity is how an individual "understands his or her relationship to the world, how that relationship is constructed across time and space, and how the person understands possibilities for the future".

Dörnyei and Ushioda's more recent work (2011) extends the notion of self and identities into an interpretative foreign language (L2) motivation model. Three components are identified: the 'ideal' L2 self (which involves more integrative and instrumental motives), the 'ought-to' L2 self (which focuses on more extrinsic instrumental motives) and the L2 learning experience (which focuses on the situatedness of the learning context including the classroom, the teacher, activities and perceived successes). This approach constitutes a *complex dynamic systems* perspective combining motivation, cognition and affect. It suggests that the way individuals feel about themselves and others, the ways in which they appraise their achievements, set within specific L2 learning contexts, will have a significant impact on their learning. The relation between what students want to become and what students actually become may be mediated by what students feel they are able to become (Pizzolato 2006: 59).

Therefore, from a review of the literature and more recent studies in motivation in modern language settings, two key aspects of motivation emerge, i.e. affect or self and the learning environment. These two principles are at the core of my own investigations and contribute significantly to the underlying theoretical principles. They highlight interactions between classroom learning environments, learner experiences of using language both in the present and future, the nurturing of positive and motivational challenges and engagement with evaluation of those experiences – all of which encourage successful learning. Crucially, a focus on the 'here and now' in the daily enactments of (language) learning are pivotal to past experiences and future goals so that the continual interaction and flow between learner engagement and purposeful learning significantly contribute to motivating an individual (Ushioda 2010).

There is tension, however, between what individuals achieve, what learners gain from these experiences and what is measured – all of which impact on learner engagement and sense of self (Coyle 2011a). The usual practice in schools is for learner achievements to be 'evidenced' through measuring attainment such as test scores. However, achievement can also be conceptualised from an alternative perspective which is not embedded in 'performance' discourse, i.e. where it captures and understands 'value-added' in terms of cognitive, social and personal gains of individuals within the school context (Stelfox 2008). To understand 'pupil gains' involves gathering evidence of what the main players – classroom learners and their teachers – regard as successful learning rooted in the classroom context, alongside pedagogic interactions, learner engagement, and deepening learner awareness of self. This kind of evidence is what Simons et al. (2003) define as 'practice-based evidence', seen from teacher and learner perspectives in terms of 'what works' (see also Doiz, Lasagabaster, & Sierra in this volume) and predicated on a shared understanding of practices in CLIL/language classrooms. It is in contrast to evidence-based practice which has a pre-determined and often externally imposed set of criteria for evaluating achievement. Situated in the qualitative inquiry paradigm, practice-based evidence captures the experiences and practices of learners and teachers in their own classrooms.

'Successful learning'

Taking account of different stages involved in constructing a 'motivational climate' over time is particularly relevant for sustaining motivation and connects to analysing and owning learning in the 'here and now'. Several conceptual models have been developed: Ushioda's model (2001) brings together the learning process, external pressures and learner dispositions; Noel's model (2001) similarly exposes inherent intrinsic L2 experiences with extrinsic and integrative positioning of learners' self; and Dörnyei's (2000) Motivational Process Model led to identifying four different stages of motivational teaching practice: (1) creating the basic motivational conditions, (2) generating initial motivation, (3) maintaining and protecting motivation, and (4) encouraging 'positive introspection' (Guilloteaux & Dörnyei 2008: 59). The challenges posed by the last two stages (i.e. sustaining motivation and encouraging positive introspection), have been drivers in working towards a deeper understanding of the necessary conditions and practices which impact on extending high quality learning at the micro level of the classroom itself. In particular, I focus on the conditions which bring together both of these into an interconnected space which nurtures and develops 'successful learning'. Note: 'successful learning' in this context denotes a consensual definition of learner gains agreed between learners and teachers in different classrooms. It is owned by those individuals. However, in general terms, contributory factors constantly emerge from research (Coyle 2011a) which identify teacher-learner consensus of 'successful' learning across a range of contexts. The two most prominent can be seen as interconnected strands: learner strategic engagement and classroom dialogue.

Strategic engagement

Social constructivist approaches to classroom learning emphasise the role of social interaction for mediating learning which foreground, for example, developing learner autonomy through co-constructed learning, collaborative problem solving and opportunities for analysing one's own learning. Learner autonomy as a construct is of course open to wide interpretation where active engagement in cognitive and meta-cognitive aspects of learning is inextricably linked with learn-ers' own sense of self-determination. Ushioda (2013:6) usefully summarises this:

> from a psychological perspective as personal agency which focuses on self-de-termined elements of motivation, and from a meta-cognitive perspective where autonomy promotes self-regulated learning, dependent on willingness to learn.

Much has been written over the years about the role of learner autonomy and self-regulation in effective language learning and using (Lewis & Vialleton 2011). Ryan and Deci (2002), for example, focus on the importance of self-agency un-derpinned by learning conditions which encourage self-regulation and learner autonomy. Constructs such as self-agency, self-regulation, self-determination and learner autonomy, each with their own discourses, underline the importance of learning environments which encourage an evolving independence for the language learner, yet by definition cannot prescribe how this will be achieved. Ushioda's work (2003, 2007, 2013) emphasises the need for interactions between motivation and meta-cognition (i.e. strategies for successful learning) which can lead learners towards developing a sense of competence and autonomy. Oxford's seminal work (2000) emphasises the development of a range of comprehensive learner strategies to support learner autonomy.

There is some disagreement with regards to theoretical definitions and the relationship between learner strategies and self-regulation (Dörnyei 2009; Cohen 2011; Oxford 2000). Cohen (2013:67) suggests a compromise position "to include self-regulation as perhaps an umbrella notion when referring to language learners and to also include the strategies that they use for both learning and performing in an L2". In the context of this chapter with its emphasis on sustaining motivation, Ushioda (2013) points out that determination and strategic resilience may not be enough if learners do not know how to deal with experienced problems and bar-riers. In a similar vein, Bardovi-Harlig and Springer (2010) raise concerns as to how learners can be strategic in their efforts to guard against attrition of L2 attain-ment. Cohen (2013) contends that viewing strategies in isolation is not as benefi-cial to learners and teachers as viewing them at the intersection of learning style preferences, motivation, and specific second-language (L2) activities. Yet, whilst different researchers interpret their work from a range of sometimes conflicting and sometimes consensual perspectives, what is shared is the pre-eminence of the learner and the necessity to conceptualise learning through the learner's lens.

I therefore find the concept of *strategic engagement* to support learner in-vestment more helpful. It includes raising awareness of learner strategies and developing self-regulation to enable learners to cope with the less motivating as-pects of sustained language learning. In this sense, the 'will and skill' (Bandura

& Schunk 1981) of self-regulated learning referred to by Ushioda (2013) focuses on the immediacy of short-term goal setting to support self-evaluation of abilities and needs based on cognitive, meta-cognitive and affective demands. However, strategic engagement is dependent on shared ownership of the learning. For learners to invest in learning it has to be rooted in their own sense of self and the environment in which they 'opt into' – where learners can think for themselves, reflect collaboratively on learning events and "dialogue is shaped to motivate and enhance learners' own sense of cognitive agency in constructing and regulating their thinking so that they become more confident, willing and able to engage with the cognitive and linguistic challenges of learning" (Ushioda 2013: 16).

The implications for creating classrooms conditions that support 'ownership' suggest that co-constructed dialogic reflection, analysis and forward planning are prerequisites. In this way, objectification of the learning process and resilience through reflection will support individuals to make sense of their own learning and develop their own increasing awareness of self-regulation and the demands and benefits of being an independent learner (Coyle 2011b). This stance will be further developed through considering the role of dialogic practices in language-medium classrooms.

Dialogic practices

Much of the research which prioritises discourse or talk as a fundamental learning tool has been carried out in L1 classrooms (e.g. Mercer 2000; Wells 1999a, 1999b). For classroom talk to make a meaningful contribution to learning it must move beyond acting out 'cognitively restricting rituals' (Alexander 2006:9). Wegerif (2006) suggests that dialogic learning involves thinking, being creative and learning to learn, all of which are also fundamental to L2-medium contexts. Drawing on Wegerif and Mercer's (1997) concept of a dialogical model of reasoning, exploratory talk allows different voices to inter-animate each other in a way which not only constructs shared knowledge but also critically assesses the quality of that knowledge. Creating opportunities for 'respectful discussions' (Giugni 2006:106) involving teachers and learners have shown that learners can articulate their own ways of knowing, and their own knowledge (Lewis & Porter 2007) as well as how they learn and under which conditions. McIntyre, Pedder and Ruddock (2005) investigated how learners could contribute to understanding their learning through a constructive focus on what supports learning. When consulted, pupils reported the following as supporting their learning (see also Doiz, Lasagabaster, & Sierra in this volume): interactive teaching for learning (teacher explanations, active involvement and a variety of approaches); contextualising learning (connecting new ideas with existing ones, tasks into closer alignment with their worlds); fostering a stronger sense of agency and ownership (autonomy and trust to make their own learning decisions and for teachers to use their time more efficiently); and a social context amenable to collaborative learning. Participation in dialogues requires learners to become more meta-cognitively aware of how they go about their own learning and thinking (Mercer & Littleton 2007: 60).

In CLIL/language classrooms there is of course another dimension: predominantly the learning does not take place in the learners' first language. It will depend on individual classrooms as to the appropriateness of the language used to enable learners to carry out 'respectful discussions'. Whilst learning conversations may be built into the language development programme, it may be that where learners share a first language, an in-depth opportunity for reflection and analysis beyond the current competence levels of the learners, provides 'time-out' to secure learner engagement. Evidence suggests that objectifying learning through respectful discussions encourages both learners and teachers to participate in a shared analysis of learning which otherwise would not take place (Coyle 2013). This will be further developed in the next section.

In essence, teachers who listen to and respond to learners' perspectives on teaching and learning as an essential aspect of their teaching practice remain open to change (Todd 2007), and can use the information obtained from 'respectful discussions' (Giugni 2006: 106) with young people to lay the foundations for shared ownership of classroom learning. Teacher preparedness to encourage dialogue with learners is fundamental to strategic engagement.

Collaborative inquiry: Learners and teachers as researchers

To summarise the arguments presented thus far leads to conceptualising a model for investigating motivation. The classroom environment, the extent to which learners are willing to engage in learning which is constructed in and grown from that environment along with the impact this has on the learner's own sense of self as a learner and competent language user, are all significant contributors to learner motivation. The ITALIC process model (Coyle 2011a) provides a conceptual tool for investigating motivation in CLIL/language learning settings.

The conceptual tool is based on the fundamental principle of collaborative inquiry where learners and teachers are researchers (Chevalier & Buckles 2013). Whilst much has been written about teachers as researchers, less work has been carried out where learners must also be involved.

A process model ~ Investigating motivation in CLIL settings

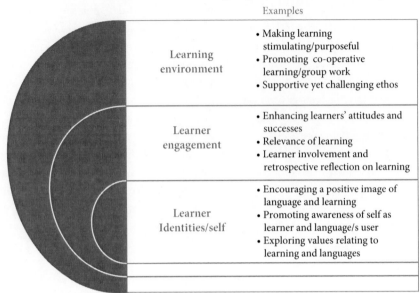

Figure 1. A process model (source: Coyle 2011a)

Carr (1995: 103) describes practitioner research as:

> A reflexive and dialectical process of critique: a process which does not eschew theory in order to improve practice, but which preserves the dialectical unity of theory and practice by understanding them as mutually constitutive elements in a dynamic developing and integrated whole.

It is not the use of *ad hoc* reflection which solves local problems. Rather, teachers have to 'buy-into' the inquiry processes and commit to risk-taking. They have to develop understanding and research skills which enable them to engage in *objectifying* the teaching and learning process and analyse its effectiveness with the learners in their particular context (Cochran-Smith & Lytle 1993). *Objectification* means that individuals can speak about their own learning and the learning of others in ways which are non-threatening, respectful and use a shared dynamic discourse. Framing practitioner research through an articulation of 'theories of practice' may provide a useful reflective tool.

> Since all teachers have a theory of teaching, at least an implicit one, the first task of curricular renewal is to invite interested teachers to examine their own theory, making it explicit […] and determine options for pedagogical action on its basis.
>
> (Van Lier 1996: 30)

According to van Lier if professional learning is to lead to understanding what motivates and engages learners, then teachers need to be encouraged and supported in making their implicit theories and beliefs into explicit ones in order for them to determine "options for pedagogical action on its basis" (1996: 28). He goes on to say that there is a need for teachers to engage in discourse with each other and with their learners in order to throw light on understanding classroom learning and interaction which:

> [...] allows us to construct a theory of teaching and curriculum which is firmly based on evidence from classrooms. The theory of learning thus will consist of learning, a theory of pedagogical interaction and a theory of instruction.
>
> (Van Lier 1996: 37)

Moreover, constructing these theories of practice involves a shift in mindset from teacher as 'provider' of knowledge to a learning environment where together teachers and their learners engage in respectful discussions and dialogue over time:

> Face to face connectedness, co-construction of meaning and emotional sharing with unpredictability of sequence and outcomes and potentially equal distribution of rights and duties, of talk as both parties initiate topics, change the direction of the lesson and relate learning to their lives.   (Van Lier 1996: 38)

Learner 'voice' in this collaborative process is fundamental to the concept of the co-construction of successful learning. In order to create interactive and successful classrooms, teachers and their learners need to engage in discourses which reflect on and build on those processes which promote deep learning – what Wegerif (2011) describes as *opening dialogic spaces* both within classrooms and between them.

The LOCIT process

Given the need to locate practitioner research in an inclusive ethos of sharing and analysing practice, of involving learners in discussing how learning happens and making explicit theories of practice based on practice-based evidence, an inclusive approach to practitioner and learner research has been developed over the last six years (Coyle 2013) which is 'owned' by teachers and learners. The LOCIT process[1] (learning-oriented critical incident technique) introduces teachers and learners to 'non-threatening' analysis. The approach is built on the principle of

---

1. For further information go to http://www.abdn.ac.uk/locit.

the *objectification* of the learning and teaching process by focussing on learning rather than teaching. Whilst it can be argued that identifying and reflecting on *learning moments* is a subjective activity, it is through sharing these ideas with others that 'learning discourse' evolves. However, what makes the LOCIT process significantly different is that it involves both teachers and learners working together in collaborative analysis and identification of *learning moments*.

Jay and Johnson (2002) propose a reflection typology of three dimensions of reflective discourse: descriptive (noticing), comparative (considering alternative perspectives) and critical (grasping new perspectives based on critical evaluation and planning future action accordingly). The LOCIT process provides opportunities and guidance for users to engage in all three levels of reflection. However, I also add another dimension: collaborative reflection. This dimension involves the teacher and the learners reflecting together on classroom learning using their video analysis to guide their reflections and impact future practice. It is respectful, inclusive and powerful.

The LOCIT process starts with the analysis of 'lived through' lessons by both learners and teachers, using 'playback' reflection and critical incident technique (CIT). According to Kain (2004), critical incidents capture events that are critical for learning – a systematic means of gathering significances others attach to events, analysing emerging patterns and drawing these together to collaboratively develop new ideas. For Tripp (2012: 8) critical incidents are

> [...] not 'things' which exist independently of an observer and are awaiting discovery like gold nuggets or desert islands, but like all data [...] are created. Incidents happen, but critical incidents are created by the way we look at a situation [...] an interpretation of the significance of an event. To take something as a critical incident is a value judgement we make, and the basis of that judgement is the significance we attach to the meaning of the incident.

In the LOCIT process (Coyle 2013) teachers and learners independent of each other analyse lessons to identify and justify incidents which they believe are *learning moments*. It is the sharing and comparing of the incidents which forms the basis of 'respectful discussions'. These discussions which grow from positive subjective judgements about learning, can lead to a more 'objective' conceptualisation of learning, which has the potential to transform classroom practice. Ultimately, LOCIT aims to mediate learner engagement in shared learning and to encourage further practitioner research shared with colleagues and learners within and across schools.

It should be noted perhaps that LOCIT starts from a different position than most practitioner research which problematises classroom practice (Dana & Yendol-Silva 2003). At the point of entry LOCIT is an analysis of 'successful learning' as perceived by teachers and learners in order to understand why it is successful and how it can be sustained and transferred to other areas of teaching and learning. A sample of lessons is video recorded with one selected for analysis which teachers and learners feel positively about in terms of evidencing 'successful learning'. The lesson is reviewed and edited in a secure digital space by the teacher and learners to select clips of say 5 minutes which capture individual or small group consensus of *learning moments*. Each clip selected is accompanied by reasons for selection. The final stage consists of a reflection lesson where learner clips and teacher clips are compared. The resonance or dissidence between clips is discussed and an action plan for 'change' or development in learning and teaching is composed by both learners and teachers working together (note here the previous reference to Jay and Johnson's (2002) reflective dimensions including descriptive, comparative, critical and then to LOCIT's collaborative reflection).

Critiques of the process may question the validity and reliability of the *learning moments* and the multitude of factors which will affect their identification. However, this misses the point. The *learning moments* themselves are triggers for collaborative reflection and discussion between the teachers and learners to encourage dialogic interaction and introspection about the learning process itself. In other words, it is this discussion which can 'grow' dialogic spaces in classrooms which focus as much on the process of learning as the outcomes of it. This does not stop at rationalising practice but instead leads towards the meta-logic collaborative reframing of shared ownership of classroom practice. For some examples of LOCIT classroom practice see Note 1.

Conclusion

Most of this chapter has focussed on the theoretical rationale for an inclusive approach to researching motivation at the micro-level of individual classrooms and the perspectives of individuals within. According to Ushioda (2013: 18) there is "far less research that narrows the focus on the more micro-level of learners' ongoing motivation experience during the day-to-day process of L2 learning, or in relation to a specific task, learning problem or critical event."

One starting point for co-constructing learning environments conducive to dialogic spaces, where learning can be openly analysed, discussed and planned for, has been suggested through the LOCIT process. It is interesting to note that the focus is on 'successful learning' or 'learning moments' as the criterion for selection of incidents. Yet as collaboration and trust develops, as learners and teachers develop their own ground rules and confidence in articulating 'successful learning' and by omission less successful learning, what emerges are rich data that signify the conditions for learning in a particular classroom which motivate particular learners. It is also about nurturing professional confidence in teachers to acknowledge that 'practice is more than knowledge: practice humanises theory' (Phelps 1991:883).

There remains, however, the question concerning the kind of data the process yields and how this is framed in the ITALIC process model. The power and use of the data lies with those who own the process, act upon it and use it for future learning. However, to share some of the findings, I can draw upon the ITALIC research in eleven secondary CLIL classrooms in England and Scotland using French, German or Spanish (Coyle 2011a), and ILC (Coyle 2011b) in 6 Gaelic-medium primary schools on a Scottish island.

Successful learning in individual schools consists of clips featuring the following examples:

- effective teacher explanation, discussion of content, revision strategies and scaffolded writing for content knowledge construction and conceptual understanding
- teacher correction and language skill practice for lexical understanding
- opportunities for using known language to access new content and new language for new content
- visual and written scaffolded questions/answers/oral explanations for learning content
- repetition/memorisation/practising/comparison with L1/recording vocabulary/body language/speaking for practising new language
- celebrating individual successes through games, songs, miming, kinaesthetic activities, quiz, interactive whiteboard use and humour
- when 'our teacher explains things clearly, listens to us, makes a task hard but not too hard'
- interactive lessons when learners genuinely communicate, are challenged, are engaged in learning meaningful new things; use familiar language and construct their own talk i.e. 'what we want to know'

Critical incidents such as these can be summarised as focussing on cognitive engagement, interaction, language using, communication, meaningful content, new learning (content and language), scaffolded activities, real dialogue and a sense of owning learning and expressing opinions about that learning in a 'listened to' way. The critical incidents also revealed that young learners were also very much aware of the effectiveness at different times of teacher-mediated learning, learner-mediated learning, co-constructed peer learning and whole class learning.

On reading a selection of *learning moments*, the reader may be tempted to conclude that there is 'nothing new' in these findings. I would argue that these data must be interpreted in each individual classroom – i.e. in the context in which they are constructed, understood and analysed. These examples are the result of co-constructed discussion of 'lived through' enactments of learning in the here and now, researched by learners and their teachers to identify successful examples of their own language mediated learning and to act upon the findings to enhance future learning. This is ownership, this is collaborative inquiry and this is micro-analysis of classroom learning owned by those who matter.

From the teacher's perspective, co-researching with learners also provides a challenging yet motivating opportunity to engage in professional learning, to analyse practices and situate them within an evolving articulation of a personal Theory of Practice.

> This kind of deep reflection can be integrated into professional learning for con-structing rationalised and theorised individual teaching and learning practices.
>
> (Van Lier 1996)

The processes suggested in this chapter, therefore, can be described as offering teachers an approach to understanding how to motivate an individual class of learners. These are based in the here and now, co-ownership of learning, accom-modating the 'self' of individual learners and optimising links to support strategic engagement and learner investment through objectifying, celebrating and acting upon 'successful learning' in language classrooms.

References

Alexander, R. (2006). *Towards dialogic teaching: Rethinking classroom talk* (3rd ed.). Cambridge: Dialogos.

Bandura, A., & Schunk, D. (1981). Cultivating competence, self-efficacy, and intrinsic interest through proximal self-motivation. *Journal of Personality and Social Psychology*, 41, 586–598. DOI: 10.1037/0022-3514.41.3.586

Bardovi-Harlig, K., & Stringer, D. (2010). Variables in second language attrition: Advancing the state of the art. *Studies in Second Language Acquisition*, 32(1), 1–45. DOI: 10.1017/S0272263109990246

Bradford, A. (2007). Motivational orientations in under-reserched FLL contexts. *RELC Journal*, 38, 302–323. DOI: 10.1177/0033688207085849

Carr, W. (1995). *For education: Towards critical educational inquiry*. Buckingham: Open University Press.

Chevalier, J.M., & Buckles, D.J. (2013). *Participatory action research: Theory and methods for engaged inquiry*. London: Routledge.

Cochran-Smith, M., & Lytle, S.L. (1993). *Inside/outside: teacher research and knowledge*. New York NY: Teachers College Press.

Cohen, A.D. (2011). L2 learner strategies. In E. Hinkel (Ed.), *Handbook of research in second language teaching and learning, Vol. II – Part V. Methods and instruction in second language teaching* (pp. 681–698). Abingdon: Routledge.

Cohen, A.D. (2013). Strategies: The interface of styles, strategies, and motivation on tasks. In S. Mercer, S. Ryan, & M. Williams (Eds.), *Language learning psychology: Research, theory, and pedagogy*. Basingstoke: Palgrave Macmillan.

Coyle, D. (2011a). *ITALIC Final Research Report, Investigating Student Gains: Content and Language Integrated Learning*. <http://www.abdn.ac.uk/italic> (14 May 2013).

Coyle, D. (2011b). Innovative Teacher Communities: an investigation in Gaelic medium schools into pupils teacher research analysing classroom practices. Paper presented at *SERA conference*, November 2011.

Coyle, D. (2013). Listening to Learners: An investigation into successful learning across CLIL contexts. *International Journal of Bilingual Education and Bilingualism*, 16(3), 244–266. DOI: 10.1080/13670050.2013.777384

Dana, N.F., & Yendol-Silva, D. (2003). *The reflective educator's guide to classroom research: learning to teach and teaching to learn through practitioner inquiry*. Thousand Oaks, CA: Corwin Press.

Department for Education and Science (2002). *Languages for all: Languages for life – a strategy for England, the Nuffield Report*. London: DFES.

Dooley, M., & Eastman, D. (Eds.). (2008). *How we're going about it: Teachers' voices on innovative approaches to teaching and learning languages*. Newcastle upon Tyne: Cambridge Scholars.

Dörnyei, Z. (2000). Motivation in action: towards a process-oriented conceptualisation of student motivation. *British Journal of Educational Psychology*, 70, 519–38. DOI: 10.1348/000709900158281

Dörnyei, Z. (2002). The motivational base of language learning tasks. In P. Robinson (Ed.), *Individual differences and instructed language learning* (pp. 137–158). Amsterdam: John Benjamins. DOI: 10.1075/lllt.2.10dor

Dörnyei, Z. (2007). *Research methods in applied linguistics: Quantitative, qualitative and mixed methodologies*. Oxford: Oxford University Press.

Dörnyei, Z. (2009). *The psychology of second language acquisition*. Oxford: Oxford University Press.

Dörnyei, Z., & Otto, I. (1998). Motivation in action: A process model of L2 motivation. *Working Papers in Applied Linguistics*, 4, 43–69.

Dörnyei, Z., & Ushioda, E. (2011). *Teaching and researching motivation*. Harlow: Pearson Education.

Evans, M., & Fisher, L. (2009). *Language learning at Key Stage 3: The impact of the KS3 Modern Languages Framework and changes to the curriculum on provision and practice*. HMSO: Department for Children, Schools and Families Final Report Research Report DCSF-RR127. <https://www.education.gov.uk/publications//eOrderingDownload/DFE-RR052.pdf> (10 June 2011).

Gardner, R.C. (1985). *Social psychology and second language learning: The role of attitudes and motivation*. Baltimore, MD: Edward Arnold.

Giugni, M. (2006). *Contemporary Issues in Early Childhood*, 7(2), 97–108.

Guilloteaux, M.J., & Dörnyei, Z. (2008). Motivating language learners: A classroom-oriented investigation of the effects of motivational strategies on student motivation. *TESOL Quarterly*, 42(1), 55–77.

Jay, J.K., & Johnson, K.L. (2002). Capturing complexity: a typology of reflective practice for teacher education. *Teaching and Teacher Education*, 18(1), 73–85. DOI: 10.1016/S0742-051X(01)00051-8

Kain, D. (2004). Owning significance: the critical incident technique in research. In K. de Marrais, & D. Lapan (Eds.), *Foundations for research: methods of Inquiry and the social sciences* (pp. 69–85). Mahwah, NJ: Lawrence Erlbaum Associates.

Lasagabaster, D. (2011). English achievement and student motivation in CLIL and EFL settings. *Innovation in Language Learning and Teaching*, 5, 3–18. DOI: 10.1080/17501229.2010.519030

Lewis, A., & Porter, J. (2007). Research and pupil voice. In L. Florian (Ed.), *Handbook of Special Education* (pp. 222–232). London: Sage.

Locke, E., & Latham, G. (2002). Building a practically useful theory of goal setting and task motivation: A 35-year odyssey. *American Psychologist*, 57, 705–717. DOI: 10.1037/0003-066X.57.9.705

Lorenzo, F., Casal, S., & Moore, P. (2010). The effects of content and language integrated learning in European education: key findings from the Andalusian bilingual sections evaluation project. *Applied Linguistics*, 31(3), 418–442. DOI: 10.1093/applin/amp041

Lewis, T., & Vialleton, E. (2011). The notions of control and consciousness in learner autonomy and self-regulated learning: A comparison and critique. *Innovation in Language Learning and Teaching*, 5(2), 205–219. DOI: 10.1080/17501229.2011.577535

McCombs, B., & Marzano, R.J. (1990). Putting the self in self-regulated learning: The self agent in integrating will and skill. *Educational Psychologist*, 25(1), 51–69. DOI: 10.1207/s15326985ep2501_5

McIntyre, D., Pedder, D., & Ruddock, J. (2005). Pupil voice: Comfortable and uncomfortable learnings for teachers. *Research Papers in Education*, 20(2), 149–168. DOI: 10.1080/02671520500077970

Mercer, N. (2000). *Words and minds: How we use language to think together*. London: Routledge. DOI: 10.4324/9780203464984

Mercer, N. & Littleton, K. (2007). *Dialogue and the development of children's thinking: A sociocultural approach*. London: Routledge.

Noels, K.A., Pelletier, L.G., Clément, R., & Vallerand, R.J. (2000). Why are you learning a second language? Motivational orientations and self-determination theory. *Language Learning*, 50, 57–85. DOI: 10.1111/0023-8333.00111

Norton, B. (2000). *Identity and language learning: Gender, ethnicity and educational change*. Harlow: Longman.

Oxford, R.L. (2000). Language learning strategies for ESL and EFL: A synthesis of theory and research. In R. Carter, & D. Nunan (Eds.), *English language teaching handbook*. Cambridge: Cambridge University Press.

Pae, T.-I. (2008). Second language orientation and self-determination theory. A structural analysis of the factors affecting second language achievement. *Journal of Language and Social Psychology*, 27, 5–27. DOI: 10.1177/0261927X07309509

Pizzolato, J.E. (2006). Achieving college student possible selves: navigating the space between commitment and achievement of long-term activity goals. *Cultural Diversity and Ethnic Minority Psychology*,12(1), 57–69. DOI: 10.1037/1099-9809.12.1.57

Phelps, L. (1991). *Practical wisdom and the geography of knowledge in composition. College English*, 53(8), 399–422.

Ryan, R.M., & Deci, E.L. (2002). Overview of self-determination theory: An organismic dialectical perspective. In E.L. Deci & R.M. Ryan (Eds.), *Handbook of self-determination research* (pp. 3–33). Rochester, NY: University of Rochester Press.

Seikkula-Leino, J. (2007). CLIL learning: Achievement levels and affective factors. *Language and Education*, 21(4), 328–341. DOI: 10.2167/le635.0

Sierra, J.M. (2011). CLIL and project work: Contributions from the classroom. In Y. Ruiz de Zarobe, J.M. Sierra, & F. Gallardo del Puerto (Eds.), *Content and Foreign Language Integrated Learning: Contributions to Multilingualism in European Contexts* (pp. 211–239). Bern: Peter Lang.

Simons, H., Kushner, S., Jones, K., & James, D. (2003). From evidence-based practice to practice-based evidence: the idea of situated generalisation. *Research Papers in Education*, 18(4), 347–364. DOI: 10.1080/0267152032000176855

Stelfox, K. (2008). *Pupil Gains: a contested concept*. Unpublished presentation at the University of Aberdeen seminar on STNE 18.09.2008. <http://www.abdn.ac.uk/stne/index.php?id= 24&top=5> (18 December 2012).

Todd, E.S. (2007). *Partnerships for inclusive education: A critical approach to collaborative working*. London: Routledge Monographs.

Tripp, D. (2012). *Critical Incident Technique, developing professional judgement*. London: Routledge.

Ushioda, E. (2001). Language learning at university: Exploring the role of motivational thinking. In Z. Dörnyei & R. Schmidt (Eds.), *Motivation and second language acquisition* (pp. 93–125). Honolulu, HI: University of Hawaii Press.

Ushioda, E. (2003). Motivation as a socially mediated process. In D. Little, J. Ridley, & E. Ushioda (Eds.), *Learner autonomy in the foreign language classroom: Teacher, learners, curriculum and assessment* (pp. 90–120). Dublin: Authentik.

Ushioda, E. (2007). Motivation, autonomy and socio-cultural theory. In P. Benson (Ed.), *Learner autonomy 8: Teacher and learner perspectives* (pp. 5–24). Dublin: Authentik.

Ushioda, E. (2010). Motivation and SLA: bridging the gap. *EUROSLA Yearbook*, 10, 5–20. DOI: 10.1075/eurosla.10.03ush

Ushioda, E. (2013). Motivation, autonomy and meta-cognition: exploring their interactions. Paper presented at the *UPV/EHU Symposium on Motivation in the L2 Classroom: From Theory to Practice*, 10. May 2013.

van Lier, L. (1996). Interaction in the language curriculum: awareness, autonomy and authenticity. *Applied Linguistics and Language Study Series*. London: Longman.

Vandergrift, L. (2005). Relationships among motivation orientations, meta-cognitive awareness and proficiency in L2 listening. *Applied Linguistics*, 26(1), 70–89. DOI: 10.1093/applin/amh039

Wegerif, R., & Mercer, N. (1997). A dialogical framework for investigating talk. In R. Wegerif & P. Scrimshaw (Eds.), *Computers and Talk in the Primary Classroom* (pp. 49–65). Clevedon: Multilingual Matters.

Wegerif, R. (2006). Towards a dialogic understanding of the relationship between teaching thinking and CSCL. *International Journal of Computer Supported Collaborative Learning*, 1, 143–157. DOI: 10.1007/s11412-006-6840-8

Wegerif, R. (2011). Towards a dialogic theory of how children learn to think. Thinking skills and creativity. <http://dx.doi.org/10.1016/j.tsc.2011.08.002> (18 December 2012).

Wells, G. (1999a). *Dialogic inquiry: Towards a socio-cultural practice and theory of education*. Cambridge: Cambridge University Press. DOI: 10.1017/CBO9780511605895

Wells, G. (1999b). *Towards a sociocultural practice and theory of education*. Cambridge: Cambridge University Press. DOI: 10.1017/CBO9780511605895

Williams, M., & Burden, R. (1997). *Psychology for language teachers*. Cambridge: Cambridge University Press.

CHAPTER 4

Motivating language teachers

Inspiring vision

Magdalena Kubanyiova

Recent theorising in research on language teachers' conceptual change has suggested that transforming language classrooms into engaging learning environments begins with teachers' vision (Kubanyiova 2012). This chapter considers the significance of this finding through the lens of practical proposals for motivating language teachers' deep reflection on their praxis. Situating the discussion in the wider domain of language teacher cognition research, this chapter adopts a theoretical framework of language teachers' possible selves and outlines three key processes involved in inspiring language teachers' vision: the teachers' reflection on the *who* (i.e. the person doing the teaching), engagement with the *why* (i.e. the bigger purposes guiding language teachers' work), and the construction of the *image* (i.e. a visual representation of desired teaching selves).

Keywords: teacher vision, possible selves, language teacher cognition

Introduction

L2 motivation research has firmly embraced the construct of L2 vision, that is, a learner's vivid and realistic image of his or her successful L2 speaking future self, as one of the most powerful forces that shape language learners' engagement in the learning process (Dörnyei 2005). This theorising, backed up by growing empirical evidence (Dörnyei & Ushioda 2009; Henry 2010; Papi & Abdollahzadeh 2012), has led to generating a range of novel motivational techniques for the language classroom (Dörnyei & Kubanyiova 2014; Hadfield & Dörnyei 2013; Magid & Chan 2012). Yet, parallel to these developments is a growing understanding that transforming classrooms into engaging environments for language learning demands more than a repertoire of innovative principles and techniques; it requires teachers who will be motivated to put the knowledge into practice.

The rationale for this chapter builds on recent research on language teachers' conceptual change (Kubanyiova 2012) which has suggested that in order to create engaging learning environments and help students to discover and pursue their L2 visions, teachers need to start with a deeper reflection on who *they* are, who *they* want to become and, ultimately, what kind of language learning environments *they* envisage for their students. Rather than focusing on techniques for "motivating" teachers in the traditional sense (e.g. Pastoll 2009), therefore, I will consider approaches, recently summarised in Dörnyei and Kubanyiova (2014), which seek to inspire language teachers' vision. I first outline theoretical developments in the language teacher cognition research. Situating the discussion in the theoretical framework of language teachers' possible selves, the remainder of the chapter discusses three key processes involved in inspiring language teachers' vision, including the teachers' reflection on the *who* (i.e. the person doing the teaching), engagement with the *why* (i.e. the bigger purposes guiding language teachers' work) and the construction of the *image* (i.e. a visual representation of desired teaching selves).

The "problem" of impact

The relationship between teacher education and teacher learning has always been recognised as a complex one in both general and language teacher education research. While some studies have been able to demonstrate significant influence of teacher education programmes on language teachers' beliefs, practices, or both (Bodur 2012; Lamie 2004; Lee 2010), others seem to have been more cautious in claiming impact (Borg 2011; Kubanyiova 2006; Watzke 2007). Yet others have gone as far as to conclude that teacher education represents a largely insignificant intervention in producing effective teachers (see review in Grossman 2008).

The reasons for such disparate outcomes are too many to outline here and range from a variety of contextual factors, teachers' individual differences and cognitions through to conceptual and methodological approaches adopted for operationalizing and measuring such an impact. Yet, the following account of a secondary school English as a Foreign Language (EFL) teacher who reflects on her participation in a yearlong teacher development course on motivating language learners seems to represent a fairly common experience among teachers who have engaged in various forms of professional development:

> The trainer, when she speaks about it, it's so clear, I'm so enthusiastic that if they asked me to do something, I would do it. But as soon as the door closes and I'm at home, it's gone. I think that maybe I'm not enthusiastic enough, maybe I'm not

convinced about it. They work using those methods and they are successful, but maybe I'm not that convinced about it so I don't go for it. And maybe it's the same with [this teacher development course]. Yes, this is true, we should do it this way, but then you return home and you say to yourself: It's much more comfortable to do it the old way.   (Kubanyiova 2012:158)

This and other teachers' experiences have been the subject of Kubanyiova's (2012) in-depth longitudinal study of how language teachers mobilise (or not) their internal resources when they engage with latest research presented in teacher education or teacher development programmes. This chapter considers its theoretical findings through the lens of practical proposals for motivating language teachers' deep engagement with new pedagogical ideas and approaches. It is hoped that this discussion will also be important in informing the content and processes of a range of language teacher professional development tools, such as classroom observations (Lasagabaster & Sierra 2011) or teacher development groups (Farrell 2014).

Theoretical background

In his exploration of the relationship among second language acquisition (SLA), teacher education and classroom pedagogy, Ellis (2010) has proposed two key tasks that, he believes, need to be undertaken by SLA researchers to address the often glaring divide between SLA research and classroom practice. He has urged researchers to explore ways in which technical knowledge generated through their research inquiry can be made available to teachers in ways that impact on their practices. The related second task invites the researchers to ponder how "what teachers know and do [can] inform the theories that researchers seek to build" (p. 186). This latter proposal, also echoed in Ortega's (2012) call to produce research in synergy with teacher knowledge, reflects a more general recognition within SLA and applied linguistics more broadly of the need to account more fully for the role of teacher as "the practical link between SLA research and classroom practice" (Crookes 1997:93). It was this shift from investigating whether teachers' observable behaviours correspond with the latest research to considering why teachers do what they do and what shapes their practices that led to the development of a new line of inquiry in applied linguistics, now commonly referred to as *language teacher cognition*.

Language teacher cognition research

The term *language teacher cognition* refers to "the unobservable cognitive dimension of teaching", traditionally summed up as what teachers "know, believe, and think" (Borg 2003:81). This domain of inquiry is primarily concerned with a deeper understanding of the teachers' mental lives and how these shape their classroom practices. In the relatively short life span of this field of research, which was launched in the 1990s, a vast range of theoretical concepts embracing language teachers' mental lives have been explored, expanding well beyond the original definition of language teacher cognition. These include teachers' beliefs (Basturkmen 2012; Wan, Low, & Li 2011), conceptions (Freeman 1991; Mangubhai, Marland, Dashwood, & Son 2005), emotions (Golombek & Johnson 2004), identities (Abednia 2012; Farrell 2011; Gao 2012; Kanno & Stuart 2011; Tsui 2007), images (Feryok & Pryde 2012; Johnson 1994), knowledge (Golombek 1998; Mullock 2006; Woods & Çakır 2011), maxims (Tsang 2004), metaphors (Warford & Reeves 2003), moral values (Akbari & Tajik 2012; Mangubhai 2007), possible selves (Hiver 2013; Kubanyiova 2009; Kumazawa 2013), principles (Breen, Hird, Milton, Oliver, & Thwaite 2001), religious beliefs (Varghese & Johnston 2007; Wong 2013) and theories (Efstathia 2008).

While the above list is far from exhaustive, the collective findings that the language teacher cognition research has generated attest to highly complex dynamics which underlie teachers' classroom practices in general and their understanding, interpretation and implementation of new theoretical ideas in their teaching in particular. It has been found that language teachers' practices are shaped in complex, unique and often unpredictable ways by the *invisible* dimension of their knowledge of language, language pedagogy, context, students and themselves, their prior beliefs about how languages are learned and how they should or should not be taught, and the diverse images and models of teaching that teachers have internalised throughout their careers. These cognitions are, in turn, a reflection of teachers' unique personal and language learning histories and language teacher education experiences, as well as the personal values they hold, future identities they envisage, educational philosophies they espouse and identity development trajectories they have travelled, all of which is moulded by the interplay of teachers' agency and the specific educational, sociocultural, political and historical contexts in which they do their work.

It appears, therefore, that whether teachers transform their language classrooms into effective learning environments as a result of attending a teacher development course, talking to colleagues, or reading about the latest research findings in SLA depends on a rather intricate tapestry of multiple influences. Yet, amidst this complexity, an important finding has emerged from research on language teachers' conceptual change which lends itself to more concrete proposals for facilitating meaningful teacher development: teachers' future visions of themselves, conceptualised as language teachers' *possible selves*, seem to play a critical role in their in-depth engagement with new ideas and, consequently, their development (Kubanyiova 2012). In other words, who teachers strive to become and, even more precisely, who they *see* when they imagine themselves in the future appears to occupy centre stage in the multifaceted and complex network of language teachers' cognitions.

Possible selves and language teacher development

The construct of possible selves was first introduced by Markus and Nurius (1986) in social psychology to explain human motivation and self-regulation. Serving as bridges between individuals' present and imagined future states, the images of people's self-related future hopes, aspirations or fears have been found significant in motivating their action in the effort to either attain the desired future selves or avoid the feared ones. Although most empirical research to date has focused on the role of possible selves in students' motivation and achievement (as discussed in the introduction to this chapter), some recent work has begun to apply this theoretical construct to gain a deeper understanding of teaching and teacher development (Hamman, Gosselin, Romano, & Bunuan 2010; Hiver 2013; Horn, Nolen, Ward, & Campbell 2008; Kubanyiova 2009; Kumazawa 2013; Ronfeldt & Grossman 2008).

For example, to explain the process of language teachers' development, Kubanyiova (2012) has proposed an empirically-grounded theoretical model of Language Teacher Conceptual Change (LTCC) which highlights language teachers' cognitive representations of their ideal, ought-to and feared future selves in relation to their work as language teachers as central cognitions shaping the ways in which they approach their professional development. In line with the L2 motivation conceptualisation (e.g. Dörnyei 2005), language teachers' possible selves have been operationalised in LTCC as *Ideal Language Teacher Self*, which represents the teacher's images of future selves that she would ideally like to attain, such as identity-relevant goals, hopes and aspirations. *Ought-to Language Teacher Self* refers to the language teacher's images of who she believes she should become, or, in other words, her visual self-relevant representation of responsibilities, obligations and normative pressures with regard to her work, which come from a variety of sources, including students' expectations, the school's official policies as well as latent norms, the wider sociocultural context or the requirements of a specific teacher training course. And, finally, the teacher's vision of the negative consequences and fears for the future has been conceptualised as *Feared Language Teacher Self* which represents a vision of who the teacher could become if she does not live up to her ideal or ought-to images.

One of the most significant contributions of LTCC is in its explanation of why new theoretical input on teacher education or development programmes, however compelling and pedagogically relevant it may be, does not necessarily translate into teachers' conscious and sustained effort to act on it. One of the reasons, whose practical implications are the subject of this chapter, is that such ideas, techniques or materials do not resonate with those professional self images that are salient in the teacher's current self-concept. Put differently, the teacher may appreciate the ideas and perhaps even try them out in the classroom if there is a temporary expectation of her to do so (e.g. as part of observed teaching practice), but because they do not represent the kind of teacher she would ideally like to become, there is no genuine incentive for her to engage with them at a deeper level and take further action once the external pressure to perform has ended. This developmental path, the so called "Nice-but-not-for-me" route of LTCC (Kubanyiova 2012: 110), has been eloquently summarized in the earlier quote by the secondary EFL teacher.

The remainder of this chapter takes a closer look at the key implication that has emerged from this theorising, which suggests that in order for teacher education programmes and teacher development initiatives to facilitate meaningful development, they need to create opportunities for teachers to *see* the kinds of educators they could become and the learning environments they could facilitate in their language classrooms in relation to the teacher education input. In other words, motivating language teachers' meaningful development begins with inspiring vision.

Inspiring language teachers' vision

The previous discussion has highlighted the development of language teachers' vision as one of the central tasks of language teacher education. The key question that requires further reflection, however, concerns the processes involved in this enterprise. In other words, what kind of vision is needed to inspire learners' engagement in language learning and how do teacher educators, in turn, inspire such vision in language teachers? There is no straightforward answer to either of these crucial questions and only limited empirical evidence has been gathered so far in the language teacher cognition domain directly addressing such issues. However, a careful scrutiny of what current theory and research in as well as outside applied linguistics have to say about what vision is, what it consists of and how it comes about provides a number of vital clues. Drawing on this body of scholarship, the next three sections will consider three processes that have been identified as essential in inspiring productive images of ideal language teacher selves: (1) a deeper understanding of the person they have become through their gifts, passions and past experiences (*who*), (2) a reflection on the bigger purposes guiding their work as language teachers (*why*), and (3) a construction of a visual representation of their desired teaching selves (*image*).

Understanding the "who"

> Your vision will become clear only when you can look into your own heart.
> Who looks outside, dreams; who looks inside, awakes.   (Carl Jung)

In order to *see* with clarity and conviction the future person one wants to become, language teachers, like learners (cf. Dörnyei & Kubanyiova 2014), need to examine their past as well as current experiences as potential sources of their vision and reflect on images of good practice which come from existing theories of teaching and learning, teachers' own intuitions or past role models. The purpose of this reflection, however, is neither to identify an idealised fantasy image of a language classroom that may never exist, nor to impose an externally-defined vision that is not the teacher's own. Rather, the aim of this exercise is to enable the teacher to respond to new theoretical input by developing a personally meaningful possible vision that is congruent with the person that he or she is and which is germane to the context in which his or her work is located. Such a process is in line with theorising grounded in self-determination theory which suggests that promoting new visions must not occur at the expense of suppressing teachers' authentic voices (cf. Assor, Kaplan, Feinberg, & Tal 2009).

Sadly, we know all too well that however passionate people may have been about choosing teaching as a career, their initial enthusiasm is often stifled by external pressures, bureaucratic demands, an unsupportive school culture and imposed visions that are usually in stark contrast with the teachers' original aspirations, ideals and voices (Crookes 2009; Hammerness 2003; Kubanyiova 2006). While an unsupportive system has frequently been blamed for the widespread phenomena of teacher demotivation and burn out, Palmer (2007: 21) has argued that the roots are even deeper and come from a more profound psychological detachment:

> Academics often suffer the pain of dismemberment. On the surface, this is the pain of people who thought they were joining a community of scholars but find themselves in distant, competitive, and uncaring relationships with colleagues and students. Deeper down, this pain is more spiritual than sociological: it comes

from being disconnected from our own truth, from the passions that took us into
teaching, from the heart that is the source of all good work.

It appears, therefore, that the "problem" of impact does not merely stem from
the fact that teacher education programmes, teacher development initiatives or
educational reforms do not always let the teachers' voices be heard. An even more
profound reason for teachers' lack of motivation may be that those voices are no
longer remembered. Understanding or, if necessary, reconnecting with the *who* is
therefore the single most important component of the vision building agenda for
language teachers. One way of achieving this is to enable teachers to gain a firm
grasp of their existing gifts and passions; something that teacher education programmes rarely encourage teachers to reflect on, but which, as Casbon, Shagoury,
and Smith (2005: 346) have argued, is fundamental to meaningful teacher development:

> We are all revitalized by recollections of our teaching in our own voices. And we
> hear stories from our colleagues that reflect a range of possibilities of teaching
> that are genuine and show integrity. This kind of work involves the cultivation
> of what is already present. If teachers are to teach who they are in ways that are
> convincing to their students, in ways that engage young people in learning, then
> they must do so with a firm grasp of their own gifts. Students respond almost
> naturally to people who are willing to share their talents and passions with others.

A number of tasks have been suggested by Dörnyei and Kubanyiova (2014) which
are aimed at facilitating such reflection on teacher education programmes or in
informal teacher development groups and a brief example is offered in Illustration 1. This and similar tasks contribute to a critical process in the agenda for
motivating language teachers which is reflected in the following principle summarising this section: *helping teachers to inspire others begins with helping them to
see who they are.*

Engaging with the "whys": Values, moral purposes, and teaching philosophies

> Without a narrative, life has no meaning.
> Without meaning, learning has no purpose.
> Without a purpose, schools are houses of detention, not attention.
>
> (Postman 1996: 7)

What we see when we imagine ourselves as language educators largely depends
on what we believe the teaching and teachers are for, why and how languages
matter, and the kinds of interactions we wish our students to have with each other

On a piece of paper, brainstorm your gifts and passions, drawing on your current interests, childhood memories or interactions with family and friends, reflecting on questions such as:

- What are you good at? What kind of achievements in the past have earned you positive feedback? What would be the characteristics that colleagues or friends would mention when they praise you? If you were allowed to highlight only three of your strengths, what would these be? When in the past did you feel you were doing yourself real justice?
- What do you really enjoy? When did you feel in the past that you were genuinely 'in your element'? What activities cause you a 'flow' experience (i.e. total blissful absorption)? What complex tasks do you find (perhaps surprisingly) easy to complete?
- What are your passions? What makes you unique? What do people remember you for? What can you get enthusiastic about? If you were allowed to be the member of only one club, what would it be?

Process your list by sharing it with your peer group or selected colleagues/friends, and by reflecting on it in a journal. Then, think about a time when you were able to bring some of your gifts and passions to your language teaching. Share the stories with the group.

Illustration 1. A sample task for facilitating teachers' understanding of who they are (from Dörnyei & Kubanyiova 2014: 127)

and with the world around them. The key premise of this section, therefore, is that there is much more to a vision than a mere pursuit of teachers' personal aspirations. This, in turn, implies that encouraging language teachers to engage with the broader moral fabric of their teaching is crucial in developing the kinds of ideal language teacher selves which could energise teachers' deeper engagement with the values, meanings and practical implications of new theoretical ideas in relation to their own practices situated in the specific educational and socio-political settings.

Data-based research on the moral foundations of language teachers' knowledge base is scarce within the language teacher cognition domain (but see e.g. Akbari & Tajik 2012; Mangubhai 2007), possibly because research investigating language teachers' beliefs and knowledge has traditionally focused on the more narrowly defined pedagogical dimension. Compelling evidence is emerging from more in-depth explorations of teachers' cognitions, however, of the critical role of language teachers' moral knowledge base in guiding their teaching and teacher learning. For example, Mori's (2011) study revealed that teachers' corrective feedback practices were grounded in broader, value-oriented goals and ideals which were concerned with how the teachers can enable their students to achieve a fuller and more meaningful participation in the classroom life.

This finding is in line with more extensive research in the general teacher education domain which has produced abundant evidence of values that underpin teachers' work. Examples include studies, such as Borrero's (2011) examination of pre-service teachers of urban youth whose visions centred around the desire to promote social justice and bring about positive change in their communities, or Kennedy's (2006) exploration of the bases for teachers' visions. Although the findings indicated that theoretical knowledge may partly contribute to the construction of these images, it was, first and foremost, the teachers' sense of purpose that formed the foundations of their visions for teaching. Interestingly, it has been found that when such purposes and broader moral concerns are missing from the teachers' considerations, there is little chance of meaningful teacher development that would have significant consequences for students' learning (Kubanyiova 2009, 2012). In short, a growing consensus is emerging among language teacher educators and researchers that developing teachers' "ethical knowing" (Scarino 2005: 33), which includes reflection on the philosophies, values, and moral purposes that guide their practices, constitutes one of the key tasks of preservice and inservice language teacher education.

In practical terms, the above conclusion implies a more systemic inclusion on teacher education and teacher development programmes of tasks which require teachers or student teachers to probe the philosophical, ethical and value dimensions of their images of ideal language teacher selves. Illustration 2 offers an insight into a novice Chinese language teacher's moral vision which she began to articulate as a response to a journal writing task on a postgraduate teacher education programme, entitled "The Language Teacher I Would Ideally Like to Become."

Tasks such as this enable teachers to begin the process of construction and articulation of their ideal language teacher selves. In some cases, as in the example above, these statements already incorporate a compelling articulation of purpose and values, which can be built on when discussing the broader purposes of language education on teacher education programmes. Other statements, in contrast, may not yet bear evidence of an ethical base for the teachers' visions and more groundwork may be required in those cases. Useful tasks include probing images of other teachers for what these can reveal about the purposes that may be worth pursuing in the language classrooms (see some useful resource materials in Johnston 2003; Mendelsohn 1999), engaging more explicitly with specific philosophies of education with the view to construct a personally meaningful statement of purpose (see a comprehensive overview in Crookes 2009), or examining existing research on topical subjects, such as internationalisation, multilingualism and English-medium education (Doiz, Lasagabaster, & Sierra 2011), language, culture and power (Sharkey & Johnson 2003), or the role of religious beliefs as a source for moral vision for teaching (Kubanyiova 2013).

I would like to be a teacher who can inspire my students to discover and explore their world and make some changes to the world. I chose to be an English teacher because English is a global lingua franca. Young people in China are able to know more current world if they master English, not only in terms of academic issues but also political issues and global dimension. Learning English is one way to access the world out there. Because of censorship, the majority of youth in China are not able to critically analyse what's going on in their country or in the world if they do not have a chance to get resources from the rest of world. I want to share information with my students in class. I wish that I could be not only their language teacher, but also a friend who can share information with them. I have experienced a traditional teaching approach, which was teacher centred and textbook-based, in my primary, secondary and high school. It was suffering for me because I could not enjoy learning languages. Hopefully, I can introduce some new ideas, or even big ideas, to where I am going to work. I want to create a dynamic creative learning environment for students. I want my students to become not only successful language learners, but also individual critical thinkers. The aim of learning other languages is not just for academic progress or employment, it should benefit to students themselves in terms of their self-development. I want for my language lessons in school not to be just subjects, but also a way for students to think differently about other subjects.

Illustration 2. "The Language Teacher I Would Ideally Like to Become": A journal entry by a Chinese language teacher (published with permission)

These and similar tasks can serve as an important step in helping teachers to construct their own visions which are a result of a critical inquiry into the purposes and philosophies of education that are relevant to the language teaching domain, responsive to the contexts in which the teachers' work takes place and resonant with who the teachers are. The second principle for inspiring teacher vision can therefore be summarised as follows: *helping teachers to inspire learning in their language classrooms means helping them to see themselves as moral agents of change.*

Generating images of ideal language teacher selves

> We must have new eyes – the eyes of our heart enlightened. That means that we must see essential realities vividly. We must have our imagination captured. [Some say] that conduct is three-fourths of life. But it isn't. Getting your imagination captured is almost the whole of life. The minute the eyes of your heart are enlightened, the minute your imagination gives you the picture of your path, your goal, your aim – it is as good as done.
>
> (Rufus Jones, cited in Walters 2001:84)

One of the essential characteristics of possible selves which sets them apart from mere abstract future goals is their sensory quality. The power of this "vividness" is evident in the following account of an EFL teacher who recalls her enjoyment of her English language teaching methodology classes as part of her university degree because she could "imagine the theory in practice". Her example illustrates how new ideas can acquire an entirely new dimension for those teachers able and willing to "live and breathe" the future teacher selves that those ideas represent.

> Most of my classmates didn't like the [language teacher methodology] courses, they [said that they] were too theoretical. Yes, there was theory, but I could always imagine the theory in practice. It was perhaps also the fact that by that time I was thinking of doing it in the future. Maybe it was boring for them precisely because they didn't have this prospect of teaching English one day. But for me, it was interesting, because I wanted to try all those things in practice. I remember that I literally lived and breathed [teaching]!
>
> (Kubanyiova, unpublished data from teacher interviews)

The focus on images of teaching is not new in the teacher education literature. For instance, Johnson (1994) and, more recently, Golombek (2009) have included the construct of *images of teaching* in their discussion of language teacher knowledge and beliefs, while Goodman (1988) has explored *guiding images* as visual representations of pre-service teachers' philosophies of teaching derived from their images of past experiences as children, pupils, student teachers and their future expectations. Although we have yet to gather systematic empirical evidence on how teachers construct language teacher selves, the available research suggests some promising future directions. It has been found, for example, that teachers routinely generate images of themselves when reflecting on their practice (Feryok & Pryde 2012). What is more, there is intriguing evidence that visualisation can be an effective technique for facilitating student teachers' development and enhancing their resiliency (e.g. Fletcher 2000). And, finally, research has found that the more vivid, specific and coherent images the teachers construct, the more likely they are to develop their practices in desired directions as they embark on their teaching career (McElhone, Hebhard, Scot, & Connie 2009).

Along with extensive research in the possible selves literature in psychology, this expanding empirical base in teacher education seems to suggest that although reflecting on the person the teacher is and on the moral purposes that inform his/her teaching is critical to constructing an effective language teacher vision, it is the image, that is, the actual sensory experience of the vision, that ultimately energises the teacher's action to transform dreams into reality. What Crookes (2010: 344) has noted about critical pedagogy seems true more generally: "the imagination, and an entire realm of the imaginary, is what finally is needed to help dreams become reality AND enhance the practicality and relevance of critical pedagogy in our field, in our time" (original emphasis). This argument is in line with the widely recognised notion that imagination plays a central part in motivating action, as illustrated by Liu and Brandon (2009: 8) in the following statement:

> The general assumption is that a will to act must precede imagination – that you decide to do something before you imagine what it is. The reality is that imagination comes first. It must. Until and unless we have the emotional and intellectual capacity to conceive of what does not yet exist, there is nothing toward which we are to direct our will and our resources.

It appears, therefore, that the question no longer is whether imagination is essential in the vision building agenda for language teachers. Rather, one of the key concerns for language teacher educators relates to how we can assist language teachers in their "journey of imaginative development" (Fettes 2005: 3) and help them to generate vivid and compelling images of their future selves. A whole range of imagery tasks have been proposed by Dörnyei and Kubanyiova (2014) with the aim to cultivate both people's capacity to dare to imagine (i.e. the attitude) and their ability to do so (i.e. the actual imagery skills). Some examples include:

- *Guided imagery*, such as "Socratic" imagery (i.e. open-ended questions which invite the teachers to imagine the details of their ideal scenarios; for an example, see Illustration 3), scripted imagery (i.e. detailed narratives guiding teachers to visualise specific images), or image streaming (i.e. with simple verbal prompts, teachers are encouraged to self-generate images of their ideal language classrooms);
- *Photovoice*, i.e. a visual approach to teacher ethnography whereby teachers are asked to take pictures of situations, events, places and people that matter to them as persons and language teachers. They make a selection of the most important images and describe why they matter to them and in what way they represent the kind of language teacher they wish to become in an oral/written narrative or in a dialogue with their colleague, mentor or fellow participant on a teacher development course;
- *Vision boards* and *image portfolios* which encourage teachers to construct visual displays of their teaching visions, using photos, magazine pictures, newspapers cuttings, etc.;
- *Written narratives*, such as narrating future histories (i.e. describing future in the past tense as if it had already happened) or writing a future letter to oneself from a former student;
- *Story telling*, such as narrating autobiographical stories about teachers' past, present and future selves or retelling stories involving critical incidents;
- *Visual rehearsals*, such as lesson planning visualisations (Arnold 1999; Thornbury 1999) and resilience visualisations (Fletcher 2000);

Imagine that you are taking me on a tour around your ideal classroom. You can look around the room and you can hear and see the activities going on …

- What do you see, feel and hear when you walk around your ideal classroom?
- What are you doing in your ideal classroom? What is your role? Why?
- What are your students doing in this ideal classroom? What role(s) do the students play? Why?
- What kinds of things are the students learning in your ideal classroom? For instance, what activities, topics or texts are they working on? Why are those important for them to learn?
- What is the relationship between what goes on in your ideal classroom and the kind of society you would like to see in the twenty-first century?

Illustration 3. A sample task for generating images of Ideal Language Teacher Selves (adapted from Hammerness 2006)

- *Video self-modelling* (cf. Dowrick 2012), i.e. success video montage made up of clips of a teacher performing at his or her best;
- *Transportation into narrative worlds* through reading books or watching films about inspirational teachers.

The previous discussion has highlighted the importance of paying explicit attention to imagination on teacher education programmes and enabling teachers to imagine language teaching, language classrooms and themselves as language teachers in new ways. The final principle for motivating language teachers from the vision building perspective is therefore as follows: *helping teachers to become inspirational practitioners means helping them to dare to imagine.*

Conclusion

Although the past 25 years of inquiry into language teachers' cognitions has transformed our understanding of the language teaching and teacher learning activity, the traditional notions of teacher learning and knowledge continue to shape current models of second language teacher education practice (Tedick 2009; Wright 2010). The reasons for such a state of affairs are far too many to review here. It could be argued, however, that reinvigorating the research domain's agendas and approaches could contribute to producing a more robust evidence-base which may inspire a more widespread uptake of language teacher education practices that support the development of effective language education professionals.

One promising direction in current research has been the subject of this chapter. Researchers are beginning to understand that what teachers think, believe, and know, that is, the traditional concerns of the language teacher cognition research (Borg 2003), is inextricably linked with what they are passionate about, who they yearn to become, how they imagine teaching and themselves as language teachers, and how they resist imposed visions and normative pressures in their teaching worlds. The future of this domain of research therefore seems to lie in extending the inquiry to include the focus on the emotional, moral, motivational and imaginative dimensions of language teachers' work. The questions that are likely to gain greater prominence in future research and inform language teacher education pedagogy include inquiry into what images of desired language teacher selves teacher education programmes will need to cultivate in order to engage teachers in deep learning, and how language teacher educators can facilitate teachers' development of a moral vision for language teaching, which will contribute to transforming classrooms into places of learning. The principles for motivating language teachers through vision outlined in this chapter will hopefully contribute to both initiating productive new lines of research inquiry and developing powerful language teacher education interventions that will enable teachers to (re)connect with who they are, engage with the ethical dimension of language teaching and develop imaginative capacity and courage to conceive of what does not yet exist.

References

Abednia, A. (2012). Teachers' professional identity: Contributions of a critical EFL teacher education course in Iran. *Teaching and Teacher Education*, 28, 706–717.
DOI: 10.1016/j.tate.2012.02.005

Akbari, R., & Tajik, L. (2012). Second-language teachers' moral knowledge base: A comparison between experienced and less experienced, male and female practitioners. *Journal of Moral Education*, 41, 39–59. DOI: 10.1080/03057240.2011.630384

Arnold, J. (1999). Visualization: Language learning with the mind's eye. In J. Arnold (Ed.), *Affect in language learning* (pp. 260–278). Cambridge: Cambridge University Press.

Assor, A., Kaplan, H., Feinberg, O., & Tal, K. (2009). Combining vision with voice: A learning and implementation structure promoting teachers' internalization of practices based on self-determination theory. *Theory and Research in Education*, 7, 234–243.
DOI: 10.1177/1477878509104328

Basturkmen, H. (2012). Review of research into the correspondence between language teachers' stated beliefs and practices. *System*, 40, 282–295. DOI: 10.1016/j.system.2012.05.001

Bodur, Y. (2012). Impact of course and fieldwork on multicultural beliefs and attitudes. *The Education Forum*, 76, 41–56. DOI: 10.1080/00131725.2011.627981

Borg, S. (2003). Teacher cognition in language teaching: A review of research on what language teachers think, know, believe, and do. *Language Teaching*, 36, 81–109. DOI: 10.1017/S0261444803001903

Borg, S. (2011). The impact of in-service teacher education on language teachers' beliefs. *System*, 39, 370–380. DOI: 10.1016/j.system.2011.07.009

Borrero, N. (2011). Entering teaching for and with love: Visions of pre-service urban teachers. *Journal of Urban Learning, Teaching, and Research*, 7, 18–26.

Breen, M.P., Hird, B., Milton, M., Oliver, R., & Thwaite, A. (2001). Making sense of language teaching: Teachers' principles and classroom practices. *Applied Linguistics*, 22, 470–501. DOI: 10.1093/applin/22.4.470

Casbon, C.H., Shagoury, R., & Smith, G.A. (2005). Rediscovering the call to teach: A new vision for professional and personal development. *Language Arts*, 82, 359–366.

Crookes, G. (1997). SLA and language pedagogy. *Studies in Second Language Acquisition*, 19, 93–116. DOI: 10.1017/S027226319700106X

Crookes, G. (2009). *Values, philosophies, and beliefs in TESOL: Making a statement*. Cambridge: Cambridge University Press.

Crookes, G. (2010). The practicality and relevance of second language critical pedagogy. *Language Teaching*, 43, 333–348. DOI: 10.1017/S0261444809990292

Doiz, A., Lasagabaster, D., & Sierra, J.M. (2011). Internationalisation, multilingualism and English-medium instruction. *World Englishes*, 30, 345–359. DOI: 10.1111/j.1467-971X.2011.01718.x

Dörnyei, Z. (2005). *The psychology of the language learner: Individual differences in second language acquisition*. Mahwah, NJ: Lawrence Erlbaum Associates.

Dörnyei, Z., & Kubanyiova, M. (2014). *Motivating learners, motivating teachers: Building vision in the language classroom*. Cambridge: Cambridge University Press.

Dörnyei, Z., & Ushioda, E. (Eds.). (2009). *Motivation, language identity and the L2 self*. Bristol: Multilingual Matters.

Dowrick, P.W. (2012). Self modeling: Expanding the theories of learning. *Psychology in Schools*, 49, 30–41. DOI: 10.1002/pits.20613

Efstathia, P. (2008). Voices from the Greek community schools: Bilingual pedagogy and teachers' theories. *Innovation in Language Learning and Teaching*, 2, 189–205. DOI: 10.1080/17501220802158909

Ellis, R. (2010). Second language acquisition, teacher education and language pedagogy. *Language Teaching*, 43, 182–201. DOI: 10.1017/S0261444809990139

Farrell, T.S.C. (2011). Exploring the professional role identities of experienced ESL teachers through reflective practice. *System*, 39, 54–62. DOI: 10.1016/j.system.2011.01.012

Farrell, T.S.C. (2014). *Reflective practice in ESL teacher development groups: From practices to principles*. Basingstoke: Palgrave Macmillan.

Feryok, A., & Pryde, M. (2012). Images as orienting activity: Using theory to inform classroom practices. *Teachers and Teaching: theory and practice*, 18, 441–454. DOI: 10.1080/13540602.2012.696045

Fettes, M. (2005). Imaginative transformation in teacher education. *Teaching Education*, 16, 3–11. DOI: 10.1080/1047621052000341572

Fletcher, S. (2000). A role for imagery in mentoring. *Career Development International*, 5, 235–243. DOI: 10.1108/EUM0000000005361

Freeman, D. (1991). 'To make the tacit explicit': Teacher education emerging discourse, and conceptions of teaching. *Teaching and Teacher Education*, 7, 439–454. DOI: 10.1016/0742-051X(91)90040-V

Gao, F. (2012). Teacher identity, teaching vision, and Chinese language education for South Asian students in Hong Kong. *Teachers and Teaching: theory and practice*, 18, 89–99. DOI: 10.1080/13540602.2011.622558

Golombek, P.R. (1998). A study of language teachers' personal practical knowledge. *TESOL Quarterly*, 32, 447–464. DOI: 10.2307/3588117

Golombek, P.R. (2009). Personal practical knowledge in L2 teacher education. In A. Burns & J.C. Richards (Eds.), *The Cambridge guide to second language teacher education* (pp. 155–162). Cambridge: Cambridge University Press.

Golombek, P.R., & Johnson, K. E. (2004). Narrative inquiry as a mediational space: Examining emotional and cognitive dissonance in second-language teachers' development. *Teachers and Teaching: Theory and practice*, 10, 307–327. DOI: 10.1080/1354060042000204388

Goodman, J. (1988). Constructing a practical philosophy of teaching: A study of pre-service teachers' professional perspectives. *Teaching and Teacher Education*, 4, 121–137. DOI: 10.1016/0742-051X(88)90013-3

Grossman, P. (2008). Responding to our critics: From crisis to opportunity in research on teacher education. *Journal of Teacher Education*, 59, 10–23. DOI: 10.1177/0022487107310748

Hadfield, J., & Dörnyei, Z. (2013). *Motivating learning*. Harlow: Pearson.

Hamman, D., Gosselin, K., Romano, J., & Bunuan, R. (2010). Using possible-selves theory to understand the identity development of new teachers. *Teaching and Teacher Education*, 26, 1349–1361. DOI: 10.1016/j.tate.2010.03.005

Hammerness, K. (2003). Learning to hope, or hoping to learn? The role of vision in the early professional lives of teachers. *Journal of Teacher Education*, 54, 43–56. DOI: 10.1177/0022487102238657

Hammerness, K. (2006). *Seeing through teachers' eyes: Professional ideals and classroom practices*. New York, NY: Teachers College Press.

Henry, A. (2010). Contexts of possibility in simultaneous language learning: Using the L2 Motivational Self System to assess the impact of global English. *Journal of Multilingual and Multicultural Development*, 31, 149–162. DOI: 10.1080/01434630903471439

Hiver, P.V. (2013). The interplay of possible language teacher selves in professional development choices. *Language Teaching Research*, 17, 210–227. DOI: 10.1177/1362168813475944

Horn, I.S., Nolen, S.B., Ward, C., & Campbell, S.S. (2008). Developing practices in multiple worlds: The role of identity in learning to teach. *Teacher Education Quarterly*, 35, 61–72.

Johnson, K.E. (1994). The emerging beliefs and instructional practices of preservice English as a second language teachers. *Teaching and Teacher Education*, 10, 439–452. DOI: 10.1016/0742-051X(94)90024-8

Johnston, B. (2003). *Values in English language teaching*. Mahwah, NJ: Lawrence Erlbaum Associates.

Kanno, Y., & Stuart, C. (2011). The development of L2 teacher identity: Longitudinal case studies. *The Modern Language Journal*, 95, 236–252. DOI: 10.1111/j.1540-4781.2011.01178.x

Kennedy, M.M. (2006). Knowledge and vision in teaching. *Journal of Teacher Education*, 57, 205–211. DOI: 10.1177/0022487105285639

Kubanyiova, M. (2006). Developing a motivational teaching practice in EFL teachers in Slovakia: Challenges of promoting teacher change in EFL contexts. *TESL-EJ. Special Issue: Language Education Research in International Contexts*, 10, 1–17. Retrieved from <http://www.tesl-ej.org/ej38/a5.pdf>

Kubanyiova, M. (2009). Possible selves in language teacher development. In Z. Dörnyei & E. Ushioda (Eds.), *Motivation, language identity and the L2 Self* (pp. 314–332). Bristol: Multilingual Matters.

Kubanyiova, M. (2012). *Teacher development in action: Understanding language teachers' conceptual change*. Basingstoke: Palgrave Macmillan.

Kubanyiova, M. (2013). Towards understanding the role of faith in the development of language teachers' identities: A modest proposal for extending the research agenda. In M.S. Wong, C. Kristjánsson, & Z. Dörnyei (Eds.), *Christian faith and English language teaching and learning: Research on the interrelationship of religion and ELT* (pp. 85–92). New York, NY: Routledge.

Kumazawa, M. (2013). Gaps too large: Four novice EFL teachers' self-concept and motivation. *Teaching and Teacher Education*, 33, 45–55. DOI: 10.1016/j.tate.2013.02.005

Lamie, J.M. (2004). Presenting a model of change. *Language Teaching Research*, 8, 115–142. DOI: 10.1191/1362168804lr137oa

Lasagabaster, D., & Sierra, J.M. (2011). Classroom observation: desirable conditions established by teachers. *European Journal of Teacher Education*, 34, 449–463. DOI: 10.1080/02619768.2011.587113

Lee, I. (2010). Writing teacher education and teacher learning: Testimonies of four EFL teachers. *Journal of Second Language Writing*, 19, 143–157. DOI: 10.1016/j.jslw.2010.05.001

Liu, E., & Noppe-Brandon, S. (2009). *Imagination first: Unlocking the power of possibility*. San Francisco, CA: Jossey-Bass.

Magid, M., & Chan, L. (2012). Motivating English learners by helping them visualise their Ideal L2 Self: Lessons from two motivational programmes. *Innovation in Language Learning and Teaching*, 6, 113–125. DOI: 10.1080/17501229.2011.614693

Mangubhai, F. (2007). The moral and ethical dimensions of language teaching. *Australian Journal of Education*, 51, 178–189. DOI: 10.1177/000494410705100206

Mangubhai, F., Marland, P., Dashwood, A., & Son, J.-B. (2005). Similarities and differences in teachers' and researchers' conceptions of communicative language teaching: does the use of an educational model cast a better light? *Language Teaching Research*, 9, 31–66. DOI: 10.1191/1362168805lr153oa

Markus, H., & Nurius, P. (1986). Possible selves. *American Psychologist*, 41, 954–969. DOI: 10.1037/0003-066X.41.9.954

McElhone, D., Hebhard, H., Scot, R., & Connie, J. (2009). The role of vision in trajectories of literacy practice among new teachers. *Studying Teacher Education*, 5, 147–158. DOI: 10.1080/17425960903306682

Mendelsohn, D.J. (Ed.). (1999). *Expanding our vision*. Toronto: OUP.

Mori, R. (2011). Teacher cognition in corrective feedback in Japan. *System*, 39, 451–467. DOI: 10.1016/j.system.2011.10.014

Mullock, B. (2006). The pedagogical knowledge base of four TESOL teachers. *The Modern Language Journal*, 90, 48–66. DOI: 10.1111/j.1540-4781.2006.00384.x

Ortega, L. (2012). Language acquisition research for language teaching: Choosing between application and relevance. In B. Hinger, E.M. Unterrainer, & D. Newby (Eds.), *Sprachen lernen: Kompetenzen entwickeln? Performanzen (über)prüfen* (pp. 24–38). Wien: Präsens Verlag.

Palmer, P.J. (2007). *The courage to teach: Exploring the inner landscape of a teacher's life* (10th ed.). San Francisco, CA: Jossey-Bass.

Papi, M., & Abdollahzadeh, E. (2012). Teacher motivational practice, student motivation, and possible L2 selves: An examination in the Iranian EFL context. *Language Learning*, 62, 571–594. DOI: 10.1111/j.1467-9922.2011.00632.x

Pastoll, G. (2009). *Motivating people to learnand teachers to teach*. Bloomington, IN: Author-House.

Postman, N. (1996). *The end of education: Redefining the value of school*. New York, NY: Vintage.

Ronfeldt, M., & Grossman, P. (2008). Becoming a professional: Experimenting with possible selves in professional preparation. *Teacher Education Quarterly*, 35, 41–60.

Scarino, A. (2005). Introspection and retrospection as windows on teacher knowledge, values, and ethical dispositions. In D.J. Tedick (Ed.), *Second language teacher education: International perspectives* (pp. 33–52). Mahwah, NJ: Lawrence Erlbaum Associates.

Sharkey, J., & Johnson, K.E. (Eds.). (2003). *The TESOL Quarterly dialogues: Rethinking issues of language, culture, and power*. Alexandria, VA: TESOL.

Tedick, D.J. (2009). K-12 language teacher preparation: Problems and possibilities. *The Modern Language Journal*, 93, 263–267. DOI: 10.1111/j.1540-4781.2009.00860_2.x

Thornbury, S. (1999). Lesson art and design. *ELT Journal*, 53, 4–11. DOI: 10.1093/elt/53.1.4

Tsang, W.K. (2004). Teachers' personal practical knowledge and interactive decisions. *Language Teaching Research*, 8, 163–198. DOI: 10.1191/1362168804lr139oa

Tsui, A.B.M. (2007). Complexities of identity formation: A narrative inquiry of an EFL teacher. *TESOL Quarterly*, 41, 657–680.

Varghese, M.M., & Johnston, B. (2007). Evangelical Christians and English language teaching. *TESOL Quarterly*, 41, 5–31.

Walters, K. (Ed.). (2001). *Rufus Jones: Essential writings*. Maryknoll, NY: Orbis Books.

Wan, W., Low, G.D., & Li, M. (2011). From students' and teachers' perspectives: Metaphor analysis of beliefs about EFL teachers' roles. *System*, 39, 403–415. DOI: 10.1016/j.system.2011.07.012

Warford, M.K., & Reeves, J. (2003). Falling into it: Novice TESOL teacher thinking. *Teachers and Teaching: Theory and Practice*, 9, 47–65. DOI: 10.1080/1354060032000049904

Watzke, J.L. (2007). Foreign language pedagogical knowledge: Toward a developmental theory of beginning teacher practices. *The Modern Language Journal*, 91, 63–82. DOI: 10.1111/j.1540-4781.2007.00510.x

Wong, M.S. (2013). Called to teach: The impact of faith on professional identity formation of three Western English teachers in China. In M.S. Wong, C. Kristjánsson, & Z. Dörnyei (Eds.). *Christian faith and English language teaching and learning: Research on the interrelationship of religion and ELT* (pp. 11–30). New York, NY: Routledge.

Woods, D., & Çakır, H. (2011). Two dimensions of teacher knowledge: The case of communicative language teaching. *System*, 39, 381–390. DOI: 10.1016/j.system.2011.07.010

Wright, T. (2010). Second language teacher education: Review of recent research on practice. *Language Teaching*, 43, 259–296. DOI: 10.1017/S0261444810000030

Studies on motivation in foreign language classrooms

CHAPTER 5

Swedish students' beliefs about learning English in and outside of school

Alastair Henry

In Sweden students' encounters with English in and out of school are very different. Spending around 20 hours per week in English-mediated environments outside of school, they are often engaged in richly meaningful activities. Consequently, many young people believe they learn as much of their English as a result of participation in English-mediated leisure time activities as they do from textbook-dominated classroom instruction. Drawing on emerging discussions on the ways in which learners' beliefs about the primacy of learning English in natural environments can have negative effects on learning behaviours in formal settings (e.g. Mercer & Ryan 2010), and how learners' beliefs about the causes of success in language learning can impact on motivation (e.g. Hsieh 2012), this chapter examines the ways in which such beliefs may impact on Swedish students' responses to classroom learning.

Keywords: informal learning, beliefs, self-regulation, motivation, gender differences

The setting

As a backdrop to the discussions that follow, three aspects of the social/societal context in which young people in Sweden grow up are worth highlighting. First, Sweden is a small linguistic community, second, levels of English language proficiency are generally high, and third, Sweden is currently the world leader in technological development and Internet access/use.

A small linguistic community

With little more than 10 million speakers of Swedish worldwide, nearly all of the foreign cultural media imported into Sweden (primarily from the US and the UK)

is broadcast and published in English. With the exception of offerings for the very youngest children, television programs are not dubbed into Swedish, instead having Swedish subtitles. Similarly, although there is an abundance of Swedish-mediated Internet sites in all imaginable fields, people in Sweden are accustomed to searching for information and carrying out business transactions and social interaction via English-mediated sites. Furthermore, since English functions as the default language in digital gaming (Waters 2007) – which, as elsewhere, is an extremely popular activity among young people in Sweden (particularly boys) – both casual and serious gaming often takes place in English.

High levels of English language proficiency

People living in Sweden are generally regarded as being good at English, and in two recent international surveys Sweden has emerged as the country with the highest levels of English language proficiency. In the European Commission's Survey on Language Competences, SurveyLang, (European Commission 2012), more 14–15 year-old students in Sweden than in any of the other 15 countries surveyed were assessed to be in the Common European Framework B2 'upper intermediate user' category for both reading and listening.[1] Similarly, in a survey assessing levels of adults' skills in English commissioned by *EF*, the language education provider, the Swedish respondents were ranked first among the 54 participating countries.[2] Not only do the vast majority of young people in Sweden gain passing grades or higher in English at secondary and upper secondary levels, but CLIL (Content and Language Integrated Learning) programs at the upper secondary level are not uncommon (Sylvén 2013) and an increasing number of university courses and programs are now being provided in English (see e.g. Airey 2009).

Technologically advanced with universal Internet use

In Sweden there is almost universal access to high-speed broadband Internet and in the World Economic Forum's 'Networked Readiness Index' (World Economic Forum, Global Information Technology Report 2012) Sweden was ranked first of 142 countries. 'Networked readiness' gauges everyday technological affordances including a society's ICT (Information and Communication Technology) uptake,

---

1. The C categories were not measured.

2. It is important to point out that contrary to the rigorous procedures of SurveyLang, EF's online survey does not meet generally accepted scientific standards in that participants are self-selected.

its preparation to make good use of an affordable ICT infrastructure, the efforts of the main social agents to increase their capacity to use ICT, ICT use in day-to-day activities, and the social impacts accruing from ICT. Ownership of a computer is common among young people in Sweden. According to the Swedish Media Council (2013), in 2012/2013 81% of 13–16 year-olds owned their own computer (with the remaining 19% having access to one in the family), and 99% of the same age group owned their own mobile phone. As the Media Council has shown, the use of the Internet is almost universal among young people, with 93% of 13–16 year-olds reporting using the Internet every day, with the remaining 7% reporting being online frequently during the week. Moreover, using the Internet – for surfing, social networking and playing digital games – was by far the most commonly reported free-time activity for all age groups (Swedish Media Council 2013).

Out-of-school encounters with English

Extent, scope and impact on language acquisition

Many of the online activities, digital games, music, and TV programs popular among young people in Sweden are mediated in English (Swedish Media Council 2013). While in some cases Swedish language alternatives do not exist, in other cases they are not as attractive. For example, the most popular TV series watched by Swedish youngsters in the 13–16 age bracket in 2012/2013 were *Family Guy* (24% watching regularly) *The Simpsons* (22%) and *How I met your Mother* (15%). All of these programs are broadcast in English with Swedish subtitles. For digital gaming, the four most popular games played by young people aged 13–16 in the same period were *FIFA* (26%), *Call of Duty* (COD) (23%), *Minecraft* (20%) and *League of Legends* (LOL) (16%), with other popular games including *Battlefield* and *World of Warcraft* (WOW), each played by 9% of boys (Swedish Media Council 2013). With the exception of *Minecraft* and *FIFA*, which can be played using Swedish language settings,[3] the other games are English mediated. All of these games are overwhelmingly played by boys, with 90% of 13–16 year-old boys playing digital games compared to only 36% of girls in the same age group (for whom *The Sims*[4] was the most popular game). For the boys 44% of 13–16 year-olds report playing digital games for more than three hours every day.

---

3. Anecdotal reports suggest that for *FIFA* in particular English language game settings are often selected.

4. *The Sims* can be played in both English and Swedish.

In gaming trends change very quickly. While, for example, *World of Warcraft* was the second most popular digital game in 2010, it is joint fifth in popularity in 2012/2013 (Swedish Media Council 2010, 2013). A noticeable trend in 2013 and 2014 has been the increased popularity of *League of Legends*, as well as two other 'action real time strategy' games, *Defence of Ancients 2 (DOTA2)* and *Heroes of Newerth (HON)*.[5] Many of the English-mediated games commonly played by 13–16 year-olds in Sweden – especially *World of Warcraft, League of Legends, Defence of Ancients 2* and *Heroes of Newerth* – put players in environments that place very high demands on understanding and communication. As revealed in recent research (e.g. Liang 2012; Peterson 2010, 2012; Reinders & Wattana 2011; Thorne 2008), playing multiplayer action and role-playing games can have a positive impact on language acquisition. Not only do such games provide rich lexical environments, the design features of 'massively multiplayer online role-playing' and 'action real time strategy' games also play an important role in developing communicative skills. As for example Peterson (2010) explains, network-based text and voice chat provide multiple communication channels for real-time interaction and feedback, challenging themes engage players in the pursuit of complex quests, while goal-based interaction encourages the development of collaborative social relationships. Further, the use of personal avatars can enhance a player's in-game immersion, reduce inhibition and facilitate risk-taking.

Mapping the amount of time students in Sweden spend in English-mediated environments, Sundqvist (2009), and Olsson (2011), asked samples of 9th grade (15-year-old) students to maintain language diaries over designated periods of time. In these diaries students recorded the amount of time they spent each day on English-mediated activities, such as watching TV, watching films, visiting Internet sites, playing digital games and listening to music. While in her study Sundqvist found that students (n = 80) spent an average of over 18 hours a week in English-mediated environments (20.8 hours per week for boys, and 16.4 hours per week for girls), in Olsson's study the average time that students (n = 74) were in contact with English was just over 20 hours per week (23 hours per week for boys, and 17.5 hours per week for girls).[6]

In Sundqvist's (2009) study (also reported on in Sundqvist & Sylvén 2012), the impact of out-of-school encounters with English on tests of students' oral

---

5. For *League of Legends* this reflects a global trend where, according its manufacturer, Riot Games, as of January 2014, it was played worldwide by 27 million people daily, 67 million monthly and had recorded peaks of 7.5 million concurrent players (*Forbes Magazine*, 2014).

6. In both studies, students also completed questionnaires asking about out-of-school contacts with English. The questionnaires revealed a substantially higher number of contacts with English. The language diaries are, however, regarded as more accurate measures.

proficiency and vocabulary skills was also investigated. In both cases positive correlations were found between the amount of time spent in English-mediated environments and students' test scores. Findings also revealed that some out-of-school activities had a greater influence on test results than others. Activities that involved a greater degree of interaction – for example digital gaming and visiting English-mediated Internet sites – were found to have more of an impact than receptive activities such as listening to music and watching films and TV. A gender effect was also found. Not only did boys spend more time than girls on interactive activities (particularly digital gaming), but for them the impact of out-of-school English-mediated activities on vocabulary and oral skills was also greater. In Olsson's (2011) study, which focused on written proficiency, similarly significant correlations were found. Here too students who were frequent users of English outside the classroom – again more boys than girls – performed better on tests of writing proficiency.

Learning English in school

Having sketched a picture of young people's encounters with English outside school, I turn now to consider the situation inside the classroom. Alongside mathematics and Swedish, English is a core subject, which most students start learning in the first grade (age 7). Although schools have discretion in allocating time to English across different stages of secondary education, by grade 6 (age 12), the average secondary school student will usually have two 50- to 60-minute lessons per week.

During the period October 2010 to February 2011, an extensive subject evaluation of English in grades 6 through to 9 was conducted by the Swedish Schools Inspectorate (2011). Structured observations of nearly 300 lessons at 22 different schools from different parts of the country were carried out. Interviews with randomly selected students and teachers of English at these schools were conducted, and questionnaires were completed by some 3000 students. In reporting on the quality of English education, a number of problems were identified.

In the majority of the classrooms visited, the inspectors describe learning environments that were secure and supportive. However the inspectors also found little evidence of activities that awakened students' interest, or provided them with any real challenge (see also Busse in this volume). Many of the lessons observed were constructed around commercially-produced learning materials, with a 'one-size-fits-all' approach being common. Instances where teachers used authentic materials were few. The tasks and questions students were given often anticipated 'right or wrong' answers, and while students would frequently be provided with texts about other countries and other cultures, rarely were they required to do more than answer questions and translate these texts into Swedish. Activities designed to accommodate students' differing interests were rarely encountered. Furthermore, in nearly half of the lessons observed, few opportunities for oral interaction were provided. Indeed, in only one fifth of all classes was English spoken consistently throughout the lesson. Worryingly, in some lessons hardly a word of English was spoken. The use of digital technologies was also extremely rare, a finding confirmed in the student questionnaire where 80% of students reported that computers were infrequently or never used in English lessons.

In many of the interviews, students talked about how the working methods used in English classes could be mundane, and learning not particularly challenging. In an otherwise demanding school day, students spoke about how English could provide a welcome opportunity to relax; the format of lessons were predictable and the demands not too high. Furthermore, a difference between English in school and English outside, particularly in the type of communication that takes place, was also identified. In particular students talked about how there were few, if any, opportunities to make use of out-of-school experiences of English in the classroom, and how they are much more comfortable using English outside school than inside.

A situation unique to Sweden?

Although the combination of a high level of technological development and the small linguistic community might suggest that the in-school/out-of-school differences in students' encounters with English found in Sweden may differ from those of students in other countries, it is interesting that similar phenomena have recently been reported in other settings. Referring to anecdotal evidence from teachers from a number of different European countries, Ushioda (2013) describes how many paint a similar picture; students seem to find English in school boring and invest little effort in classroom activities. Because students may feel a greater sense of self-confidence and self-fulfilment when communicating in English in out-of-school environments, this can mean that there are few incentives for them to work on the development of formal skills (Ushioda 2013). Looking at the situation in Romania, Taylor (2013), for example, identifies a widespread feeling among students that, in school, they are not valued as individuals and their interests are not taken into account.

Recognising fundamental differences in students' in and out-of-school experiences of English, and the negative impact that such dissonances can have on motivation, Ushioda (2013) argues that teachers working in settings where

English is part of the social fabric of young people's daily lives are now facing very real challenges in providing learning opportunities that can generate and sustain interest and motivation. As a means of addressing this challenge she emphasizes the importance of giving students possibilities to engage in personally meaningful activities where they can express their identities. As Ushioda (2011a) explains, when proper account is not taken of students' different social identities, motivation is likely to suffer. Teachers, she contends, need therefore to "invoke and orient to students' transportable identities in the classroom" and engage with their students "as 'people' rather than as simply 'language learners'". This means giving them opportunities to build their own personally relevant connections between what they do in and outside of class, and allowing them "to speak as themselves" and to "engage and express their own preferred meanings, interests and identities through the medium of the target language" (Ushioda 2011a: 17).

In a similar take on the problem, Henry (2013) has suggested that students' reluctance to engage in classroom learning can be understood in the sense that classroom activities lack authenticity. While many of the things students do in their leisure time that are English-mediated, such as digital gaming, can often provide them with meaningful, positive and identity-confirming experiences, work done in school is frequently perceived as artificial and distant from 'reality'. Because, he explains, students are likely to compare the English-mediated, identity-congruent activities they engage in outside school with the mundane and sometimes meaningless activities taking place in the classroom, their reluctance to invest in classroom work can be understood in terms of experiencing a lack of self-authenticity or feelings of "frustrated authenticity". Specifically, he contends, they lack "the scope to use the language in the same meaningful and self-relevant ways" that it is used in out-of-school environments, such as in digital gaming (Henry 2013: 146).

As both Ushioda (2011a, 2011b, 2013) and Henry (2013) suggest, it is of great importance that pedagogical practices which bridge between the worlds in and outside the classroom, and which engage students' identities, are developed. However, even if context-bridging, identity-confirming pedagogies can be developed and implemented in instruction, such initiatives may not, on their own, be sufficient to engage students' interest and generate motivation. Beliefs about the ease and efficacy of different acquisition processes are also likely to have a fundamental impact on the ways learning is approached (Mercer, Ryan, & Williams 2012). Thus, if students believe that English is most effectively learnt in naturalistic out-of-school situations, they may still be reluctant to put effort into classroom activities. It is therefore important that, in the context of the in-school/out-of-school dissonance, researchers and teachers develop an understanding of students' beliefs, the effects these can have on approaches to classroom work, and ways in which they can be addressed.

Taking data from the Swedish Schools Inspectorate's (2011) student question-naire, in the sections that follow, I examine students' beliefs about the relative value of learning English in and out of school. Drawing on different theories of self-regulation, I consider how these beliefs can impact on classroom motivation, particularly for those students – mainly boys – who believe that they learn most or nearly all of their English outside school. In attempting to generate insights into the ways in which beliefs about the relative efficacy of different acquisition contexts might impact on approaches to classroom learning, my intention is not to make any general claims, nor draw any specific conclusions. Rather, I want to explore some of the possible consequences that students' beliefs may have for classroom motivation and to identify areas that could usefully be explored in future research.

Beliefs about the effects of out-of-school encounters with English

As we have seen, students in Sweden spend substantial periods of time in En-glish-mediated environments that are often personally meaningful, identity-con-firming and in which they feel comfortable using the language. Contrasted with the rather negative experiences many have of learning English in the classroom, it is perhaps not surprising that large numbers of students believe that much of their language competence is gained in out-of-school settings. In the Swedish Schools Inspectorate's student questionnaire, one of the items asked participants (n = 2,868) to indicate where they believed that they had learnt most of their English. Of the responses received, substantially more than half believed that they had learned more, or at least as much of their English, outside of school. Further-more, 16% of all students said they believed that they had learnt most or nearly all of their English outside of school (see Figure 1).

Learner beliefs

Because they have been investigated in diverse fields, and because researchers have different agendas, learner beliefs are, conceptually, difficult to pin down. Un-like knowledge – which is based on objective 'fact' – beliefs are based on evalua-tion and judgment. This means that the researcher has to make inferences about underlying states. Beliefs are thus "inferred from what people say, intend, and do" (Pajares 1992: 314). With regard to beliefs about second language acquisition,

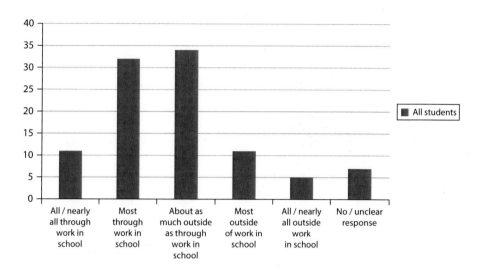

Figure 1. Responses to the question: 'Where do you believe you learned most of what you know in English?'

Barcelos (2003:8) emphasises the importance of the cultural setting and social milieu, making the point that understanding students' beliefs "means under- standing their world and their identity". Furthermore, because beliefs about SLA are variable, context-embedded and complexly interrelated, they encompass not just matters that people perceive to be true, and are sufficiently confident about to act upon, but also knowledge which is contingently accepted as true (Barcelos 2003).

Self-regulation

As Bandura (1977, 1986) has demonstrated, the beliefs people hold about their abilities and the consequences of their efforts impact not only on the ways they behave, but also on the cognitive and affective processes involved in the pursuance of different goals. Self-regulation describes the ways in which individuals *activate* and *sustain* the cognitions, affects and behaviours that are systematically oriented to learning goals (Schunk & Zimmerman 2008; Zimmerman 2000). Self-regula- tion functions thus as an overarching construct, encompassing a wide range of differing activities that, for example, include organizing and coding information to be learned, attending to and concentrating on instructions, and establishing positive conditions for learning. It also encompasses broader-based beliefs about learning, such as holding positive beliefs about the capacity to learn, beliefs about the anticipated outcomes of learning, and beliefs about the value of learning (Pintrich 2000). From the range of different theories relating to self-regulation, three seem to offer particularly interesting lenses through which to consider the motivational consequences of out-of-school encounters with English; Bandura's (1977, 1986) theory of *self-efficacy* (in SLA contexts applied by Mills, Pajares & Herron 2007), Weiner's (1992) *attribution theory* (used in SLA by Hsieh 2012), and Dweck's (1999) theory of *implicit theories of intelligence* (recently applied in SLA contexts by Mercer & Ryan 2010).

Self-efficacy beliefs

As Bandura (1986) has explained, through processes of self-evaluation, where the individual reflects upon and evaluates thoughts, feelings and experiences, people are able to condition the ways in which they think and behave. Through such processes people make judgments about their capabilities to accomplish different tasks and about the activities in which they wish to engage. Rooted in core beliefs about individual agency – the power to bring about change as a result of one's actions – self-efficacy forms the foundation for motivation. This, as Pajares (2008) explains, is because unless people believe that their actions can produce desired outcomes, they will not have the incentive to pursue particular behaviours, or to persevere when difficulties are encountered.

Expectations about future behaviours are rooted in experiences of the consequences of previous actions. Based on self-evaluation of prior experiences, choices are made about the efficacy of future courses of action. Importantly, beliefs about self-efficacy relate not to *actual* ability, but rather to what, given her/his own particular set of skills, the individual *believes* she/he can accomplish (Pajares 2008). For this reason, self-efficacy beliefs have a greater impact on the effort expended on an activity than prior successes, skills or knowledge (Bandura 1997). Individuals who hold beliefs about their self-efficacy are more focused in their learning behaviours and, as Pajares and his colleagues (Mills, Pajares, & Herron 2007; Pajares 2008; Pajares, Britner, & Valiente 2000) make clear, these beliefs can be very powerful, enabling the individual to continue with a course of action even in the face of obstacles and adversity. Moreover, when failures are experienced, individuals who believe in their own self-efficacy are more likely to attribute them to deficiencies in effort or knowledge, with setbacks less likely to impact on future effort than would be the case for less self-efficacious individuals.

Investigating self-efficacy in the context of foreign language learning in a sample of US university students studying French, Pajares and his colleagues (Mills, Pajares, & Herron 2007) found it to be a predictor of achievement. One construct in particular, *self-efficacy for self-regulation* – that is to say the perceived ability to use appropriate strategies to plan, monitor, and complete a task – was found to have a particularly strong effect. Additionally, self-efficacy for self-regulation was also found to be positively correlated with perceptions of the value of French and French culture, leading the authors to conclude that, in the classroom context, levels of self-regulation will be related to students' interest in the language and cultures associated with it. In another study examining self-efficacy and achievement in language learning, this time in a Korean context with 9th grade students learning English, Hsieh and Kang (2010) found, as anticipated, the two variables to be positively correlated.

In what sense then, in the context of Swedish students' encounters with English, might a self-efficacy perspective contribute to understanding how out-of-school experiences can impact on classroom motivation? Even if it were empirically possible to quantify the amount of English students actually acquire in leisure time activities, the important point to bear in mind is not whether beliefs about learning English outside school in fact correspond with actual acquisition, but, rather, the strength and impact that such beliefs have on learning behaviours. If students firmly believe that one of the two domains in which English is encountered – the 20 or so hours a week they spend in English-mediated environments (as opposed to the couple of hours in the classroom) – is the primary reason for increases in skills and ability, this is likely to have a negative impact on levels of self-regulated behaviour in the classroom. If students do not believe that their actions produce desired outcomes – i.e. that efforts expended in the classroom do not lead to a fluent command of English – then there will be little incentive for them to actively engage in the learning activities on offer, or to direct effort to areas of perceived difficulty, such as grammar. It is therefore important that, in settings where young people regularly encounter English in out-of-school contexts, research with a focus on students' self-efficacy beliefs in relation to the perceived value of different learning contexts is carried out.

Attributions

Attributions are beliefs about the causes of outcomes. Like self-efficacy, attributions have an important impact on self-regulation. Building on Heider's (1958) suggestions that people attribute outcomes to internal factors, such as ability and motivation, as well as to external factors in the surrounding environment, Kelley (1967) argues that, faced with a range of competing possibilities, people are selective in the attributions they make, settling on explanations that best seem to fit the event. Thus, in accounting for their successes and failures, students will attribute them to factors such as ability, effort, task difficulty and luck (Weiner 1992; Weiner et al. 1971).

Developing an understanding of students' attributions is particularly important because, like self-efficacy beliefs, they are likely to impact on decisions about where to channel effort and resources. Similarly, the accuracy of attributions is not itself important; even dubious causal attributions that fail to reflect objectively observable reasons for success or failure are sufficient to generate self-regulated learning behaviours (Weiner 2000). Further, people tend also to identify single causal factors when, in reality, reasons might be multiple. With a focus on L2 acquisition, Hsieh (2012) (see also Hsieh & Schallert 2008) offers the following explanation of how attributions can impact on learning behaviour:

> If a student believes that his or her success in learning a foreign language is due to the amount of effort he or she has put into learning (e.g., practicing speaking with a native speaker), the student will expect to do well the next time he or she approaches similar tasks assuming that effort can determine the outcome. Or, if the student fails in a language class and believes that failure is due to his or her low ability (i.e., the person believes they do not have a 'gift' for learning a foreign languages), the student may avoid similar tasks in the future so as to avoid failing again. (Hsieh 2012:91)

In the context of the two different learning environments identified by the students in the Swedish Schools Inspectorate's survey, *locus*, that is to say whether the attribution is internal or external to the individual, is likely to have a particular bearing on the attributions students make. As Schunk (2008) explains, locus impacts on learners' affects and emotions in the sense that greater achievement satisfaction is generated when development is attributed to internal, as opposed to external causes. Because of the reciprocal relationship between affect and attributions – we are more likely to make attributions that make us feel good – there may be a tendency among the students surveyed to attribute successes to the natural acquisition of skills as a result of spending time in English-mediated environments (an *internal* locus), as opposed to the effects of classroom-based learning and focused instruction (an *external* locus). Thus there may exist a dissonance between the actual effects on proficiency of out-of-school encounters with English, and what students *attribute* to such experiences. As with self-efficacy beliefs, research is needed on the nature and effects of the attributions students make in relation to the English language skills they develop, with studies focusing on affective factors being particularly important.

Self-theories of intelligence

As Dweck and her associates (Dweck 1999; Dweck & Leggett 1988) have demonstrated, the views that students hold about intelligence impact on their willingness to engage in, self-regulate and generate motivation for different learning activities. Most individuals hold one of two general views about intelligence. Some, so-called 'entity theorists', believe that intelligence is a deep-seated commodity, more or less innate in nature, and which changes little, if at all, over time. Others, 'incremental theorists', believe that intelligence is malleable and can develop over time as a result of focused learning and effort (Dweck 1999; Dweck & Master 2008). For students who subscribe to an entity view of intelligence, appearing smart is more important than learning, while students who hold incremental views are focused on learning new things, even when there is a risk of losing face. For the former group, success involves being smarter than others, while for the latter, the development of knowledge and skills is the primary aim. When it comes to the effort invested in study, clear differences have been found between the two types of learners. For entity theorists, natural ability is regarded as the key to success and effort is equated with low intelligence. Incremental theorists however see effort in a different way. For them, hard work leads to learning and generates intelligence. If failure occurs, it is put down to insufficient effort and not, like entity theorists, low intelligence. Because entity theorists believe that if you are good at something, hard work should not be necessary, and that if you do have to work hard at something you are probably not very good at it, the central goal in education is to exert the minimum amount of effort (Blackwell, Trzesniewski, & Dweck 2007; Dweck & Master 2008).

In making the case for SLA applications of implicit theories of intelligence (or 'mindsets' as they are also referred to) Mercer and Ryan (Mercer & Ryan 2010; Ryan & Mercer 2011, 2012) identify two different types of what they call 'language learning mindsets'. A *fixed language learning mindset*, they explain, describes a person who holds the belief that successful language learning is attributable to natural talent or to an innate ability. Someone, on the other hand, who holds the belief that language skills can be developed as a result of effort and practice is said to have a *growth language learning mindset*. In developing these ideas, Mercer and Ryan argue that strong beliefs about the efficacy of acquisition in the naturalistic setting of a study abroad context – often entirely separate from classroom learning in the students' home countries – can have negative consequences in terms of demotivating and disempowering learners in the classroom. In pointing to the negative effects of EFL study abroad experiences, particularly for students with fixed language learning mindsets, Ryan and Mercer make the point that, in the Japanese and Austrian contexts in which their studies have been carried out, countries where English is spoken remain "a constant background presence in foreign language learning" (Ryan & Mercer 2011:166). For such learners, they argue, time spent abroad may negate the need for effortful learning at home and compensate for any perceived deficiencies in talent. In extreme cases, learners may take the view that the language development that takes place in naturalistic settings can never be achieved through classroom learning (Ryan & Mercer 2011).

If, as these findings seem to suggest, periods of study abroad can diminish the learner's sense of individual agency, trigger demotivation and impact negatively on approaches to classroom learning, what then of a situation where, as in Sweden, it is not just TL (Target Language) countries or TL cultures that form a "constant background presence", but all the TL-mediated activities engaged in as soon as the school day ends, on weekends and during school holidays? In that English is an indissociable part of the social fabric in Sweden, ever-present in some of the most important social/cultural practices where young people's identity work takes place (for a discussion see Henry & Goddard in press), this might mean that (i) more learners of English are likely to possess a 'fixed language learning mindset' than those in other countries, and (ii) that the strength of the beliefs undergirding such mindsets may be stronger and more resistant to mindset-changing interventions (Ryan & Mercer 2012) than elsewhere.

Mercer and Ryan's language learning mindset theory offers a particularly interesting angle of interpretation when considering the effects of students' beliefs about the relative value of the different contexts in which English is learnt. Given that the range of responses to the questionnaire item on students' beliefs about the efficacy of different learning contexts would seem to indicate the existence of both 'fixed' and 'growth' second language learning mindsets, the use of either longitudinal or retrodictive designs (retrodiction being a strategy by which the usual research direction is reversed, where the researcher starts at the end with the outcomes and then traces things back to see why these outcomes came about (see e.g. Chan, Dörnyei, & Henry 2015; Dörnyei 2014)), could shed light on the developmental trajectories leading to these different mindset types.

Gender differences in beliefs about learning English

In the questionnaire data (n = 2,868) it is interesting to note that the responses of girls and boys differ in noticeable ways. As shown in Figure 2 (below), substantially more girls (48%) than boys (37%) believed that they learnt most or all of their English in school. While the proportion believing that they learnt equally much English as a result of school work as they did outside school was roughly similar (girls 35%, boys 33%), striking differences can be seen in the categories

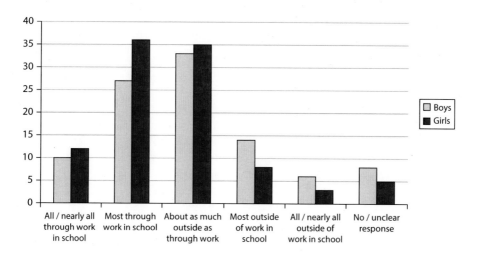

Figure 2. Responses to the question: 'Where do you believe you learned most of what you know in English?'

'learn most of my English outside school' (girls 8%, boys 14%) and 'learn all, or nearly all of my English outside school' (girls 3%, boys 6%). Given that in a recent study Henry and Cliffordson (2013) failed to find any gender-related differences in Swedish 9th grade students' ideal English-speaking/using selves, the rather dramatic divergences in students' beliefs about *learning* English warrant further investigation. In the sections that follow the theories previously discussed are revisited, this time considering whether gender-related differences generally found in self-efficacy, attribution and self-theory research have the potential to shed light on differences in girls' and boys' beliefs about learning English.

Self-regulation and gender

In common with other constructs in psychology where gender differences have been found, differences in females' and males' self-regulated learning tend to be domain related. Overall, studies indicate that girls make greater use of self-regulation strategies than boys, that they tend to be more self-disciplined, and that they exercise more conscious control over their learning (see e.g. Dweck 1999). Indeed, as Meece and Painter (2008) report, data across a range of studies indicate that girls' cognitive investment in learning activities often reaches deeper levels than boys'. Consequently the differences in girls' and boys' beliefs about the relative efficacy of different sites for learning English, and the impact on motivation mediated by such beliefs, may stem from deep-rooted differences in levels of investment in classroom learning generally.

Self-efficacy beliefs

Self-efficacy beliefs form a field where a considerable amount of gender-related research has been carried out, and where domain-related differences often emerge. Numerous studies have shown how in mathematics, science and computing, boys tend to report stronger self-efficacy beliefs than girls. In arts subjects the reverse is often found, where girls' self-efficacy beliefs can be stronger (Meece & Painter 2008). In their study of the self-efficacy and other motivational self-beliefs of college learners of French as a foreign language, Mills, Pajares and Herron (2007) found that, in addition to placing a higher value on French, having a greater interest in the language, and deriving greater enjoyment from learning French and about French culture, female students also had a stronger sense of self-efficacy. In considering factors that could explain this and similar findings (see e.g. Pajares & Valiante 2001), Pajares (2008:124) suggests that one reason could be due to "differences in the beliefs that students hold about their gender rather than by their gender per se". That is to say, gender differences might be a function of gender stereotypic beliefs, themselves rooted in differing educational expectations for girls and boys, where boys are expected to be good at mathematics and girls are expected to be good at languages (Pajares & Valiante 2001).

In terms of the contexts in which English is learnt, gender-related differences, as we have seen, are found not just in students' beliefs, but also the extent to which they participate in English-mediated activities and the type of activities they engage in. Largely the result of their interest in digital gaming, boys spend more time engaged in English-mediated activities (Sundqvist 2009). However, in the context of students' self-efficacy beliefs, whether or not those who claim to learn more of their English outside of the classroom actually *do* develop most of their skills in this way, is not in itself important (see e.g. Nisbett & Ross 1980). Because the individual *believes* this to be true, even in the face of contradictory evidence – such as the tangible results of school-based learning – this can impact on motivation, effort and focus (Bandura 1997; Pajares 2008). In this respect it is interesting to note that, in Sundqvist's (2009) study, where the amount of time 9th grade students spent in English-mediated environments outside of school was compared with measures of oral proficiency and vocabulary levels, although statistically significant positive correlations were found, the coefficients were relatively small ($rs = .31$ and $rs = .35$ respectively), indicating that the effect of out-of-school activities on proficiency might not be that substantial.

Nevertheless, regardless of the accuracy of the belief, a reciprocal relation can arise; if proportionately more boys than girls *believe* that they learn more English outside school – for example by playing digital games – they may be less likely to exert themselves in the classroom. Reinforced by messages in popular discourse that boys become good at English through playing lots of digital games, these beliefs can provide the underpinning for an emerging stereotype of the young male who, safe in the knowledge he can effortlessly gain English from everyday digital activities, does not need to take classroom learning particularly seriously. Thus the gender gap in self-regulated learning strategies and motivated learning behaviour generally noticed in school may be further accentuated in settings such as Sweden where, in digital gaming, many boys spend substantial periods of time in environments they perceive as to be particularly conducive to language acquisition.

Attributions

As Meece and Painter (2008) explain, in studies of causal attribution gender differences have been found in varying educational domains. Generally, girls are less likely than boys to attribute their successes to natural talent (Eccles-Parsons, Adler, & Meece 1984; Meece & Painter 2008). However these results have been found to vary across domains. While in masculine sex-typed subjects, such as mathematics and science, girls are more likely to attribute success to effort and hard work, in arts and language subjects, gender differences have not been as apparent (Meece & Painter 2008).

The reasons underlying the gender differences in Swedish students' beliefs about the efficacy of different sites in which English is learnt are likely to be many in number and closely interrelated. One aspect of attributions though that may have a particular bearing on differences in students' beliefs is the locus dimension, that is to say whether girls' and boys' internal and external success attributions differ. Analogous to the idea that people who hold a belief that they lack a gift for foreign languages might feel that it is meaningless to put effort into learning (cf. Hsieh 2012), a belief that English can best be acquired without effort in naturalistic contexts might result in similar approaches. In particular, if more so than girls, boys attribute successes in English to out-of-school learning – language skills being a naturally acquired by-product of engagement in personally meaningful activities such as digital gaming (an internal locus) – they may be less motivated to engage in classroom learning activities.

Self-theories of intelligence

While the effects of gender on self-efficacy beliefs and attributions have been widely studied (Meece 2006; Meece & Painter 2008), relatively little research has focused on differences in females' and males' self-theories of intelligence. Of the work that has been carried out, in a sample of US 8th grade students Leggett (1985) (cited in Dweck 1999; see also Dweck & Leggett 1988) found striking gender differences, with girls being significantly more likely than boys to hold an entity theory of intelligence. Further, among all students holding entity theories, girls were found to be much more likely to choose tasks that provided safe options, thus avoiding the risk of mistakes and failure. Similar results have been obtained by Licht and Shapiro (1982) (as cited in Dweck 1999), who found that academically-gifted girls preferred tasks on which they felt they were likely to do well, and Chen and Pajares (2010) who found that, in relation to science, boys reported slightly higher incremental views of ability than girls. Consequently, Dweck (1999) suggests that not only do academically-gifted girls attribute failures to entity-causes – i.e. a lack of intelligence – but in many educational domains they have lower estimates of ability and lower expectations of success. This, she argues, stems from "a diet of early success and praise" (Dweck 1999: 124), meaning that in subsequent stages of education, girls operate in a framework "in which challenge is a threat and errors are a condemnation" (Dweck 1999: 55).

In adapting Dweck's theories to language learning, Ryan and Mercer (2012), as we have seen, explain that a *fixed language learning mindset* describes the belief that success in language learning is attributable to innate ability, while a *growth language learning mindset* involves the belief that language learning abilities can be developed as a result of effort, practice and hard work.[7] Because implicit theories of intelligence are domain-specific and are likely to vary across cultures, findings of gender differences in one domain and from one particular culture may not translate to other domains or settings. Thus the entity theories of intelligence found generally to be held by girls in US junior high school (Dweck & Leggett 1988; Leggett 1985; Licht & Shapiro 1982) may not have any direct bearing on the

---

7. In addition to the central role of natural talent, Ryan and Mercer (2011: 166) also incorporate an element which they identify as a unique feature of language learning mindsets, namely "beliefs about the importance or necessity of time spent in a country where the language is widely spoken and the relative 'naturalness' of the language learning process". Therefore, when considering whether previous research on gender differences in implicit theories of intelligence (Dweck 1999; Dweck & Leggett 1988; Leggett 1985) can contribute in accounting for possible gender differences in language learning mindsets, it is important to bear in mind that these would only relate only to the conceptual core of the construct, that is to say beliefs about natural talent.

belief that successful language learning is attributable to the 'talent' of being able to acquire the language in natural settings (which, as we have seen, in a Swedish context may be more strongly held by boys). Because mindsets offer a potentially rewarding lens through which to examine classroom motivation in settings where English constitutes "a constant background presence" (Ryan & Mercer 2011: 166), research focusing on the role played by gender in the development of language learning mindsets would be of particular value.

Conclusion

In this chapter I have described how, in its recent evaluation of the quality of learning environments in English classrooms, the Swedish Schools Inspectorate (2011) found that little account was taken of students' out-of-school encounters with English. A picture is painted of classrooms where teachers fail to integrate students' interests into the activities on offer and where students do not feel particularly challenged, tending to regard English lessons as providing a welcome opportunity for rest and relaxation. I have also described how young people in Sweden spend substantial amounts of time in English language environments, often engaged in personally-meaningful activities, such as digital gaming. Examining students' responses to a questionnaire item on beliefs about the relative efficacy of in and out-of-school learning environments, I have shown how many students hold the belief that they learn as much if not more English outside the classroom, with substantially more boys than girls believing that they learn most or nearly all of their English outside school. Examining these results through a self-regulation lens, I have suggested that theories about the effects of self-efficacy beliefs, attributions and self-theories of intelligence on learning and motivation can all provide useful perspectives from which to understand the phenomenon of students lacking the enthusiasm to engage with English in school currently witnessed in Sweden and, it would seem (Ushioda 2013), is also emerging elsewhere in Europe.

Even if the situation I have sketched out may be dissimilar to that in other social/educational contexts (for example in parts of Asia), given that English is continuing to entrench its position as a global lingua franca (Canagarajah 2007; Graddol 2006) and that, across the globe, young people are enjoying ever greater access to digital medias (many English-mediated), the situation currently seen in Sweden could well develop in other parts of the world. To avoid the consequences of a situation where, because they believe English is best acquired in the naturalistic environments of out-of-school encounters, students fail to benefit from instruction in the formal elements of language and risk losing out on skills important for higher education and future professional communication, it is important that both students and teachers are made aware of the consequences such beliefs can have on motivation and learning.

However, before work can be carried out investigating ways in which, in pedagogical interventions, awareness can be raised, beliefs modified and learning behaviours altered, the nature, origin and effects on motivation of students' language learning beliefs need to be properly investigated. Thus, in addition to qualitative studies into beliefs about learning in natural and instructed contexts held by different types of students, in different social/cultural/educational contexts, and for different languages (see e.g. Busse in this volume for a study on German as an FL), studies that consider the impact of learning beliefs on students' classroom motivation are also needed. Given that gender roles and gender stereotyping might be highly implicated in the formation of beliefs about learning English, particular focus should be directed to the ways in which female and male learners might differently view the relative efficacy of in and out-of-school contexts and the ways in which these beliefs may have an impact on motivation.

References

Airey, J. (2009). *Science, language and literacy: Case studies of learning in Swedish university physics*. Uppsala: Uppsala Dissertations from the Faculty of Science and Technology.

Bandura, A. (1977). Self-efficacy: Toward a unifying theory of behavioural change. *Psychological Review*, 84, 191–215. DOI: 10.1037/0033-295X.84.2.191

Bandura, A. (1986). *Social foundations of thought and action: A social cognitive theory*. Englewood Cliffs, NJ: Prentice Hall.

Bandura, A. (1997). *Self-efficacy: The exercise of control*. New York, NY: Freeman.

Barcelos, A.M.F. (2003). Researching beliefs about SLA: A critical review. In P. Kalaja & A.M.F. Barcelos (Eds.), *Beliefs about SLA: New research approaches* (pp. 7–33). New York, NY: Springer.

Blackwell, L.S., Trzesniewski, K., & Dweck, C.S. (2007). Implicit theories of intelligence predict achievement across an adolescent transition: A longitudinal study and an intervention. *Child Development*, 78, 246–679. DOI: 10.1111/j.1467-8624.2007.00995.x

Canagarajah, A.S. (2007). The ecology of global English. *International Multilingual Research Journal*, 1(2), 89–100. DOI: 10.1080/15257770701495299

Chan, L., Dörnyei, Z., & Henry, A. (2015). Learner archetypes and signature dynamics in the language classroom: A retrodictive qualitative modelling approach to studying L2 motivation. In Z. Dörnyei, P.D. MacIntyre, & A. Henry (Eds.), *Motivational dynamics in language learning*. Bristol: Multilingual Matters.

Chen, J.A., & Pajares, F. (2010). Implicit theories of ability of grade 6 science students: Relation to epistemological beliefs and academic motivation and achievement in science. *Contemporary Educational Psychology*, 35, 75–87. DOI: 10.1016/j.cedpsych.2009.10.003

Dörnyei, Z. (2014). Researching complex dynamic systems: 'Retrodictive qualitative modelling' in the language classroom. *Language Teaching*, 47(1), 80–91.

Dweck, C.S. (1999). *Self-theories: Their role in motivation, personality and development*. Hove: Psychology Press.

Dweck, C.S., & Leggett, E.L. (1988). A social-cognitive approach to motivation and personality. *Psychological Review*, 95, 256–273. DOI: 10.1037/0033-295X.95.2.256

Dweck, C.S., & Master, A. (2008). Self-theories motivate self-regulated learning. In D.H. Schunk, & B.J. Zimmerman (Eds.), *Motivation and self-regulated learning: Theory, research and applications* (pp. 31–51). New York, NY: Lawrence Erlbaum Associates.

Eccles-Parsons, J., Adler, T.F., & Meece, J.L. (1984). Sex differences in achievement: A test of alternative theories. *Journal of Personality and Social Psychology*, 46, 26–43. DOI: 10.1037/0022-3514.46.1.26

European Commission (2012). *SurveyLang: The European Survey on Language Competencies*. Brussels: European Commission.

Forbes Magazine (2014). <http://www.forbes.com/sites/insertcoin/2014/01/27/riots-league-of-legends-reveals-astonishing-27-million-daily-players-67-million-monthly/> (28 January 2014).

Graddol, D. (2006). *English next: Why global English may mean the end of 'English as a foreign language'*. London: British Council.

Henry, A. (2013). Digital games and ELT: Bridging the authenticity gap. In E. Ushioda (Ed.), *International perspectives on motivation: Language learning and professional challenges* (pp. 133–155). Houndmills: Palgrave MacMillan.

Henry, A., & Cliffordson, C. (2013). Motivation, gender and possible selves. *Language Learning*, 63(2), 271–295.

Henry, A., & Goddard, A. (in press). Bicultural or hybrid? The second language identities of students on an English-medium university program in Sweden. *Journal of Language, Identity and Education*.

Heider, F. (1958). *The psychology of interpersonal relations*. New York, NY: Wiley. DOI: 10.1037/10628-000

Hsieh, P.H. (2012). Attribution: Looking back and ahead at the 'why' theory. In S. Mercer, S. Ryan & M. Williams (Eds.), *Psychology for language learning* (pp. 90–102). Clevedon: Multilingual Matters.

Hsieh, P.H., & Kang, H.S. (2010). Attribution and self-efficacy and their interrelationship in the Korean EFL context. *Language Learning*, 60, 606–627. DOI: 10.1111/j.1467-9922.2010.00570.x

Hsieh, P.H., & Schallert, D.L. (2008). Implications from self-efficacy and attribution theories for an understanding of undergraduates' motivation in a foreign language course. *Contemporary Educational Psychology*, 33, 513–532. DOI: 10.1016/j.cedpsych.2008.01.003

Kelley, H.H. (1967). Attribution theory in social psychology. In D. Levine (Ed.), *Nebraska Symposium on Motivation* (Vol. 15, pp. 192–238). Lincoln, NE: University of Nebraska Press.

Leggett, E.L. (1985). Children's entity and incremental theories of intelligence: Relationship to achievement behaviour. Paper presented at *the annual meeting of the Eastern Psychological Association*, March, Boston.

Liang, M.Y. (2012). Foreign ludicity in online role-playing games. *Computer Assisted Language Learning*, 25(5), 455–473. DOI: 10.1080/09588221.2011.619988

Licht, B.G., & Shapiro, S.H. (1982, August). Sex differences in attributions among high achievers. Paper presented at *the meeting of the American Psychological Association*, Washington DC.

Meece, J.L. (2006). Introduction to special issue. Explaining women's math and science related career choices at the end of the20th century: Large scale and longitudinal studies from four nations. In H.M.G. Watt & J.S. Eccles (Eds.), *Educational Research and Evaluation*, 12, 297–304.

Meece, J.L., & Painter, J. (2008). Gender, self-regulation, and motivation. In D.H. Schunk & B.J. Zimmerman (Eds.), *Motivation and self-regulated learning: Theory, research and applications* (pp. 339–368). New York, NY: Lawrence Erlbaum Associates.

Mercer, S., & Ryan, S. (2010). A mindset for EFL: Learners' beliefs about the role of natural talent. *ELT Journal*, 64, 436–444. DOI: 10.1093/elt/ccp083

Mercer, S., Ryan, S. & Williams, M. (2012). Introduction. In S. Mercer, S. Ryan, & M. Williams (Eds.), *Psychology for language learning* (pp. 1–9). Clevedon: Multilingual Matters. DOI: 10.1057/9781137032829

Mills, N., Pajares, F., & Herron, C. (2007). Self-efficacy of college intermediate French students: Relation to achievement and motivation. *Language Learning*, 57, 417–422. DOI: 10.1111/j.1467-9922.2007.00421.x

Nisbett, R., & Ross, L. (1980). *Human inference: Strategies and shortcomings of social judgment*. Engelwood Cliffs, NJ: Prentice Hall.

Olsson, E. (2011). *'Everything I read on the Internet is in English': On the impact of extramural English on Swedish 16-year-old pupils' writing proficiency*. Licenciate thesis, Faculty of Humanities, University of Gothenburg, Sweden.

Pajares, F. (1992). Teachers' beliefs and educational research: Cleaning up a messy construct. *Review of Educational Research*, 62, 307–332. DOI: 10.3102/00346543062003307

Pajares, F. (2008). Motivational role of self-efficacy beliefs in self-regulated learning. In D.H. Schunk & B.J. Zimmerman (Eds.), *Motivation and self-regulated learning: Theory, research and applications* (pp. 111–140). New York, NY: Lawrence Erlbaum Associates.

Pajares, F., & Valiante, G. (2001). Gender differences in writing motivation and achievement of middle school students: A function of gender orientation? *Contemporary Educational Psychology*, 26, 366–381. DOI: 10.1006/ceps.2000.1069

Pajares, F., Britner, S.L., & Valiante, G. (2000). Relation between achievement goals and self-beliefs of middle school students in writing and science. *Contemporary Educational Psychology*, 25, 406–422. DOI: 10.1006/ceps.1999.1027

Peterson, M. (2010). Massively multiplayer online role-playing games as arenas for second language learning. *Computer Assisted Language Learning*, 23(5), 429–439. DOI: 10.1080/09588221.2010.520673

Peterson, M. (2012). Learner interaction in a massively multiplayer online role playing game (MMORPG): A sociocultural discourse analysis. *ReCALL*, 24(3), 361–380. DOI: 10.1017/S0958344012000195

Pintrich, P.R. (2000). An achievement goal theory perspective on issues in motivation terminology, theory, and research. *Contemporary Educational Psychology*, 25, 92–104. DOI: 10.1006/ceps.1999.1017

Reinders, H., & Wattana, S. (2011). Learn English or die: The effects of digital games on interaction and willingness to communicate in a foreign language. *Digital Culture and Education*, 3(1), 4–28.

Ryan, S., & Mercer, S. (2011). Natural talent, natural acquisition and abroad: Learner attributions of agency in language learning. In G. Murray, X. Gao, & T. Lamb (Eds.), *Identity, motivation and autonomy in language learning* (pp. 160–176). Clevedon: Multilingual Matters.

Ryan, S., & Mercer, S. (2012). Implicit theories: Language learning mindsets. In S. Mercer, S. Ryan, & M. Williams (Eds.), *Psychology for language learning* (pp. 74–89). Clevedon: Multilingual Matters. DOI: 10.1057/9781137032829

Schunk, D. (2008). Attributions as motivators of self-regulated learning. In D.H. Schunk & B.J. Zimmerman (Eds.), *Motivation and self-regulated learning: Theory, research and applications* (pp. 245–266). New York, NY: Lawrence Erlbaum Associates.

Schunk, D.H., & Zimmerman, B.J. (2008). *Motivation and self-regulated learning: Theory, research and applications.* New York, NY: Lawrence Erlbaum Associates.

Sundqvist, P. (2009). *Extramural English matters: Out-of-school English and its impact on Swedish ninth graders' oral proficiency and vocabulary.* Karlstad: Karlstad University Studies.

Sundqvist, P., & Sylvén, L.K. (2012). World of VocCraft: Computer games and Swedish learners' L2 English vocabulary. In H. Reinders (Ed.), *Digital games in language learning and teaching* (pp. 189–208). Basingstoke: Palgrave Macmillan.

Sylvén, L.K. (2013). CLIL in Sweden – why does it not work? A metaperspective on CLIL across contexts in Europe. *International Journal of Bilingual Education and Bilingualism, 16*(3), 301–320. DOI: 10.1080/13670050.2013.777387

Swedish Media Council. (2010). *Ungar och medier 2010: Fakta om barns och ungas användning och upplevelser av medier* (Young people and the media 2010: Facts on children and young people's media use and experiences). Stockholm: Statens Media Råd.

Swedish Media Council. (2013). *Ungar och medier 2012/2013: Fakta om barns och ungas användning och upplevelser av medier* (Young people and the media 2012/2013: Facts on children and young people's media use and experiences). Stockholm: Statens Media Råd.

Swedish Schools Inspectorate. (2011). *Kvalitetsgranskning: Engelska i grundskolans årskurser 6–9.* (Quality evaluation: English in secondary school grades 6–9). Stockholm: Swedish Government.

Taylor, F. (2013). Listening to Romanian teenagers: Lessons in motivation and ELT methodology. In E. Ushioda (Ed.), *International perspectives on motivation: Language learning and professional challenges* (pp. 35–60). Houndmills: Palgrave MacMillan.

Thorne, S.L. (2008). Transcultural communication in open Internet environments and massively multiplayer online games. In S.S. Magnan (Ed.), *Mediating discourse online* (pp. 305–330). Amsterdam: John Benjamins. DOI: 10.1075/aals.3.17tho

Ushioda, E. (2011a). Motivating learners to speak as themselves. In G. Murray, X. Gao, & T. Lamb (Eds.), *Identity, motivation and autonomy in language learning* (pp. 11–24). Clevedon: Multilingual Matters.

Ushioda, E. (2011b). Language learning motivation, self and identity: Current theoretical perspectives. *Computer Assisted Language Learning, 24*(3), 199–210. DOI: 10.1080/09588221.2010.538701

Ushioda, E. (2013). Motivation and ELT: Global issues and local concerns. In E. Ushioda (Ed.), *International perspectives on motivation: Language learning and professional challenges* (pp. 1–18). Houndmills: Palgrave MacMillan. DOI: 10.1057/9781137000873

Waters, J.K. (2007). On a quest for English. *T. H. E. Journal, 34*(10), 26–32.

Weiner, B. (2000). Attributional thoughts about consumer behaviour. *Journal of Consumer Research, 27*(3), 382–387. DOI: 10.1086/317592

Weiner, B. (1992). *Human motivation: Metaphors, theories, and research.* Newbury Park, CA: Sage.

Weiner, B., Frieze, I.H., Kukla, A., Reed, L., Rest, S., & Rosenbaum, R.M. (1971). *Perceiving the causes of success and failure.* Morristown, NJ: General Learning Press.

World Economic Forum. (2012). *Global Information Technology Report*. Geneva, Switzerland: WEF.

Zimmerman, B.J. (2000). Attainment of self-regulation: A social cognitive perspective. In M. Boekaerts, P. Pintrich, & M. Zeidner (Eds.), *Handbook of self-regulation* (pp. 13–39). Orlando, FL: Academic Press. DOI: 10.1016/B978-012109890-2/50031-7

CHAPTER 6

Giving voice to the students

What (de)motivates them in CLIL classes?

Aintzane Doiz, David Lasagabaster and Juan Manuel Sierra

As a result of the widespread implementation of the CLIL approach in the educational system across European countries, research on its effects has become a much debated topic. Yet there is a dearth of studies on the role of motivation in CLIL. Many studies on motivation have focused on *why* students are (de) motivated to learn. We will paid heed to *what* makes them feel (de)motivated. In our study students express their opinions about what they like most and least in their CLIL classes, and the advantages and disadvantages they associate with this curricular proposal. The analysis of 221 participants' answers allows us to end up with a set of recommendations which may help CLIL teachers to boost their students' motivation.

Keywords: CLIL, methodological aspects, mixed-ability classes, secondary students' reflections

Introduction

It is an undeniable fact that English has become the hegemonic foreign language in the vast majority of European education systems (Eurydice 2006), up to the point that it is negatively affecting the interest and motivation to learn other foreign languages (Csizér & Lukacs 2010; Henry 2012). While "global English makes the transition from 'foreign language' to basic skill" (Graddol 2006: 118), in many European education systems CLIL (Content and Language Integrated Learning) has blossomed during the last decade as the most popular approach among the diverse initiatives undertaken to overcome the weaknesses found in the traditional teaching of English as a foreign language (EFL) (Lasagabaster 2008; Ruiz de Zarobe, Sierra, & Gallardo 2011). The preeminence of English in CLIL is such that Dalton-Puffer (2011: 183) states that often "CLIL effectively means CEIL, or content-and-English integrated learning". It is worth mentioning that approaches that integrate content and language are commonly labelled Content-based language instruction (CBI) or Content-based second language teaching in North America (Tedick & Camarata 2012), whereas the label CLIL is most commonly used in Europe (Coyle 2007; Coyle, Hood, & Marsh 2010).

CLIL implementation revolves around the idea that this approach may help students to learn both content and English, as its advocates claim that not only the specific content is learnt, but students' foreign language competence is also significantly improved. Nevertheless, in her review of CLIL research Dalton-Puffer (2011:195) concludes that this "two for one" belief still needs further research: "But how far this catalyst role of CLIL will actually go and how necessary it depends on the contingencies of individual contexts: Contrary to many people's expectations, CLIL is not a panacea".

Motivation is one of the CLIL-related aspects that demands further attention. The research void in this area is especially remarkable when one notices the lack of studies that aim to provide teachers with recommendations on how to improve motivation in CLIL classes based on students' reflections. There is a need to fill this gap, as CLIL programs have little chance to succeed if students do not feel motivated. What Breidbach & Viebrock (2012:11) state about the German context can be applied to the vast majority of other European contexts: "Motivation is among the marginally examined concepts in German-speaking CLIL research."

Different studies (Chambers 1999; Williams, Burden, & Lanvers 2002) conclude that foreign language learning motivation is usually negatively affected as a result of what students find as monotonous language activities in the EFL classroom, a state of demotivation that many teachers find frustrating. One possible explanation for students' lack of motivation could lie in the different perceptions that teachers and students have of the most adequate and motivating courses of action to improve language learning. As Kern (1995) points out, the beliefs of teachers and students are important for understanding the process of learning, because they can help us to prevent those conflicts that may augment frustration, anxiety and lack of motivation on the part of the student, or even their giving up the learning of the foreign language.

But hopefully students' motivation can be recovered and fuelled if they face new positive and motivating experiences such as a new teacher, challenging topics, more opportunities to use the foreign language outside the classroom, or a new teaching approach such as CLIL. Since many foreign language teachers complain that their students find their classes boring and unchallenging, a study on motivation in CLIL contexts may shed some light on the alleged motivational benefits of this approach.

CLIL and motivation

In contexts as diverse as Spain (Doiz, Lasagabaster, & Sierra 2014; Lasagabaster 2011; Lorenzo, Casal, & Moore 2010) and Finland (Seikkula-Leino 2007), researchers have observed that CLIL students seem to be more motivated to learn the foreign language than their EFL counterparts, but there is a need to understand better what particular factors help to spark students' motivation. The available evidence from CLIL experiences indicates that the use of the L2 as a means of communication for content learning (what Lorenzo terms as academic classroom communication, see Lorenzo in this volume) boosts motivation among all students, creates an atmosphere that facilitates L2 use, and allows students to make progress according to their learning styles and different learning rhythms.

A review of the literature on motivation reveals that many studies are quantitative in design and hinge on instruments such as questionnaires and language tests. Qualitative research on second language motivation is scant, although in the last few years there is an increasing trend to carry out qualitative studies (see for example the different chapters included in the recent volume edited by Murray, Gao, & Lamb 2011). In the research field of motivation most theories have been "concerned more with the general than the particular, with statistical averages and relations rather than rich descriptive analysis" (Ushioda 2011:11) and, consequently, the learners' individuality has been overlooked. Recent and influential volumes such as the one edited by Dörnyei and Ushioda (2009) also rely heavily on quantitative contributions. There is no doubt that the questionnaire has traditionally been the most widely used instrument when studying motivation, especially closed-ended questionnaires that, once filled out by the participants, are statistically analysed. However, some authors have claimed that this research tradition does not habitually yield practical implications (Kim 2006) and has paved the way to the belief that it does not help to bridge the gap between research and everyday teaching in the classroom. Nevertheless, we would like to underscore that questionnaires can also include open questions which may provide researchers with rich information about students' needs, beliefs, desires and motivation.

Although teachers may be interested in theoretical models of motivation, they are undoubtedly more willing to learn about particular strategies and activities that have a positive bearing on their students' motivation, as well as about those that reduce or diminish their motivation. Csizér and Kormos (2009) assert that language learning experiences have a very strong influence on motivation among secondary education students, which leads them to conclude that the responsibility to motivate students inevitably relies on the teacher.

Many studies on motivation have been focused on *why* students are (de)motivated to learn (e.g. because I don't like learning languages), but few have paid heed to *what* makes them feel (de)motivated (e.g. I find grammar activities extremely boring). In this chapter, we intend to delve into the motivational aspects of a CLIL approach by giving students the chance to freely express the opinions about what they like most and least in their CLIL classes, and the advantages and disadvantages they associate with this approach. Nikolov's study (2001) is relevant in this context, as its participants were unsuccessful learners who stated that their foreign language learning failure was mainly due to their negative perceptions of classroom practices. With this in mind, the analysis of our participants' answers will ideally allow us to end up with a set of pedagogical implications for CLIL programs that should help to boost students' motivation and enhance their learning experience in the classroom. As Dörnyei (2010) highlights, situated motives related to the immediate learning environment and experience exert a very significant influence on students' motivation. These motives include factors such as the impact of the teacher, the curriculum, the materials used in class, the peer group, the experience of success, and what interests us in this chapter, the type of approach – namely CLIL – implemented in the classes.

Dörnyei (2001) also indicates that in order to maintain motivation, it is important to make the learning stimulating and enjoyable and to present classroom activities in a motivating way in order to build learners' self-esteem and confidence. With this in mind, it is our objective to give voice to the students to get to know what they find (de)motivating in CLIL classes.

The study

In this section we will briefly describe the main characteristics of the participants and the instrument (a questionnaire) used to gather the data.

The participants

The participants were 221 CLIL students from five schools in the Basque Autonomous Community (Spain), 107 of whom were enrolled in the first year of compulsory secondary education (12–13 year-old students) and the remaining 114 in the third year of compulsory secondary education (14–15 year-old students). The subjects taught in English varied from school to school and they were the following: social sciences (which includes geography and history), citizenship, arts, music, religion, alternative to religion (those students who are not enrolled in religion have to take this subject), and the weekly tutorial. All the participants had 3 sessions (45 or 60 minutes each on average) of EFL, and between two and four hours of CLIL in one or two of the aforementioned subjects per week.

The instrument

The tool we utilized is part of a larger longitudinal study which also includes closed-ended questions that have been reported elsewhere (Doiz, Lasagabaster, & Sierra 2014). The participants were asked to fill out a questionnaire which included three open-ended questions; they were free to use any of their languages (Basque, Spanish or English). Those comments that were written in Basque or Spanish were translated into English by the authors of this chapter. Students were also told that there were no right or wrong answers, that they should be themselves and should not to be afraid of expressing their real feelings and beliefs. The three questions were as follows:

a. In your opinion, what are the main advantages and disadvantages of studying subjects in English?
b. What do you like most / least in your CLIL (Content and Language Integrated Learning / Subjects taught in English) classes?
c. Make any additional comments about the subjects taught in English. We may have not dealt with issues that you find interesting. Please feel free to write down any comment.

Procedure

This chapter investigates the advantages and disadvantages of the CLIL experience for first- and third-year students and what they liked the most and the least of that experience, as well as their additional comments on their learning process. In order to address these three questions, we followed the three-step procedure for the creation of categories put forward by Garrett and Gallego (2011): firstly, we identified the discrete ideas in the students' answers; secondly, we classified these ideas under the general themes of advantages or disadvantages, and what they liked the least and the most of the CLIL experience; finally, we clustered the ideas into broader categories of dis/advantages and what they liked the most/the least.

Results

First open question

Table 1 provides an overview of the students' stance of the perceived advantages and disadvantages of taking CLIL classes.

Table 1. Number of advantages and disadvantages

	1st year (107 students)		3rd year (114 students)		Total (221 students)	
	tokens	average	tokens	average	tokens	average
Advantages	162	1.51	191	1.67	353	1.59
Disadvantages	100	0.93	112	0.98	212	0.95

A first glance at the results presented in Table 1 shows that, in general, the students believe that their CLIL experience has more advantages than disadvantages (a total of 353 tokens of positive comments provided by first- and third-year students vs. a total of 212 negative comments). When the results are classified by the students' school year, the data reveal that third-year students are slightly more positive than their first-year peers as the former provide an average of 1.67 advantages per student in contrast to 1.51 in the case of the latter. As for the disadvantages, both groups seem to have had a similar experience and mention an average of almost 1 disadvantage per student (0.93 and 0.98, first- and third-year students respectively).

The classification of the students' positive ideas led to the positing of 14 different categories within the topic of advantages. Table 2 contains the list of the categories, the tokens or the number of the students' ideas that are included in each category and the corresponding percentage of the students whose ideas belonged in each category (see Appendix 1 for an explanation of the categories). By way of an example, consider the first category, *learning English*, in Table 2. This advantage was referred to 49 times in the case of first-year students and 62 times in the case of third-year students. In other words, 45.7% of first-year students and 54.3% of third-year students believed that having CLIL lessons helps them to improve their learning of English.

The data (see Table 2) reveal that, out of the 14 categories which were created, there are 3 which are the most frequently mentioned by both groups. The categories are: *learning English, future* and *communicate*; that is to say, the students' belief that their CLIL experience is beneficial for learning English, for their future studies and/or career prospects, or for the improvement of their ability to communicate with people from other countries. The following quotes illustrate these categories in turn:

> "You improve your level of English and you acquire more vocabulary"
>
> (student 74)

> "You can have a good job if you learn English"   (student 22)

> "You can travel and talk with people from other countries"   (student 27)

Table 2. Categorization of the advantages of CLIL

1st year (107 students)			3rd year (114 students)		
category	tokens	%	category	tokens	%
Learning English	49	45.7	Learning English	62	54.3
Future	46	42.9	Future	34	29.8
Communicate	28	26.1	Communicate	29	25.4
Vocabulary	12	11.2	Vocabulary	15	13.1
Enjoy	9	8.4	Culture	11	9.6
Understand TV, etc.	5	4.6	Multilingualism	8	7
Multilingualism	4	3.7	Learn two things	7	6.1
Culture	4	3.7	Motivation	6	5.2
Learn two things	3	2.8	Enjoy	6	5.2
Motivation	2	1.8	Computers	4	3.5
			Easier content	3	2.6
			Miscellaneous	3	2.6
			Understand TV, etc.	2	1.7
			Native teachers	1	0.8
Total	162			191	

It is interesting to note that the first two categories, namely, *learning English* and *future*, were mentioned by a similar percentage of first-year students (45.7% and 42.9%), whereas in the case of third-year students, a higher number of them singled out the benefits of CLIL within the category of *learning English* as opposed to the category of *future* (54.3% vs. 29.8%). The remainder of the advantages, with the exception of *learning vocabulary*, are reported by less than 10% of the students and include: enjoying the classes (*enjoy*); having the opportunity of learning about other countries and communicating with foreign students as a result of the school's participation in a European project (*culture*); being able to learn two things at the same time (*subject-matter and English*); learning other languages (*multilingualism*); being able to understand TV series, the Internet, songs, etc. (*understand TV, etc.*); having *easier content*, using *computers*; having *native speakers* as language assistants in class; or experimenting an increase in the motivation to learn English (*motivation*).

The analysis of the students' responses regarding the disadvantages of the CLIL experience resulted in 12 categories. The categories, the number of tokens for each one and the corresponding percentages are provided in Table 3 (see Appendix 2 for a description of all the categories).

Once again, the data reveal a consensus among first- and third-year students with regards to the top two categories. The highest number of students in both groups stated that the CLIL classes were more difficult due to their limited

Table 3. Categorization of the disadvantages of CLIL

1st year (107 students)			3rd year (114 students)		
category	tokens	%	category	tokens	%
Difficult	33	30.8	Understand	30	26.3
Understand	14	13	Difficult	27	23.6
Hard work	14	13	Mix languages	11	9.6
Boring	11	10.2	Takes more time	8	7
Mix languages	8	7.4	Hard work	8	7
Takes more time	6	5.6	Worse results	8	7
Learn grammar	5	4.6	Lower content level	6	5.2
Students' low level	4	3.7	Learn grammar	4	3.5
Lower content level	3	2.8	Unprepared teachers	4	3.5
Worse results	2	1.8	Boring	3	2.6
			Miscellaneous	2	1.7
			Anxiety	1	0.8
Total	100			112	

command of English (*difficult*) and that their understanding of the teacher's lectures or the class materials was also impaired by the use of English (*understand*):

> "Some things are more difficult to learn because you have to study and memorize them in English" (student 112)

> "It is harder to study in English and we are not used to studying whole paragraphs in English" (student 115)

> "Sometimes I do not understand the subject as well as I would if it were in Basque or Spanish" (student 89)

However, there are some differences between the two groups' responses. In the first-year students' opinion, the most frequently mentioned disadvantage of the CLIL experience is clearly the *difficulty* of the classes. Thus, 30.8% of all the younger students believe that the use of English as a medium of instruction makes the study of the content of the subjects more complex and restricts their participation in the class discussions. At a distant second place on the list of disadvantages with 13% of the students' responses are the categories of having difficulties in *understanding* the content and having to *work hard* ("You have to work harder" (student 197)).

In contrast, third-year students single out mainly the fact that CLIL classes pose *understanding* difficulties (26%). They worry that they may miss information from the teacher's explanations or from the texts, they are concerned about their limited understanding of the subject, and are very much aware of the fact that if the subject were taught in their first language, they would gain a deeper understanding of the subject-matter. In a close second place, 23.6% of the students believe that it is *difficult* to study the subjects in English since it is much harder to study a subject in a language they do not know that well; furthermore, this difficulty is increased in the case of subjects which would already be difficult even if the medium of instruction was their L1. Regarding the issue of difficulty, it is interesting to note that some students with a good command of English empathise with the fellow students whose command of English is low:

> "For those students who do not have a good command of English these subjects in English may be very difficult"   (student 122)

Finally, it is also worthwhile commenting on two categories, *boring* and *mixing languages*. In particular, 10.2% of first-year students believe that the CLIL classes are boring for different reasons: some students do not like the topics they work on during the classes, and, interestingly for the theme of this chapter is the fact that other students complain that the teachers have to repeat the same ideas to ensure students' understanding, which is bound to cause boredom. The category of mixing languages takes the third place on the list of third-year students (9.6%) and the fourth place (7.4%) in the case of first-year students. It is an umbrella category coined to include the students' thoughts which refer to their L1, such as the fact that there is an English-only policy in their CLIL classes; the students' realization that although they learn new English words, they may not have the chance to learn the equivalent in their L1; or the danger that English instruction poses for minority languages, such as Basque (some of the students' L1). It also includes some students' complaints about experiencing language interference or mixing languages when they speak:

> "You study in a different language instead of in your mother tongue"   (student 137)

Second open question

Table 4 exhibits an overview of the participants' comments on what they like the most and the least in their CLIL classes.

The results indicate that the students produced many more comments on what they liked most than on what they liked least (a total of 338 positive tokens vs. a total of 184 negative tokens). This trend is maintained regardless of the students' school year. We can also see that it is the younger students who provided significantly more answers than the older students, both positive (1.76 vs. 1.30) and negative (1.10 vs. 0.58).

Table 4. Number of comments related to students' likes and dislikes

	1st year (107 students)		3rd year (114 students)		Total (221 students)	
	tokens	average	tokens	average	tokens	average
Like most	189	1.76	149	1.30	338	1.53
Like least	118	1.10	66	0.58	184	0.83

Table 5. Categorization of what students liked the most

1st year (107 students)			3rd year (114 students)		
category	tokens	%	category	tokens	%
Language improvement	44	41.1	Language improvement	45	39.4
Different activities	32	29.9	Group activities	23	20.1
Watch films	28	26.1	Computers	18	15.7
Group activities	26	24.3	Projects	16	14
Enjoy	13	12.1	Native teachers	10	8.7
Native teachers	10	9.3	Learn two things	8	7
Projects	9	8.4	Easier content	8	7
Oral presentations	9	8.4	Enjoy	5	4.3
Computers	5	4.6	Watch fims	3	2.6
Learn two things	4	3.7	Individual work	3	2.6
Class atmosphere	4	3.7	Different activities	3	2.6
PowerPoint	1	0.9	PowerPoint	2	1.7
Easier content	1	0.9	Oral presentations	2	1.7
Teacher's explanations	1	0.9	Class atmosphere	2	1.7
Book	1	0.9	Teacher's explanations	1	0.8
Exam	1	0.9			
Total	189			149	

Following the procedure used in the case of the students' perception of advantages and disadvantages, the categorization of what the students liked the most yielded 16 different categories. Table 5 shows these categories, the tokens related to each category and the corresponding percentage of the students whose comments belonged in each category (see Appendix 3 for complete descriptions of the 16 categories).

The data indicate a consensus for 1st and 3rd year students regarding what they found more congenial: *language improvement* (41.1% and 39.4%) and *group activities* (24.3% and 20.1%). The first category indicates that the students enjoyed learning English through subject-matter instruction and therefore were aware of the benefits of the CLIL approach in terms of improvement of their vocabulary, fluency and communicative skills. This is in line with two of the most mentioned advantages (*learning English* and *communicate*) previously analysed in Table 2. Examples of students' comments related to language improvement are the following:

| "What I like most is that I improve my English" | (student 189) |
| "What I like most is that you learn more English" | (student 195) |

As for *group activities*, the participants expressed their preference for group work as the following quotes attest:

| "The thing I like the most is group work" | (student 174) |
| "What I like is working in groups" | (student 3) |

First-year and third-year students coincided in giving less importance (below 10%) to learning content and English (*learn two things*), the presence of native teachers in the program (*native teachers*), the use of PowerPoint presentations by the teacher (*PowerPoint*), the preparation and the implementation of oral presentations on the part of the students (*Oral Presentations*), the fact that the content of the subjects is less difficult in the CLIL classes (*easier content*), learning in a comfortable environment (*class atmosphere*) or their *teacher's explanations*. Textbooks (*Book*) or the use of exams (*exam*) were met with far less enthusiasm by all the participants.

When comparing the younger students' with the older students' likes, we observed an interesting contrast. Whereas 1st-year students acknowledged the variety of activities used in the CLIL program (*different activities*) as one of the aspects they liked most (29.9%), their 3rd year counterparts did not identify this as one of their preferences (2.6%). A similar contrast is established when it comes to seeing films in original version in the classroom (*watch films*), an activity more appreciated in our data by the younger students (26.1%) than their older counterparts (2.6%): this may be due to the nature of the subjects taken by the third-year students (in social sciences, for example, films in the original version may not be used very frequently). Finally, the enjoyment the students experienced during the learning process (*enjoy*) was perceived much differently: 12.1% of the younger students' answers versus 4.3% of the older ones. On the contrary, third-year students valued the use of computers in the classroom (*computers*) (15.7%), whereas first-year students did not consider this category as one of their favourite ones (4.6%). As for doing projects in class with their classmates and/or with other schools (*projects*), we can also perceive a difference between older and younger students. However, in this case the contrast is not so marked (14% versus 8.4%, respectively).

Table 6. Categorization of what students liked the least

1st year (107 students)			3rd year (114 students)		
category	tokens	%	category	tokens	%
Exams	26	24.3	Activities	14	12.2
Activities	23	21.5	Difficult	12	10.5
Difficult	15	14	Boring	10	8.7
Theory	12	11.2	Exams	7	6.1
Subjects in English	8	7.4	Grammar	6	5.2
Boring	8	7.4	Textbook	4	3.5
Teacher	8	7.4	Teacher	3	2.6
Oral presentations	7	6.5	Subjects in English	2	1.7
Grammar	5	4.6	Oral presentations	2	1.7
Too many students	3	2.8	Only English	2	1.7
Lower content level	1	0.9	Few hours	2	1.7
Only English	1	0.9	Theory	1	0.8
No grammar	1	0.9	Lower content level	1	0.8
Total	118			66	

The analysis of the students' answers with regard to what they liked the least in the CLIL program led to the setting of 17 categories. The categories, the number of tokens for each one of them and the corresponding students' percentages are provided in Table 6 (see Appendix 4 for a description of these categories).

The results presented in Table 6 indicate that the participants produced fewer responses about what they liked the least (45.6% less) than in the case of what they liked the most (Table 5). This clear trend is observed both in first- and third-year students, although the older students made significantly fewer comments (56% vs. 37.6%). It is noticeable that third-year students' responses are below 10%, with the exception of the different activities that the students did not like (*activities*) and their impression that studying a subject in English is harder (*difficult*). These two categories are also among the top three categories for the younger students, although they are represented with a much higher percentage (21.5% and 14% respectively). The following quotes illustrate them:

> "It's more difficult"   (student 195)
>
> "I don't like some book activities"   (student 26)

As regards 1st year students' dislikes, the testing of the students' knowledge and skills (*exams*) represents the highest percentage (24.3%). The theoretical content of the different subjects (*theory*) is slightly higher than 10% (11.2%). These two categories get much lower percentages among the older students (6.1% and 0.8%, respectively). Two of the most conspicuous comments follow:

> "I don't like the theory exam in English"   (student 163)
>
> "What I like least is theory and grammar"   (student 166)

Many of the categories receive very few comments by all the students (below 10%). For example, the students' dislikes of subjects (*subject in English*), the preparation and implementation of oral presentations in the classroom (*oral presentations),* the studying of the linguistic code (*grammar),* boredom in the classroom due mainly to repetition (*boring)* ("The teacher repeats the same stuff over and over again" student 81), or their dislike of the teacher and their explanations (*teacher).* Even less attention (below 3.5%) is given to simplification of the subject content taught in English (*lower content level),* the fact that the content of the subject is delivered only in English may become a problem in the future (*only English),* the lack of attention paid to the linguistic code (*no grammar),* the suggestion of using less boring books (*textbook),* and the advisability of having more subjects in English (*few hours).*

Third open question

In the case of the third question, in which students were asked to make additional comments about the subjects taught in English (CLIL), out of the 107 first-year students, more than half (53.3%) made additional comments on their CLIL experience. The total number of statements produced by the 57 first-year students regarding the third open question was distributed across 8 categories (see Appendix 5 for a description of these categories). Some students referred to more than one category.

Out of the 114 third-year students, only 35 of them (37.75%) made any additional comments on their CLIL experience and their comments were distributed across 7 categories. Table 7 presents the categories, the sentences produced by the participants and the percentage these sentences represent.

Two categories (*methodology* and *learning English*) clearly stand out representing more than 60% of the participants' responses. Nearly half of all the statements refer to methodological aspects such as opinions about the implementation of subjects, project work, group work, topics, teachers, exams, classroom climate or enjoyment, and specific proposals to improve the implementation of the CLIL programs. The students highlighted the importance of these two categories, as can be seen in the following quotes:

> "The tutorial lessons are very boring sometimes. I want to do more interesting things. For example, choose more interesting topics for the tutorials, like doing written projects in groups"   (student 148)

Table 7. 1st and 3rd year students' statements categorization regarding the third open question

Category	1st year		3rd year	
	statements	%	statements	%
Methodology	31	45.6	19	44.1
Learning English	16	23.5	9	20.9
Cultural dimension	8	11.7	3	6.9
Positive experience	5	7.3	3	6.9
Better future	4	5.9	2	4.6
Difficulty	2	2.9	1	2.3
Learning in general/content	1	1.5	6	13.9
CLIL for all	1	1.5		
Total	68		43	

> "To play games to learn English more easily. To carry on with the projects because they are good fun and the theory exams should be easier"
> (student 217)

> "The experience is very good and I want to continue next year because you learn more English"   (student 2)

> "I think it is a good way to learn more English as compared to the non-CLIL classes. I think we should continue with the multilingual experience in Baccalaureate"   (student 155)

Some students elaborated on the benefits of learning English and meeting English speaking people when it comes to understanding a different culture:

> "I feel very glad when I understand a lot of things in the films or when the teacher speaks in English. It's also very nice to understand what famous people say"   (student 158)

> "I like that people from other countries who speak English come to our school"   (student 26)

Less representative are the participants' views about their positive impression of the CLIL program (*positive experience*), their expectations of finding a job (*better future*), their difficulties during the CLIL instruction (*difficulty*), and their wishes for a generalized implementation of the CLIL programs. These categories are illustrated in turn:

> "It has been excellent for me because teachers have done it very well and the lessons have been fun. The teachers have made the topics easier" (student 188)

> "I think the multilingual experience is great. We have a higher level of English and it's an opportunity for us to learn more English and have a better future"
>
> (student 159)

> "It's more difficult than in Primary school"   (student 13)

> "It would be better if all the classes could do the multilingual experience because there are only 18 students in my class and there could be more people in it"
>
> (student 152)

Once again, the main difference between the two age groups has to do with the importance they attach to the category *learning in general/learning content*, as the older students make many more comments (13.9%) than the younger ones (1.5%). The following quotes illustrate the 3rd year students' perspective:

> "You improve your level of English but you learn less content" (student 221)

> "I enjoy these classes and I like them more than the English classes, because we don't just learn English, we learn other things using English" (student 55)

> "This new experience has been very satisfactory because of all the new things I have learnt. It has been easier for me to learn geography in English than in Basque because, being taught in a different language, I pay more attention"
>
> (student 107)

These three quotations reflect a double perspective. On the one hand, the first student perceives that the improvement in English is at the cost of the subject content; on the other hand, the other two respondents point out that learning through English is more alluring, boosts their motivation and, therefore, they learn even more.

Discussion

Overall, it can be stated that both first- and third-year students perceive the advantages of having CLIL outnumbering the disadvantages, although older students are slightly more positive than their younger peers. In addition, both groups of students agree on the relevance of the CLIL approach for the development of their abilities to communicate with people from other countries and cultures. However, some interesting differences arise between the two groups. As stated above, the older students offer greater consensus as to the main advantage of CLIL, namely, its benefits for learning English. In addition, they provide a wider range of advantages which may be a consequence of their more developed level of maturity or a different CLIL experience, such as having the opportunity to practice with native teachers and using computers, neither of which are mentioned by younger students.

The older students are more concerned than the younger students about the loss of content or information due to their language limitations (*understand*). The former single out other academic issues, such as having *worse results, lower content*, and having *unprepared teachers*. By contrast, the younger students are more concerned about the *difficulty* of learning through English (language hurdles), and, to a lesser extent, about the *hard work* involved and the difficulty in *understanding* the content. These results are in line with those obtained in the closed-item questionnaire (Doiz, Lasagabaster, & Sierra 2014), where it was observed that third-year students were significantly less anxious as they seem to get accustomed to having English-medium instruction programs as they progress in their studies. However, it is also worth noting that the older students are still worried about language difficulty.

As for the second question (what they liked most/least), the trend is very similar since the participants were more inclined to note the positive aspects of the CLIL approach. Once again, they stress the benefits of CLIL regarding English improvement (the younger slightly more than the older ones). As for the differences, younger students value *different activities* and *watching films*, whereas older students favour *computers* and *projects*.

From the students' additional comments it has to be noted that their contributions are mainly focused on methodology. They include not only judgements about the different aspects of the methodology implemented but also some methodological proposals to improve the CLIL programs. This leads us to the following section, the pedagogical implications.

Conclusion

In her recent state-of-the-art article on CLIL, Dalton-Puffer (2011) underscores that although CLIL classrooms are often considered to be motivating, students' actual commitment seems to vary enormously from context to context, especially when it comes to using the target language. In this chapter we have endeavoured to pinpoint the aspects of CLIL classes that students find motivating (advantages/the ones they like most) or demotivating (disadvantages/the ones they like least), in the belief that teachers can take advantage of students reflections and adapt their teaching to students' demands.

Despite the fact that students clearly state that learning subjects in English is difficult, requires an additional effort to understand the content, and involves more work, they are nevertheless highly motivated by the CLIL approach. In fact, they think they learn more English, they find it extremely useful for their future and they believe it enables them to communicate with foreign people. Therefore, teachers should be aware that the hard work involved in CLIL programs does not put off students, as they are willing to expend the necessary effort if they feel that the results are worth it. This is the first main implication.

However, with the recent generalization of CLIL programs it is important to consider that there is a need to cater to the increasing variety of students participating in such programs. For example, when CLIL programs were first established in the Basque Autonomous Community, most of them were implemented with selected students, namely students with good levels of English and Basque. Nowadays, however, these programs are open to all students with the result of more mixed-ability classes. In fact, our data show that:

a. Some students argued that it is important to choose the CLIL courses carefully, because some subjects are already too difficult in their native languages (e.g. social sciences), let alone in English.
b. Some students were ready to take the challenge and asked for more subjects in English, including difficult ones such as geology or biology.
c. Other students claimed that the CLIL classes may seem difficult at the beginning, but eventually they manage to overcome it.
d. Finally, some believed that these classes were easier, because they are forced to pay more attention than when they are taught in Spanish or Basque, that is to say, this approach sparked their motivation to face the challenge.

A clear implication is that teachers need support to deal with the heterogeneity found in their classes (the four perspectives above being a very good case in point), which is why the educational administration should provide the necessary means and training for teachers involved in these programs.

The final implications concern methodological aspects. One has to do with the fact that participants are clearly motivated by group work as opposed to some traditional book activities and individual work. Another is centered on their preference for varied activities, as they complain about the boredom brought about by repetition, which some students seem to perceive as one of the main demotivating factors in their CLIL experience. One of the great challenges for CLIL teachers is to support the conceptual contents of the subject matter without students having the feeling that the same idea is repeated over and over again. Therefore, teachers should rely on different strategies and materials to help students grasp and reinforce the content delivered in English, so that students find such learning and reinforcement of the learning as a challenge rather than as a burden. Many educational systems involved in the setting up of CLIL programs have experienced the difficulties to provide practitioners with adequate textbooks and materials, and official efforts have been made to try to help teachers produce materials that are suitable to their academic context (see Lorenzo in this volume for the Andalusian experience in Spain).

Last but not least, a word of caution is in order. What is felt as (de)motivating varies from student to student, which is why it is difficult for teachers to respond adequately to every student's preferences. However, our results reveal that there are some common trends experienced by the vast majority of the students participating in our study and which, therefore, can be addressed.

As for further research, it would be interesting to carry out similar studies in different contexts with a view to exploring whether students' preferences and motivation in CLIL settings can be transferrable across different cultural settings. It may be the case that in areas such as Scandinavia (see Henry in this volume), where the dubbing of films and television is non-existent – in sharp contrast with Spain where all films and TV programs are dubbed –, the activities that (de)motivate students vary when compared with the results obtained in the present study. Pan-European research projects may help to shed some light on this issue.

Acknowledgements

The results presented in this chapter are part of the following research projects: FFI2012-34214 (Spanish Ministry of Economy and Competitiveness), IT311-10 (Department of Education, University and Research of the Basque Government), and UFI11/06 (UPV/EHU). We would also like to thank the school management, the staff and the students who participated in the study.

References

Breidbach, S., & Viebrock, B. (2012). CLIL in Germany: Results from recent research in a contested field of education. *International CLIL Research Journal*, 1, 1–16.

Chambers, G.N. (1999). *Motivating language learners*. Clevedon: Multilingual Matters.

Coyle, D. (2007). Content and language integrated learning: Towards a connected research agenda for CLIL pedagogies. *International Journal of Bilingual Education and Bilingualism*, 10, 543–562.

Coyle, D., Hood, P., & Marsh, D. (2010). *CLIL: Content and Language Integrated Learning*. Cambridge: Cambridge University Press.

Csizér, K., & Kormos, J. (2009). Learning experiences, selves, and motivated learning behavior: A comparative analysis of structural models for Hungarian secondary and university learners of English. In Z. Dörnyei & E. Ushioda (Eds.), *Motivation, language identity and the L2 self* (pp. 98–119). Bristol: Multilingual Matters.

Csizér, K., & Lukács, G. (2010). The comparative analysis of motivation, attitudes and selves: The case of English and German in Hungary. *System*, 38, 1–13. DOI: 10.1016/j.system.2009.12.001

Dalton-Puffer, C. (2011). Content-and-language integrated learning: From practice to principles? *Annual Review of Applied Linguistics*, 31, 182–204. DOI: 10.1017/S0267190511000092

Doiz, A., Lasagabaster, D., & Sierra, J.M. (2014). CLIL and motivation: The effect of individual and contextual variables. *Language Learning Journal*, 42(2), 209–224. DOI: 10.1080/09571736.2014.889508

Dörnyei, Z. (2001). *Motivational strategies in the language classroom*. Cambridge: Cambridge University Press.

Dörnyei, Z. (2010). Researching motivation: from integrativeness to the Ideal L2 self. In S. Hunston, & D. Oakey (Eds.), *Introducing applied linguistics: Concepts and skills* (pp. 74–83). London: Routledge.

Dörnyei, Z., & Ushioda, E. (Eds.). (2009). *Motivation, language identity and the L2 self*. Bristol: Multilingual Matters.

Eurydice. (2006). *Content and Language Integrated Learning (CLIL) at school in Europe*. Brussels: The Eurydice European Unit.

Garrett, P., & Gallego, L. (2011). Perceptual shapes of international universities and implications for minority languages: views from university students in Catalonia and Wales. Paper presented at *the Symposium on Multilingual and International Universities: Policies and Practices*. 11–12 November 2011, University of Lleida, Spain.

Graddol, D. (2006). *English next*. London: British Council.

Henry, A. (2012). *L3 motivation*. PhD thesis. Göteborg, Sweden: University of Gothenburgh.

Kern, R.G. (1995). Students'and teachers' beliefs about language learning. *Foreign Language Annals*, 28, 71–92. DOI: 10.1111/j.1944-9720.1995.tb00770.x

Kim, T.-Y. (2006). Interview method development for qualitative study of ESL motivation. *Foreign Language Education*, 13, 231–256.

Lasagabaster, D. (2008). Foreign language competence in content and language integrated learning courses. *The Open Applied Linguistic Journal*, 1, 30–41. DOI: 10.2174/1874913500801010030

Lasagabaster, D. (2011). English achievement and student motivation in CLIL and EFL settings. *Innovation in Language Learning and Teaching*, 5(1), 3–18. DOI: 10.1080/17501229.2010.519030

Lorenzo, F., Casal, S., & Moore P. (2010). The effects of content and language integrated learning in European Education: Key findings from the Andalusian bilingual sections evaluation project. *Applied Linguistics*, 31, 418–442. DOI: 10.1093/applin/amp041

Murray, G., Gao, X., & Lamb, T. (Eds.). (2011). *Identity, motivation and autonomy in language learning*. Bristol: Multilingual Matters.

Nikolov, M. (2001). A study of unsuccessful language learners. In Z. Dörnyei, & R. Schmidt (Eds.), *Motivation and Second Language Acquisition* (pp. 147–172). Honolulu, HI: University of Hawaii Press.

Ruiz de Zarobe, Y., Sierra, J.M., & Gallardo del Puerto, F. (Eds.). (2011). *Content and foreign language integrated learning: Contributions to multilingualism in European contexts*. Bern: Peter Lang.

Seikkula-Leino, J. (2007). CLIL learning: Achievement levels and affective factors. *Culture and Education*, 21, 328–341.

Tedick. D.J., & Cammarata, L. (2012). Content and language integration in K-12 contexts: Student outcomes, teacher practices, and stakeholder perspectives. *Foreign Language Annals*, 45, 28–53. DOI: 10.1111/j.1944-9720.2012.01178.x

Ushioda, E. (2011). Motivating learners to speak as themselves. In G. Murray, X. Gao, & T. Lamb (Eds.), *Identity, motivation and autonomy in language learning* (pp. 11–24). Bristol: Multilingual Matters.

Williams, M., Burden, R., & Lanvers, U. (2002). 'French is the language of love and stuff': Student perceptions of issues related to motivation in learning a foreign language. *British Educational Research Journal*, 28, 503–528. DOI: 10.1080/0141192022000005805

Appendices

The categories and a student's quote next to each category by way of an illustration of the category are provided in each of the appendices.

Appendix 1: Advantages

1. **Future**: It is good for your future studies/career. You will be able to get a better job.
2. **Communicate**: you can travel and be able to communicate with foreign people.
3. **Vocabulary**: you learn a lot of new vocabulary.
4. **Learn English**: you learn/improve your level of English. You improve your fluency, reading, writing, spelling, pronunciation in English.
5. **Learn two things**: you learn content at the same time that you are improving your English.
6. **Enjoy**: you have a good time, lessons are funny, entertaining, more amusing than regular lessons.
7. **Culture**: we learn things about other countries, we take part in European projects.
8. **Understand TV, etc.**: you understand TV series, films, internet, songs, etc. in English.
9. **Multilingualism**: You learn new languages.
10. **Easier content**: as it is in English the level of the subject is lower, so it's easier to study.
11. **Motivation**: since the lessons are more interesting you are more motivated. Also because your level of English is higher and you see your progress.
12. **Native teachers**: you have the opportunity to practice English with native speakers.
13. **Computers**: you use computers a lot and that's useful and also entertaining.

Appendix 2: Disadvantages

The categories that resulted from the analysis and a student's quote next to each category by way of illustration are provided below:

1. **Difficult**: the level is high, it is difficult to study because of the language, it is difficult to explain things in the foreign language and also to speak in front of the class.
2. **Understand**: you miss things because you don't understand the teacher or the text. Sometimes you don't understand because the variety of English is not the one you learn at school.

3. **Hard work:** you have to study a lot (language and content), we work harder than the students who do not take content-subjects in English.
4. **Boring:** some topics are boring/ we get bored in class/ the teacher has to repeat the same things so many times that it's boring.
5. **Mixing languages:** as you are learning several languages at the same time, you can have problems when speaking and make mistakes. Besides, the classes are only in English, so we are losing Basque, and when we get to Baccalaureate we will not take content-subjects in English and we will not know the technical language in Spanish or Basque.
6. **Learn grammar & theory:** we have to learn language rules (grammar) to be able to explain things correctly/ we have to study too much theory.
7. **Takes time/money:** In order to learn a language correctly you need to invest a long time and your parents a lot of money.
8. **Worse results:** if your English is not very good you may get worse results in the subject
9. **Lower content level:** as it is in English the content level gets lower.
10. **Unprepared teachers:** our teachers are not good, they don't have a good level of English
11. **Smaller class:** the class is smaller and we can't be with our friends. Everybody should enjoy this experience.
12. **Students' low level:** some of my classmates have a very low level of English and thus the lessons get slower more boring and the content gets too easy.

Appendix 3: The most liked

1. **Learn two things:** I like that we learn English at the same time that we are learning content.
2. **Group activities:** working in groups is more entertaining.
3. **Improve:** we learn English, improve vocabulary, fluency, listening, speaking, writing…
4. **English subject:** I love English.
5. **Native teachers:** You have the opportunity to practice English with native speakers.
6. **Projects:** I do a project in class with my classmates and/or with other schools.
7. **PowerPoint:** I like the presentations the teacher shows us.
8. **Watch films:** I like watching films in original version.
9. **Oral presentations:** I like preparing them and presenting them in front of the class.
10. **Easier content:** it's easier to study as the content is easier than in non-CLIL classrooms.
11. **Individual work:** I like working on my own.
12. **Class atmosphere:** I like the group, we meet new students and we are a big group.
13. **Teacher's explanations:** they repeat things a lot and the explanations are clear.
14. **Enjoy:** We do interesting activities and topics and learning in English is fun.
15. **Book:** It's very good (also other materials such as photocopies).
16. **Computers:** I like the Media Workshop (subject), Information technology in English and working with the computer in general.
17. **Different activities:** in this program we do new and varied activities: posters, excursions, debates, games…
18. **Exam:** there should be fewer and easier exams or no exams at all.

Appendix 4: The least liked

1. **Activities:** I don't like book activities because they are very boring.
2. **Subjects in English:** I don't like the subject and I would prefer other subjects to be in English instead.
3. **Oral presentations:** preparing them and presenting them in front of the class.
4. **Grammar:** I don't like "studying" the language.
5. **Boring:** some topics are boring/we get bored in class/the teacher has to repeat the same things so many times that it's boring.
6. **Teacher:** I don't like the teacher and/or their explanations.
7. **Exam:** there should be fewer and easier exams or no exams at all.
8. **Textbook:** we should use other books because these are very boring.
9. **Theory:** I don't like studying theory and I prefer practical activities.
10. **Lower content level:** we are missing content because of the language, the content is simplified.
11. **Only English:** too many English lessons, the content only in English can be a problem for the future when we have to study in Spanish or Basque…
12. **Worse results:** If your English is not very good you may get worse results in the subject.
13. **Too many students:** the classroom is small for the big number of students.
14. **No grammar:** we don't study grammar, importance of content over language.
15. **Few hours:** I like it a lot and think we should get more lessons in English.
16. **Difficult:** It is harder for me to study a subject in English/ vocabulary is difficult/ we find it difficult to understand the teacher or the texts…
17. **Speaking:** oral activities, doing exercises orally.

Appendix 5: Additional comments

1. **Methodology:** More games, more group activities and less exams.
2. **Learning English:** Because you have the opportunities to improve your level of English.
3. **Cultural dimension:** I like it so much because we meet people from the United Kingdom. It's very interesting.
4. **Positive experience:** It's a good experience and I'm so happy. I'm learning a lot and I enjoy so much in these classes.
5. **Better future:** I think it is positive because you learn a lot and in the future it is easier to find a job if you speak English.
6. **Difficulty:** I think that it is difficult to study some subjects in English, like Geography, Science or Maths.
7. **Learning in general/learning content:** I like it because we learn a lot of different things.
8. **CLIL for all:** It would be better if all the classes could do the multilingual experience.

CHAPTER 7

Motivation meets bilingual models

Goal-oriented behavior in the CLIL classroom

Francisco Lorenzo

Content and Language Integrated Learning appeared in Europe as a long-await-ed alternative to unsubstantiated foreign language approaches, which fell short of meeting the multilingual standards of a society marked by language diversity. Because of L2 content being programmed as content teaching rather than lan-guage teaching in CLIL and also because of the ensuing curriculum and method implications, students' response to CLIL are more positive and engaging than in EFL. This chapter explores the reasons why CLIL mobilizes students' attitudes, goals and responses – as an ultimate evidence of motivated behavior – and shows examples of CLIL material design that are explanatory of students being involved in a new language experience.

Keywords: CLIL, methodological aspects, mixed-ability classes, secondary students' reflections

Introduction

Around the mid-twentieth century, elite bilingual models appeared in Europe as a contemporary version of millennial bilingual education. By the turn of the cen-tury, bilingual programs reached public school networks and non-majority Eu-ropean languages became vehicular in mainstream education. Masterminded by European language policies, programs incorporated a new brand name: content and language integrated learning (CLIL).

Considered within the larger frame of bilingual education – a stance taken by García (2010) or Lorenzo, Trujillo, and Vez (2011) – CLIL stands in formal oppo-sition to foreign language teaching. CLIL vs. EFL, or in more lay terms *teaching in English* as opposed to *teaching English*, represents essentially differentiated ap-proaches to language learning and produce different outcomes both in the learn-ing process and in L2 achievement.

CLIL has, practically from its inception, claimed gains in overall language competence (see Dobson, Pérez, & Johnstone 2010; Lorenzo, Casal, & Moore 2010). Claims related to language processing, however, have often not gone beyond theorizing or accidental report. One among them is motivation, a global construct that bears immediate links to overall competence. Of late, Lasagabaster (2011) has brought this issue to the fore and reported positive correlations between CLIL and motivation. His study concludes that motivation rises in three dimensions: *interest and instrumental orientation, attitudes towards learning situation* and *effort*. This implies that students showed better results not only in attitudinal dimensions (off-task dimensions that may or may not be ultimately reflected in the act of learning) but also in tangible on-task settings, what will surely affect learning cognitive behavior and language processing strategies.

With all this, this chapter intends to give an account of the reasons why CLIL actually triggers goal-orientated behavior more so than mainstream EFL language classes. I will first briefly review L2 motivation within the context of instructed second language teaching. On this, the chapter will hold that motivational models have often been more geared to achieve theoretical or statistical robustness than to the study of actual classroom environments. Secondly, and constituting the bulk of the study, CLIL teaching will be broken down in some of their methodological components and will be discussed as motivational enhancers. Finally in a third section, actual instances of CLIL material will be shown as well as its potential effect on students' linguistic and cognitive behavior.

Motivation in instructed second language acquisition

Motivation has been thought to be key in language learning. Several strands in linguistics picture learners as human beings wired with a language faculty from birth, genetic in its origin, which remains operational for the development of a second language. Not acquiring the language is just unnatural if proper input is facilitated: Maslow's theory of needs, Rogers's classical humanism (see Arnold 1999 for a review) or Tomasello's usage-based theory of language (2003) are in tune with that approach. More particular motivational research has looked at motivation as an engine mobilizing cognitive and conative behavior and has offered results with cross-construct correlations. Gardner, Tremblay and Masgoret (1997) provide evidence that motivation mobilizes learning strategies, self-confidence and directly causes achievement, hence foregrounding motivation as a direct booster of second language acquisition.

For all its merit, this social model of motivation revolving, as other chapters of the book explain (see Busse and Ushioda in this volume), around the concept of *integrativeness*, gave an insufficient account of L2 motivation in educational settings. Further research filled that gap, primarily through Dörnyei's contributions over the years, which has ended in his *Motivational Self System* (see also Dörnyei et al. in this volume). This is meant as a construct replacing integrativeness and consisting of three subsystems: the ideal self, the ought-to and the learning experience. The *ideal self* looks to the future, whatever goal the learner wants to consider as a booster for engagement, the *ought-to system* is focused on duties and obligations imposed by external authorities. The learning experience acts as a buffer that filters behavior.[1] A notable consequence of this approach – also dubbed the *educational turn* in the study of motivation – was that teachers, and educationalists in general, found themselves as a major cause in motivational enhancement. With the social aspects overemphasized in Gardner's integrative model, teachers around the world had been left without a proper diagnosis of their students' disengagement. Students were thought to develop an instrumental motivation to the language situation, i.e., engage in language learning for the practical purposes of it (internationalization, reward systems as evaluation, parental pressure, etc.) or rather seeking integration, i.e. taking an integrative stance and intending to become part of the L2 language community. Integrativeness implied the individual's appreciation of the cultural components of the L2 community and a willingness to participate and reconsider oneself in terms of cultural identity (see Lorenzo 2004 and Lorenzo 2006 for a global overview of motivation in second language acquisition). In a way, then, motivation has not been a research topic, it was demotivation that was observed, an apparent illogical outcome in the realm of intellectual paradoxes: i.e. the exploration of the reasons why language did not thrive in individuals when conditions were ripe for learning.

For practitioners, however, motivation was a much more mundane issue. Whereas the academic debate struggled to develop theoretical motivational models and tested them, developed questionnaires and ran them, isolated variables (age, gender, school year, etc.) and checked their weight in learning outcomes, grassroots language teachers experienced the discontent of many students towards L2 language learning. For observers of the school system, lack of motivation was the end result of the fact that – quoting the outstanding humanist George Steiner – "students were inhaling the methane gas of tedium" (Steiner 2011: 165). It is well-known that education is usually prone to formalization, repetition, control and the establishment of traditional routines that stunt experimentation and creativity. Experimentation and creativity, together with complexity and error-making, are however crucial language development factors, and without them

---

1. MacIntyre, P.D., Mackinnon, S.P., & Clément, R. (2009) present a middle-of-the-road theory of motivation, in which both social and educational aspects are combined.

having a part in the act of teaching, motivation was logically absent or at least descending.

This is something known from the early days of second language acquisition research. Explicit language teaching was known to be ill-suited for natural language processing. In the words of Pit Corder:

> Practically everything that the SLA researchers found was extremely uncomfortable for teachers who naturally assumed that their efforts were more or less effective. They believed if you teach a person something, he or she will learn it. It seems to be true of almost anything else. It's just that language is the odd one out.
> (Corder 1990: 264, in Rossner & Bolitho 1995)

Learning follows developmental stages that are immune to formal teaching, accuracy levels are poor predictors of language competence, and learners make errors that are first steps towards the full acquisition of rules. The description of U-shaped behaviors in SLA or free and systematic variation in interlanguage makes language teaching a difficult task. The perception that the means do not secure gains in L2 acquisition may be a cause for motivation declining over the years. Moreover, lack of motivation could be the result of students' lack of perception of progress: a sensation attested in students' narratives (Lorenzo 2006).

Motivational psychology has stressed the role of goal construction in motivated behavior. Without goals human acts lack direction and strength. Sometimes goals are not well defined or are beyond control and new subgoals must be defined for motivated human action. Learning a language is such a case. The overall goal of L2 learning needs to be broken down in smaller attainable targets that sustain behavior (see Weiner 1986).

Goal oriented behavior (see also Henry in this volume) is in many ways context-dependent. Changing conditions involve serious changes on the motivational system. Within the classroom context even the slightest change in the reward system (evaluation), pedagogy (materials or activities) or dynamics (as in competitive versus collaborative teaching) alter the belief system, the attributional system and ultimately behavior. The shift from teaching English (EFL) to teaching subjects in English (CLIL) changes radically teaching conditions and students' perceptions of the learning situation. This raises the question as to why CLIL correlates with high motivation.

Content and language integrated learning: A rationale

CLIL is a communicative, integrated and interactive approach to language learning and as such is a motivational booster.

Communication in CLIL

Communicative approaches meant to bring meaning back in the act of learning. A balance was kept between *focus on meaning* and *focus on forms* so that formal aspects could develop in tandem. However, formalism is very resilient as a language approach and the attempt to straightjacket language and present it in individual language bits has occurred frequently. Even in communicative approaches, production is sentence-bound and controlled by the often compulsive occurrence of fill-in-the-blank activities. Communicativeness is a top predictor of motivated behavior. Many factors associated to communicativeness – skill diversity, language control by the student, topic breadth, focus on meaning – have proved to enhance motivation and classroom participation (on Communicative Orientation Language Test incorporating these factors see Harley, Cummins, Swain, & Allen 1990).

This communicative tradition has nourished CLIL in a very particular way. CLIL has often been related to task-based approaches, an evolution of communicative language teaching which has always claimed to be engaging to L2 students (Willis & Willis 2007). In task-based teaching, there is a clear goal which serves as the backbone of classroom programming: the development of a task, which could be a letter, a model, a sudoku, an experiment like growing seeds or a project like developing a photograph.[2] CLIL methodology incorporates tasks that make sense within the scholastic tradition of the courses taught in the L2: a model in Arts and Crafts, arithmetic problems in Maths or the production of an observation sheet of an experiment in Science. In the elaboration of tasks, attention is focused on meaning and form focus is only tangential so students – grabbed by meaning – get engaged in language processing while negotiating or producing academic content. As I have pointed out elsewhere (Lorenzo 2007), the task in CLIL provides one more chance for form-function matching, the value of grammar in operation to express meanings. In CLIL, however, the real justification for the task is learning academic content. L2 acquisition should remain a by-product of the classroom interaction when working on other subjects. It is only on this condition that language is partially seen to and is also the reason why authenticity of the CLIL approach is not challenged. Bilingual lesson planning models can

---

2. For a classical account of task-based teaching, the following comment by Ellis may prove useful: "TBLT challenges mainstream views about language teaching in that it is based on the principle that language learning will progress most successfully if teaching aims simply to create contexts in which the learner's natural language learning capacity can be nurtured rather than making a systematic attempt to teach the language bit by bit (as in approaches based on a structural syllabus)" (2003:222).

incorporate drills, restoration text techniques, opinion gap activities (as in discussions) or information gap activity (as in find the differences tasks), but the language behavior elicited is qualitatively different for the simple reason that engagement triggers cognitive resources which are dormant in trivial EFL contexts. Dörnyei (2013) calls this the Principled Communicative Approach, i.e. the creative integration of linguistic rules and lexical items.

Integration in CLIL

The application of *context of culture* to the study of motivation is key to understanding motivation in bilingual models. In an EFL or even in an ESL situation, learners are by definition external to the community, they aspire to become just another community member. They are alien to a community that lies beyond the borders of the classroom. Their *ideal L2 self system* cannot be accomplished within their setting, the classroom. The learning of an L2 in a classroom demands the definition of a new community if students are meant to engage in language learning. In relation to this, Ushioda (2011: 198) has pointed out: "… how we engage our students' social identities in their L2 interactions within and beyond the classroom now would seem to have important consequences for how they visualize themselves as users of the L2 in the future".

Students are in a milieu where language practice needs to be authentically motivated and needs to be congruent with their language contact beyond the classroom. In the foreign language classroom situation, achieving authenticity in language use is not an easy task. Without authentic motivation, communicative practice depends ultimately on learners' willingness to take part in a somewhat artificial conversational exchange. Pedagogical techniques based on the principles of communicative practice have enhanced participation by engaging students in information-gap activities or opinion gap tasks. Still, many students feel that L2 communication, particularly between non native speakers, was lacking in authenticity. This is what motivational literature labels as a breach of the *reality principle*. Further to that, language interaction implies that participants recognize one another as players that provide meaningful and relevant information and who are mutually responsive. Without these features, intersubjectivity is threatened. Van Lier (1996: 161) states that intersubjectivity exists when "participants are jointly focused on the activity and its goals, and they draw each other's attention into a common direction". CLIL is such a scenario, as CLIL environments provide intense learning experiences that make students deploy more cognitive activity, be more alert and engage in a more demanding linguistic setting. It provides real experience because, as in the real world, there is no content out of language and language cannot materialize itself out of content. Content in CLIL is not random as in EFL, in the sense that any topic would be valid as a pretext for learning the language.

Secondly, and following up from the former argument, in bilingual teaching content is academic. Psychology of Education has looked at *conceptual interest* and *situational interest* as concepts akin to motivation. In an academic setting, topics are expected to be academic and hence authentic and appropriate to the learning situation. Such authenticity leads to true communicative engagement in such a way that students are less aware of manipulating a language as such. There is a sense of flow, of language being used for content transmission. The sight of students engaged in absorbing new content through a second language bears witness as to how instrumental orientation to the language can set students in the right frame of mind and learning can be facilitated.

Interaction in CLIL

Classroom observation in CLIL has described a very realistic trade-off of interventions and students displaying conversational modes mostly alien to EFL. Bilingual research confirms the occurrence of high levels of cognitive demands: questions are mostly of a higher order type, which invites students to display divergent thinking (and speaking) modes, an unusual conversational scheme in plain foreign language situations. When operating in this mode, learners tend to produce extended discourses whose planning and execution is time-consuming, demanding and more prone to errors (Dalton-Puffer 2007). Since all involved in CLIL interaction – teachers and students alike – prioritise content over language, feedback to errors is not totally transparent: errors are mostly corrected through implicit feedback, usually through recasts, which implies that students need to be still more alert if an inappropriate formulation of the message is to be noticed (Lyster 2007). Proof of the intense cognitive engagement is that CLIL students often code-switch and use their L1. These features taken together make active processing necessary at all times (see more on interaction in bilingual or immersion settings in Dalton-Puffer 2005; Dalton-Puffer & Nikula 2006; Llinares, Morton, & Whittaker 2012).

What we see in the literature is that major features of synchronous interaction – not only realistic but real conversation – are present in CLIL. Among them: meaning negotiation, content discussion, error correction, task management, social talk, and technical action (see Liang 2010 for a discussion of these features).

Material analysis

The core of second language methodology is the classroom activity type. Drills define audiolingualism; text-reconstruction activities, communicative approaches and project-work (among others) define task-based teaching. Apart from the discussion of principles as above, practical presentation of CLIL activity types can help clarify the relationship between CLIL and motivation. This will be the focus of this section.

In many educational systems bilingual schools have had difficulties to find suitable textbooks and supplementary material. CLIL networks have grown mostly bottom-up, with individual schools making provision for bilingual teaching depending on the very individual needs of centers and students. Mainstream textbooks have not adjusted well to this, and teachers have shown frustration regarding a lack of classroom ready materials and the time and sometimes uncertainty involved in the preparation of home-grown materials. Official initiatives have often tried to take responsibilities and have compiled self-produced lessons by individual teachers or teachers' networks. Such is the case in the author's context (see Junta de Andalucía 2012), where he was commissioned for the production of a bank of CLIL materials. For the project production, a team was formed comprising a group of highly experienced primary and secondary content teachers with pedagogical and linguistic back-up from researchers and academics. The goal was that each teacher/designer (TD) would produce 6 theme-based lessons, each comprising materials for 6–8 lessons. The content subjects involved were natural and social science, technology, mathematics, music, sport and art as these are the most popular CLIL subjects in Andalusia. The resulting bank, which has been available on-line since early 2012, comprises lessons and totals over 3,000 pages of classroom-ready materials (see link at the bibliography section below, Junta de Andalucía 2012). The tasks shown below are not meant to give a full picture of the collection; the bank is open-accessed and there are studies underway to explain its structure and planning (Moore and Lorenzo forthcoming). Therefore, the tasks commented on below are part of larger lesson units. They are presented out of the context for the purpose of this paper.

It must also be said in relation to the data bank, that material developers –actual content teachers – were provided with a set of desiderata: the units should be structured around tasks – each one to contain 2–3 tasks with an appropriate number and type of pre- and post- tasks; develop a variety of skills and competences (e.g. learning to learn, computer literacy) in tandem with the content and language; employ adapted authentic input whenever possible, and provide a balance between input and output and a variety of text types and media. Teachers were

also coached to apply second language methodology along communicative principles. As can be seen in the free-access website (see Junta de Andalucía 2012),
the combination of area content and L2 methodology makes materials very in-
dividual-looking and their potential as motivational enhancers is not surprising.

The following lines intend to explore how the merging of L2 task-based methodology with course content as in History, Maths, etc. can elicit different behavior from students and hence cause motivation. The discussion will be structured
around key concepts in communicative approaches.

Information gap activities in CLIL

Information gaps are often used in instructed L2 to trigger participation, mostly
oral group work. For their completion, students must create some rapport and
negotiate meanings until the gap is filled. If students lack the proper resources, communication disruption follows and the task is not completed. One such
example is "spot the difference" type tasks, where students need to find out the
actual mismatches between similar illustrations. Normally, however, the content
of the illustration is limited and random and the skills tested are – other than
L2 – perceptual. Correct answers are given if the differences are well expressed
and the actual differences are spotted. No academic content appears. Figure 1
shows, however, a very distinct approach to this activity type. Students, browsing

Figure 1. Find the differences

Renaissance and Baroque painting in their Art course are asked to spot and comment on the differences between two illustrations showing original work. Each particular variation has a historical and artistic interpretation: the symbolic apples in the Renaissance paintings, the different size and body style of the figures responding to different canonical orders, the more or less exuberant decoration at the background. Differences observed convey artistic and historical differences in the period: the artistic canon, the expression of power in painting, the use of classical mythology, etc. As such, the task was a proper sample of content and language integration, further helped by the presence of set expressions needed for the task. The linguistic material needed mobilizes not only the content but also a number of language structures that cannot be avoided. Getting the message right is a strong motivation for language manipulation. Strategies like topic avoidance, so common in EFL, are not so successful in CLIL.

Cultural elements in CLIL

EFL has often included cultural elements that flesh out the linguistic syllabus of the courses. Notions and grammar structures were often used to revise cultural content: the London subway, the story of suffragettes or the construction of London Bridge. The presence of these topics has been mostly unsubstantiated and they often elicit unmotivated responses from students. Figure 2 shows how a cultural curriculum is reversed in CLIL. London Bridge illustrates not an EFL lesson but a CLIL Maths lesson. The activity represents integrated curriculum at its best: English grammar and cultural content serves the purpose of mathematical learning, more precisely to solve the triangle formed by the towers of the bridge and the upper deck of the construction using the law of sines and cosines. Sine and cosine are trigonometric functions: the sine of the angle gives the length of the y-component (rise) of the triangle and the cosine gives the length of the x-component (run). This content is advanced mathematics and is part of the official curriculum. This example shows how if once trivial, cultural content as in London Bridge found a reason to be part of a curriculum. The instance is instrumental in reflecting that all classroom participants relate differently to culture, content, materials and textbook in the CLIL classroom.

Role play

As said, EFL has often relied on teaching strategies that ultimately referred to some future situation, hence demanding an effort for students to detach themselves from their present reality and identity. Role play, although enjoyed by many

Figure 2. Culture in CLIL

students for involving active participation, still suffered this out-of-the-real-world flaw. EFL methodology applied to teaching content in an L2 provides an interesting integration. Figure 3 shows a role play, in which students are not policemen or children asking for help to bring their cat down from a tree – the typical EFL role play. Rather, the role play is a task integrated in a Science lesson on atomic theories. In the illustration, the nucleus is a basket, the orbits, or energy levels, for each electron will be represented by a circle of chairs; the number of chairs will change depending on the level and in reference to Bohr's model. Each energy level has a certain amount of space for the electrons to move in. Finally, each student will be an electron. Music represents energy for the moving electron: the end result is a whole class in motion and students absorbing linguistic and content input at once.

Input

Input is key for language learning and for restructuring students' interlanguage. EFL lessons had a difficult approach to input: who, when and, above all, for which

Sample of classroom set up with 18 chairs and 1 basket:

Have the students rotate

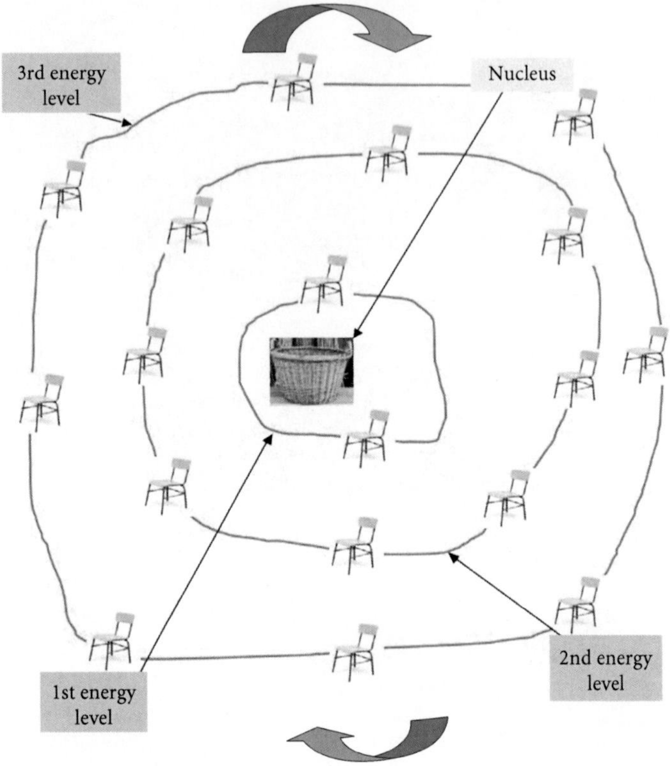

Figure 3. Role play

purpose information was provided were often unclear. Input in teacher-fronted classes could be grammatical, like metalinguistic explanation of language rules; instructional as part of classroom management or cultural. CLIL provides a differentiated sort of input. Figure 4 offers a glimpse of input in bilingual scenarios. The lesson at hand describes the scientific method. The teacher will use the graph to teach how to formulate sensible questions in science, how to convert them into hypothesis, confirm and represent results through data tables and graphs. As such, the content seems very demanding and students will need proper scaffolding to keep up with the teacher's explanation. The concept-map shows the relations between the concepts presented and outlines all the lesson content at a glance. A proper explanation would make all the verbal input redundant since the c-map is almost self-explanatory. Language processing is expected to flow without difficulties and concept understanding and language comprehension should

The scientific method.
Observe your world and come up with a question to answer using the scientific method,

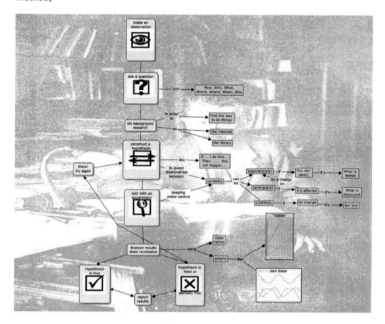

Figure 4. Input

not be compromised. If achievement triggers motivation and the other way round in a relationship of mutual dependence, students would be aware of absorbing tough academic content and experience success.

Grammar

CLIL is essentially focused on meaning. However, particular language structures even in this content-based orientation need close attention. These are the so-called *language muscles* that activate some particular content. It would be hard to explain the pulley system without a prior revision of space particles "up" and "down" and it would be easier for students to understand Mendel's laws of inheritance if duals like "both" or "either" are presented. Grammar is not totally alien to CLIL. Grammar after all is linked to meaning potential. Different grammatical forms represent significant choices about meanings. By using particular grammar choices the learner is aware of the pragmalinguistic dimension of structures in such a way that grammar becomes content. Such is the case of time relations in

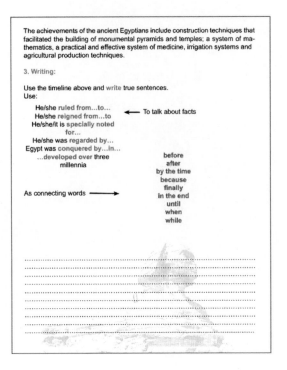

Figure 5. Grammar in CLIL

history. History is time in motion and it basically consists of the rendition of past facts. Figure 5 shows a timeline where time expressions present actions in two different moments of the past. This resource based on the use of time expressions – mostly adverbials – help present sequences and as a result cause effect relations. What makes grammar different in CLIL is that learners notice grammar items while they process content, and as such is totally motivated.

All these five features of materials make CLIL an authentic experience, at least if authenticity is interpreted as described by Nunan (1989: 102):

> For learners to authenticate materials these need minimally to fulfill two conditions. In the first place, they need to be recognized by learners as having a legitimate place in the language classroom. Secondly, they must engage the interest of the learner by relating to his interests, background knowledge and experience and, through these, stimulate genuine communication.

Conclusion

Motivation is a conative and cognitive construct. It rules behavior and also mental activity which remains invisible to the naked eye. It is also affected by beliefs and attitudes, and possibly by unintentional prejudices to the object of learning which lie far beyond conscience. This is why some of the renditions of motivation as the following have such a broad scope:

> People invariably experience their exposure to and use of the L2 in terms that relate to a deeply felt, socially grounded sense of self and normally the goal of L2 communication is to fulfil the needs of this self, in addition to any goals concerned with the direct exchange of cognitive information. (Segalowitz 2010: 186)

Goal-oriented behavior ultimately responds to the need of the self, here the need to be a sophisticated individual with an ample language repertoire. But these needs must be built upon more tangible experiences: classroom communication, more precisely, academic classroom communication as in CLIL fares better than other methods in sustaining behavior. Exposure and use of L2 are different both in amount and purpose in CLIL. Students' selves are different in bilingual programs, partly because as the CLIL literature notices, there is a mask effect that provides students with some persona, a new identity of a learner learning in a second language. Cognition is altered too, as motivation implies a new cognitive engagement with the language system. CLIL may, therefore, become a very promising approach to L2 teaching where L2 contact out of the classroom is limited. As CLIL is still in its infancy, students' emotional responses – motivation included – are still somewhat unknown. As motivation, or the lack of it has been an issue more in EFL than ESL, CLIL might well provide a solution for the lack of L2 learning engagement. If that were the case, CLIL in its actual context, mostly in Europe, could be the answer to a persisting language learning problem.

References

Arnold, J. (Ed.). (1999). *Affect in language learning.* Cambridge: Cambridge University Press.

Dalton-Puffer, C. (2005). Negotiating interpersonal meanings in naturalistic classroom discourse: directives in content and language integrated classrooms. *Journal of Pragmatics, 37,* 1275–1293. DOI: 10.1016/j.pragma.2004.12.002

Dalton-Puffer, C. (2007). *Discourse in content and language integrated learning (CLIL) classrooms.* Amsterdam: John Benjamins. DOI: 10.1075/lllt.20

Dalton-Puffer, C., & Nikula, T. (2006). Pragmatics of content-based instruction: Teacher and student directives in Finnish and Austrian classrooms. *Applied Linguistics, 27,* 241–267. DOI: 10.1093/applin/aml007

Dobson, A., Pérez. M.D., & Johnstone, R. (2010). *Bilingual education project Spain. evaluation report*. Madrid: British Council.

Dörnyei, Z. (2013). Communicative language teaching in the twenty-first century: The 'principled Communicative Approach'. In J. Arnold & T. Murphey (Eds.), *Meaningful action: Earl Stevick's influence on language teaching* (pp. 161–171). Cambridge: Cambridge University Press.

Ellis, R. (2003). *Task-based language learning and teaching*. Oxford: Oxford University Press.

García, O. (2010). *Bilingual education in the 21st century: A global perspective*. Malden, MA: Basil/Blackwell.

Gardner, R., Tremblay, P., & Masgoret, A.M. (1997). Towards a full model of second language learning: An empirical investigation. *The Modern Language Journal*, 81, 344–362. DOI: 10.1111/j.1540-4781.1997.tb05495.x

Harley, P., Cummins, J., Swain, M., & Allen, J. (1990). *The development of second language proficiency*. Cambridge: Cambridge University Press. DOI: 10.1017/CBO9781139524568

Junta de Andalucía (2012). Materiales AICLE. Available at <http://www.juntadeandalucia.es/educacion/webportal/web/portal-de-plurilinguismo/recursos-materiales/aicle-secuencias-didacticas;jsessionid=91AF894CF7665D957494F06B2A66E914.portalweb2> (2 February 2014).

Lasagabaster, D. (2011). English achievement and student motivation in CLIL and EFL settings. *Innovation in Language Learning and Teaching*, 5, 3–18. DOI: 10.1080/17501229.2010.519030

Liang, M. (2010). Using synchronous online peer response groups in EFL writing: Revision related discourse. *Language Learning & Technology*, 14, 45–64.

Llinares, A., Morton, T., & Whittaker, R. (2012). *The roles of language in CLIL*. Cambridge: Cambridge University Press.

Lorenzo, F. (2004). La motivación en el aprendizaje de una LE/L2. In J. Sánchez Lobato, & I. Santos Gargallo (Eds.), *Enseñar español como segunda lengua / lengua extranjera (L2/LE). Vademecum para la formación de profesores* (pp. 305–329). Madrid. SGEL.

Lorenzo, F. (2006). *Motivación y segundas lenguas*. Madrid: Arco-libro.

Lorenzo, F. (2007). An analytical framework of language integration in L2-content based courses: the European dimension. *Language and Education*, 21, 503–516. DOI: 10.2167/le708.0

Lorenzo, F., Casal, S., & Moore, P. (2010). The effects of content and language integrated learning in European education: Key findings from the Andalusian bilingual sections evaluation project. *Applied Linguistics*, 31, 418–442. DOI: 10.1093/applin/amp041

Lorenzo, F., Trujillo, F., & Vez, J.M. (2011). *Educación bilingüe*. Madrid: Síntesis.

Lyster, R. (2007). *Learning and teaching languages through content: A counterbalanced approach*. Amsterdam: John Benjamins. DOI: 10.1075/lllt.18

MacIntyre, P.D., Mackinnon, S.P., & Clément, R. (2009). From integrative motivation to possible selves: The baby, the bathwater and the future of language learning motivation research. In Z. Dörnyei, & E. Ushioda (Eds.), *Motivation, language identity and the L2 self* (pp. 43–65). North York, ON: Multilingual Matters.

Moore, P., & Lorenzo, F. (forthcoming). Task-based learning and CLIL classroom materials design: process to product. *Language Learning Journal*.

Nunan, D. (1989). *Designing tasks for the communicative classroom*. Cambridge: Cambridge University Press.

Rossner, R., & Bolitho, R. (1995). *Currents of change in English language teaching*. Oxford: Oxford University Press.

Segalowitz, N. (2010). *Cognitive bases of second language fluency*. London: Routledge.

Steiner, G. (2011). *Lecciones de los maestros*. Madrid: Siruela.

Tomasello, M. (2003). *Constructing a language: A usage-based theory of language acquisition*. Harvard: Harvard University Press.

Ushioda, E. (2011). Language learning motivation, self and identity: current theoretical perspectives. *Computer Assisted Language Learning*, 24(3), 199–210. DOI: 10.1080/09588221.2010.538701

Van Lier, L. (1996). *Interaction in the language curriculum: Awareness, autonomy, and authenticity*. London: Longman.

Weiner, B. (1986). *An attributional theory of motivation and emotion*. New York, NY: Springer-Verlag. DOI: 10.1007/978-1-4612-4948-1

Willis, D. & Willis, J. (2007). *Doing task-based teaching*. Oxford: Oxford University Press.

CHAPTER 8

Visible learning and visible motivation

Exploring challenging goals and feedback in language education

Vera Busse

The chapter approaches motivation from a practitioners' perspective and tries to illustrate how motivational theories can help language teachers working in higher education to gain deeper insights into students' learning behavior. Particular attention is paid to the importance of setting challenging short-term goals and providing ample opportunities for practice and feedback, in combination with nourishing long-term language goals in students' ideal self-beliefs. The chapter points towards the potential of content and language integrated learning (CLIL) in this respect, cautioning, however, that feedback becomes even more important when such a challenging teaching approach is chosen. The chapter concludes by introducing a question cycle that encourages teachers to explore their students' motivation and to identify possible motivational trouble zones.

Keywords: motivation, goal-setting, task-challenge, feedback, CLIL

Introduction

Research on student motivation is thriving, not only in mainstream education but also in L2 education. For language teachers, it can be a considerable challenge to distill from the wealth of information the pertinent aspects of research that can help to improve their teaching practice. In order to approach the topic of motivation from a practitioner's perspective, it may be useful to take a look at recent developments in the general field of education. On the basis of his landmark study from more than 800 meta-analyses encompassing 52,637 individual studies, Hattie (2009) identifies *challenge* and *feedback* as key factors underlying successful learning and teaching. With regard to challenge, Hattie notes that "goals [which] are challenging, specific and visible" (2009: 25) are of particular importance. Learning goals with a low level of challenge are less effective than those with a higher level of challenge, because, Hattie theorises, more challenging goals provide a "clearer notion of success" (2009: 164). However, if students are to meet challenging goals, *deliberate practice* in combination with *feedback* is vital. Hattie (2009: 22) notes:

> Visible teaching and learning occurs when learning is the explicit goal, when it is appropriately challenging, when the teacher and the student (…) seek to ascertain whether and to what degree the challenging goal is attained, when there is deliberate practice aimed at attaining mastery of the goal [and] when there is feedback given and sought.

While it is a truism to say that practice makes perfect, Hattie underlines that deliberate practice involves more than just allocating more time for an activity, defining it as "extensive engagement in relevant practice activities for improving performance" (2009: 30). Deliberate practice is not only necessary to provide students with the opportunity to master content, but also to reach a certain level of "fluency" (2009: 185). The latter term, one may add, can be interpreted quite literally in the case of language learning. Too often, Hattie criticises, there is practice devoid of feedback, which proves to be crucial for successful learning. It is worth pointing out that the term *feedback* is loosely defined in Hattie's work, and much emphasis is put on dialogic feedback practices, where the student plays an active role and solicits feedback (see also Hattie & Timperley 2007). However, teacher feedback still remains a most crucial variable in student learning. As Hattie (2009) points out, the more challenging the goal, the more important teacher feedback becomes not least because teacher feedback monitors and provides indicators of progress.

In order to illustrate what visible learning is about, Hattie provides the example of a cliff rescue exercise (2009: 25). Students are provided with a challenging goal (to rescue a person), with very visible success criteria and with high levels of monitoring feedback. Learners are usually active and seek feedback (as they have a high interest in how to put on a security harness), and feel excited when the challenging goal is finally met and they are safely back on the ground. One aspect of this learning experience that Hattie fails to mention in this context is the importance of practice, but one only needs to imagine how different the experience would be if students did not practice putting on the security harness before jumping down the cliff.

Hattie's study has received wide attention well beyond the scientific community, and the recently published *Visible learning for teachers* (2012) is rapidly becoming a standard reference book in educational seminars and teacher training institutions in different parts of the world. This growing interest in the educational community provides a welcome starting point to explore the importance of challenge and feedback from a motivational perspective. Against the backdrop of a longitudinal mixed-methods study involving first year students enrolled on German degree courses at two major UK universities, it will then be illustrated how insights from motivational theories can help language teachers working in higher education to improve student motivation in practice.

Theoretical background

Research shows that perceived progress is a key factor in human motivation, and it is well known that student motivation is enhanced when students perceive they are making progress (Bandura 1997; Schunk 1991). While indicators of progress are very clear in some learning situations (e.g. a child learning how to ride a bike), they may be more ambiguous in others. Language learning, in particular, is a slow process, with many ruptures, progressions and regressions, and indicators of progress may not be as easy to perceive (see Ushioda in this volume). As Hattie (2009) emphasises, reaching challenging learning goals provides students with a sense of progress and success. In other words, it makes learning visible to students. However, feedback is needed, in particular when challenging learning goals are to be met. The importance of challenge and feedback has been amply studied in motivational research. A short overview is provided below.

Challenge and goals

Conquering challenges is an important part of intrinsic motivation, which refers to the motivation that arises from the pleasure an activity produces in itself (Deci & Ryan 1985). For sustained intrinsic motivation, an optimal level of challenge is needed, which can be defined as a challenge that is slightly harder than one's skill level. Tasks that are too challenging have a detrimental effect on intrinsic motivation, as they cause students to feel incompetent and lower their self-efficacy beliefs (e.g. Boggiano, Main, & Katz 1988; Csikszentmihalyi & Nakamura 1989; Czsikszentmihalyi, Rathunde, & Whalen 1993; Danner & Lonky 1981; Harter 1974; Hunt 1966, 1975; Shapira 1976). Self-efficacy beliefs refer to people's perceptions of their ability to perform well on a given task (Bandura 1997). Conversely, tasks that are too easy may be similarly detrimental, as they fail to engage the person and result in boredom (e.g. Boggiano, Main, & Katz 1988; Csikszentmihalyi & Nakamura 1989; Czsikszentmihalyi, Rathunde, & Whalen 1993; Danner & Lonky 1981; Harter 1974; Shapira 1976).

It is also known that challenging and specific goals are linked to better performance than easy and non-specific goals. Locke and Latham provide evidence that goal-setting is strongly related to effort and that individuals with specific and challenging goals persist longer at a task than individuals with easy and vague goals, provided the goals are attainable (Latham & Locke 2006, 2007; Locke 1996; an overview of early research is provided by Locke & Latham 1990; Locke & Latham 2002). In other words, if goals are to engage students, they need to be task and situation-specific. Setting personal bests may be one way to achieve this aim, as students have a specific and challenging goal, i.e. to beat their previous achievement and to improve their personal best score (Martin 2006).

Feedback

Motivational research has also looked at the impact of feedback. It is known that feedback combined with challenging goals can enhance motivation and performance (Bandura & Cervone 1986; Becker 1978; Erez 1977; for an overview see Kluger & DeNisi 1996). Feedback also has an effect on intrinsic motivation. Feedback that is controlling and prescribes thinking and behaving in a specified way is detrimental to intrinsic motivation. Feedback that is informational and enables the learner to engage with the activity more effectively is beneficial (e.g. Anderson, Manoogian, & Reznick 1976; Deci 1971; Fisher 1978; Koestner et al. 1984; Reeve & Jang 2006; Reeve et al. 2004; Ryan 1982).

Feedback also influences self-efficacy beliefs. Bandura (1997) stresses that verbal persuasion is an important source of self-efficacy beliefs, which refers to other people's judgments of one's ability. Positive feedback from people important to learners (e.g. teachers) can heighten their sense of competence, while negative feedback or judgmental feedback can weaken perceptions of competence and hinder the development of self-efficacy beliefs (Britner & Pajares 2006; Matsui, Matsui, & Ohnishi 1990). Self-efficacy beliefs, in turn, have shown to influence a variety of academic skills, including writing performance (Pajares & Johnson 1996). There is evidence to suggest that self-efficacy beliefs may change even through a single teacher feedback (Duijnhouwer, Prins, & Stokking 2010). In view of the general importance of perceived progress for student motivation, it may not be surprising that progress feedback in particular is beneficial for student motivation, and there is evidence to show that progress feedback can influence self-efficacy beliefs for writing skills (Duijnhouwer et al. 2010; Schunk 2003; Schunk & Swartz 1993). The developing and teaching of these skills is an essential aspect of any modern foreign language course, and therefore of particular interest to language teachers working in higher education.

Challenge, goals and feedback in language learning motivation

Early studies in the field of language learning (L2) motivation focused mainly on the affective dimension involved when learning a language, looking in particular at the role students' attitudes towards a language and its culture played for long-term achievement (see Gardner 1985; Gardner & Lambert 1972). From the 1990s onward, increased attention was paid to cognitive theories which could better account for motivational processes in the classroom environment (for an overview, see Dörnyei & Ushioda 2011). The importance of learner goals for L2 motivation was duly acknowledged and existing theoretical frameworks were expanded to incorporate concepts from goal theories (e.g., Tremblay & Gardner 1995). The concept of intrinsic motivation and the notion of challenge also received increasing attention (e.g., Noels 2001), and the issue of feedback similarly shifted into focus (see, for instance, the motivational frameworks provided by Dörnyei 1994; Williams & Burden 1997).

It is worth pointing out that early motivational frameworks did not pay much attention to the interactive nature of the feedback process, with some frameworks labelling feedback generally an external factor (Williams & Burden 1997) or a teacher-specific motivational component (Dörnyei 1994). More recent approaches to feedback have shifted the interactive aspect of feedback in the spotlight (for a discussion in the context of L2 writing, see Hyland & Hyland 2006; Lantolf & Pavlenko 2001; Lee 2008), and most modern scholars would agree with Hattie (2009) that the student needs to be an active agent in the feedback process if successful learning is to take place. Nevertheless, one may say that from that time on, there was much awareness of the importance of quality teacher feedback for improving language teaching practice in L2 motivational research.

Of particular interest to practitioners may be Dörnyei and Csizér's (1998) ten commandments for motivating language learners. The authors present a list of ten macrostrategies for improving student motivation based on a survey study in which 200 Hungarian English teachers were asked to rank 51 motivational strategies according to importance and frequency of use. The items *Make tasks challenging to involve your students* and *Set up several specific learning goals* did not make it into the final ranking; but they are subsumed in commandment three: *Present the task properly*. The item *Make sure that students experience success regularly* was part of a larger self-confidence scale, just as the item *Give positive feedback and appraisal*, and the commandment *Increase the learner's self-confidence* was eventually placed on rank five.

In recent empirical investigations on L2 motivation, the issue of challenge and challenging short-term goals as well as feedback have somewhat taken a backseat. Instead, there has been a recent surge of interest in long-term goals. In particular, attention has been paid to students' conceptions of the future and how students' personal goals for their future, so-called possible selves, influence their present motivation. Dörnyei (2005, 2009) was the first to propose that the process of imagining oneself as a successful language learner is an important motivational force which influences an individual's engagement with language learning. In order to accommodate this line of thought, he introduced the *ideal L2 self*. The conceptualisation of the ideal L2 self draws on possible selves theory (e.g., Markus & Nurius 1986) and self-discrepancy theory (e.g., Higgins 1987), as motivated behaviour is hypothesised to emerge from people's desire to bridge the gap between their actual self and a desired future self, i.e. the person one would like to become. (Note that the actual/ideal dichotomy had already appeared in the literature much earlier, Rogers 1951; Rogers & Dymond 1954). If language learners have a future vision of themselves that entails speaking a foreign language, this so-called ideal L2 self serves as a motivator to learn this language, as the student desires to reduce the discrepancy between the actual and ideal self. Different pedagogical suggestions for language teachers on how to nourish L2 self beliefs have already been put forward (Arnold, Puchta, & Rinvolucri 2007; Busse 2013a; Dörnyei 2008; Dörnyei & Kubanyiova 2014; Hadfield & Dörnyei 2013; Magid & Chan 2011; Taylor et al. 2012). While these suggestions cannot be discussed here in detail, it goes without saying that reaching the long-term goal of striving towards an ideal L2 self poses a considerable challenge to students and that feedback on goal progress is much needed in this respect.

Results from a longitudinal study on language learning motivation in higher education

In order to illustrate how motivational theories can help practitioners to explore and understand their students' learning behaviour, I would like to highlight some results from my own study on language learning motivation in higher education. Methodological details have already been discussed in previous articles (Busse & Walter 2013; Busse & Williams 2010), and I shall here confine myself to summarising the main results. The study was driven by a desire to explore why Bachelor students enrolled in German degree courses at two major English universities appeared to engage less with language learning over the course of the first year. University A is a long established and highly reputable university; University B is a more recently established university, but with a similarly high academic reputation. Both universities belong to the Russell Group of twenty-four leading UK universities, and both universities have similar student intake. Students can study German either as a single subject or in combination with another language or another subject. As is common practice in the UK, the courses place emphasis on the study of literature and the first language (English) is the language of instruction for literature classes and for classes on the linguistic aspects of the second language. In addition, students at both universities receive three hours of German language instruction per week.

A mixed-methods longitudinal approach was employed and a motivational questionnaire was administered to students during language classes at the beginning and at the end of the academic year. The sample consisted of 91 students at time point 1 and their ages ranged from 18 to 20 years. Participants had studied German for an average of 6.46 years (SD 2.18). There were more women in the sample (f = 53; m = 36); however, five students did not indicate their gender. The majority of students were of British nationality (71 students), and English was the mother tongue of most of the students (81 students). At time point 2, the sample was reduced to 59 students, because fewer students attended language classes towards the end of the year and therefore did not fill in the second questionnaire. In addition, extended interviews were conducted with twelve students five times over the course of the year, and there was no attrition among interviewees.

The questionnaire data confirmed that students placed relatively less effort on language learning tasks towards the end of the academic year; at least, students rated their effort to be lower towards the end of the year. The motivational items, however, painted an interesting picture, showing that students were not simply lacking interest. On the contrary, the data suggested that students felt strongly driven by their goal to reach language proficiency. While gaining speaking proficiency was particularly important to students, reaching proficiency in other areas such as listening, reading and writing was also very important to them. Students could well imagine becoming proficient in German; in other words, students had a highly developed ideal L2 self. At the beginning of the year, they also felt highly intrinsically motivated to pursue the course of study. Over time, however, students' intrinsic motivation significantly decreased, and so did students' self-efficacy beliefs for speaking and listening to German. One may speculate that those students who did not attend classes towards the end of the year felt even less motivated than their peers. Self-efficacy beliefs for writing and reading were on the whole not very high and did not improve over the course of the year.

Student interviews shed further light on students' motivational changes. In general, there was a shared sentiment of a lack of progress. Some students felt that they were "standing still", others felt that their language skills actually declined. As one student stated frankly: "I'm not enjoying [language learning] as much as before 'cause I'm doing worse." Insufficient opportunities for practice were seen as one reason for slow progress. As mentioned before, first-year students receive only three language classes per week, and all "content" classes, i.e. linguistics and literature classes are taught in English. Students, therefore, have *de facto* relatively little exposure to the German language and relatively few opportunities to practise their language skills within the framework of university teaching. In particular, there are few opportunities for practicing speaking and listening skills, which may explain why students' self-efficacy for speaking and listening to German declined. Decreasing self-efficacy beliefs, in turn, may have hindered a further development of students' ideal L2 self. While no decline could be observed in students' ideal L2 self in the quantitative data, the interviews suggested that some students' ideal self-beliefs underwent important qualitative changes with a gradual exclusion of high language proficiency. One student, for instance, who could vividly imagine herself as proficient in the language and who could imagine working in Germany at the beginning of the year, stated towards the end of the year that she very much doubted that she would do a language specific job in her future life, as she did not have the necessary language skills. She explained: "I think you have to be very confident and very gifted in your language abilities, and I just don't have the confidence for that at the moment".

A more in-depth exploration of students' self-beliefs and the relationship between students' ideal L2 self and self-efficacy beliefs has been provided elsewhere (Busse 2013a), but it is worth pointing out that self-efficacy beliefs can play a role in whether a possible self seems attainable and therefore triggers motivated behaviour. Bandura (1997) hypothesises that self-efficacy has an effect on mental imagery, and that individuals with high levels of self-efficacy find it easier to visualise an action which, in turn, increases motivation. Recent studies in mainstream motivational research have found consistent links between self-efficacy beliefs (for more on self-efficacy, see Henry in this volume), mental imagery use and motivated behaviour (Beauchamp, Bray, & Albinson 2002; Cumming 2008; Munroe-Chandler et al. 2008; Wesch et al. 2006), and it seems plausible to assume that self-efficacy beliefs influence whether students perceive an ideal L2 self within their realistic potential and decide to invest effort into pursuing this ideal L2 self. This relationship may be taken into account when trying to understand students' declining engagement with language tasks.

Given the few opportunities for practice, it may also not be surprising that students judged many language tasks as overly challenging. For instance, students are expected to do a lot of independent reading in preparation for their literature classes. Yet reading novels in the original version proved extremely difficult, as students appeared to have had little prior experience with reading extended texts in German, and because their vocabulary size was still quite limited. There is evidence to suggest that at least ninety percent of words need to be known to in order to pose an adequate and attainable challenge (Burns 2002), although this threshold may well be higher (Gickling 1984). If the vocabulary size is too limited, students can also not derive pleasure from reading (Hirsh & Nation 1992). As a consequence, students turned to reading translations. However, by reading trans-lated versions of texts, students did not gain the sense of achievement that they themselves identified as highly important for their motivation. In students' words, they missed the sense of "gratification" when overcoming challenging tasks.

Writing tasks posed a similar problem, although an interesting twist was ob-served: students felt that German writing assignments were challenging from a linguistic point of view, because students had not had much prior writing practice and lacked vocabulary for what they wanted to say. The topics explored, howev-er, did not pose enough intellectual challenge. Particularly problematic in this respect was the fact that "language seminars", i.e. seminars aimed at teaching lan-guage skills, were not linked to "content seminars", wherein German literature is the focus. This means that the topics explored in language seminars were largely unrelated to content taught in literature seminars.

Last but not least, students expressed dissatisfaction with the feedback they received (see Busse 2013b). Some interviewees felt that there was not enough feedback, in particular towards the beginning of the academic year. When feed-back was absent, these students displayed a growing sense of insecurity and less willingness to put effort into writing assignments. Nevertheless, when feedback was received, it was often perceived as detrimental to motivation because stu-dents felt that it was not geared to their needs. An analysis of students' views on feedback and a comparison with the actual feedback they received identified the following shortcomings:

First of all, there was little selective and in-depth feedback on language prob-lems, and few clear suggestions on how to improve performance. As already dis-cussed, feedback needs to be informational in order to improve motivation (e.g., Koestner et al. 1984). Research on L2 writing also shows that more focused feed-back is better for treating L2 errors (e.g., Bitchener 2008; Bitchener & Knoch 2008, 2010a, 2010b; Ellis et al. 2008; Sheen 2007; Sheen, Wright, & Moldawa 2009). Yet feedback mostly consisted of highlighting all language mistakes.

In addition, students received almost no information about their progress. The importance of progress feedback for student motivation in general and self-efficacy beliefs in particular has already been pointed out (e.g., Duijnhouwer et al. 2010). The absence of indicators of improvement in writing feedback did certainly feed into students' missing sense of overall progress.

It was also striking that little attention was paid to sustaining students' self-ef-ficacy beliefs. Sometimes feedback was judgmental, or, as one student put it, "dis-heartening". It is known that judgmental feedback can curb intrinsic motivation (Deci & Ryan 1985), and Bandura (1997) holds that existing self-efficacy beliefs are more easily destroyed by negative feedback than restored by positive feedback.

This may have been an important factor in students' rising dissatisfaction with writing tasks. It is also worth noting in this context that there is evidence to suggest that future self-beliefs are very dynamic around the ages of 18–22 years (Dunkel & Anthis 2001; Waterman 1982) and that these self-beliefs are most sensitive to feedback from the environment (Markus & Nurius 1986). Judgmental feedback may therefore also be detrimental to students' ideal L2 selves in the long run.

Discussion and conclusion

Starting with Hattie's (2009) synthesis of meta-analyses which has drawn increased attention to goal challenge and feedback for student achievement, this chapter provided a brief overview of relevant research exploring the notion of challenge, the role of short- and long-term goals and of feedback for learning motivation. The results from my own study on language learning in higher education were used to show how motivational theories helped me to explore and understand why a group of first-year language students became disaffected with their language learning experience at university and gradually ceased to engage with language learning tasks. It was interesting to see that the factors students identified as detrimental to their motivation were surprisingly similar to the factors Hattie identifies as detrimental to achievement: students lacked a sense of progress and there were few opportunities for deliberate practice, suboptimal levels of challenge and feedback which was not geared towards students' needs. As a result, students' intrinsic motivation and their self-efficacy beliefs declined. The latter also appeared to have negatively affected some students' ideal self-beliefs.

Before jumping to conclusions about demotivational processes, we need to exercise caution and point towards the obvious limitations of these types of small-scale studies, particularly in terms of generalisability. In addition, it is worth pointing out that not all data could be discussed here, and that summaries inevitably run the risk of oversimplification. The variables discussed should also not be seen in isolation, but rather in conjunction with each other and other factors and problems specific to the particular learning environment. Neither can they be seen in isolation from the individual learner. For instance, differences in learners' motivational profiles may also influence how students react to different kinds of feedback (see, for instance, Busse 2013b; Kormos 2012; Sheen 2011), and thus lead to different motivational dynamics in individuals. Nevertheless, for the purpose of this article it might be beneficial to picture a downward spiral to show the main variables that played a role in these students' demotivational processes (see Figure 1).

Figure 1. Motivational downward spiral

The image can illustrate that by simply improving one aspect of the learning experience, we may not achieve the desired results. For example, simply raising the amount of exposure to the language will not increase student motivation unless language tasks are intellectually challenging and linguistically attainable. Careful scaffolding of language learning tasks and clear short-term goals certainly play a role in this respect (see Dörnyei et al. and Ushioda in this volume). Furthermore, student motivation may not be improved without feedback that informs students about goal progress and provides indicators of how to further improve performance and considers students' self-efficacy beliefs. This web of interrelated factors needs to be taken into account when making pedagogical suggestions.

Nevertheless, one can certainly say that in general in the language environments under consideration, more use of the target language in modern foreign language degrees is desirable, as it would give students more opportunities for deliberate practice. In the USA, where the target language is commonly used across the curriculum, the 2007 Modern Language Association report (MLA Ad Hoc Committee on Foreign Languages 2007) and follow-up articles (Byrnes 2008) reflect the internationally widening criticism of what has been termed an instrumentalist approach to teaching languages in higher education, i.e., an approach where language learning is treated as a separate skill. The need for integrated curricula is stressed, i.e., curricula where "language, culture, and literature are taught as a continuous whole" (MLA Ad Hoc Committee on Foreign Languages 2007). From a motivational perspective, such an approach is promising as it corresponds to students' long-term learning goal of gaining high levels of proficiency in the language and may thus nourish their ideal L2 self beliefs. It would also undoubtedly pose a positive intellectual challenge to language students and make learning material more relevant to them. In addition, if language acquisition is viewed as a socially constructed process (Kaplan et al. 2002; Swain 2000), providing first-year students with more possibilities to interact with their peers and their lecturers in the target language seems an appropriate thing to do.

It is interesting to see in this respect that while in European secondary education Content and Language Integrated Learning (CLIL) is steadily advancing, relatively little attention is paid to CLIL in higher education (but see, for instance, Dafouz Milne & Núñez Perucha 2010; Doiz, Lasagabaster, & Sierra 2013a; Hellekjaer 2010). However, there are not enough empirical studies to provide an informed overview of the potential and the difficulties posed by CLIL in tertiary education. In particular, it appears that modern foreign language courses which teach through the target language have not yet been systematically compared to those teaching through the native language. The scarcity of empirical evidence is quite surprising, considering that the language is also the content of classes and that proficiency is an explicit objective of all modern foreign language degree courses. It seems reasonable to assume that some of the challenges identified in the literature on English-medium instruction in higher education (see Doiz, Lasagabaster, & Sierra 2013b; Hellekjaer 2010; Shohamy 2013) can also play a role in the language learning context under consideration here. Practice examples show that a thorough reconceptualization of language learning at the university level is likely required to address these challenges and to help students reach advanced literacy skills (Byrnes, Maxim, & Norris 2010). It also goes without saying that questions of feedback will become more pressing once students learn in the target language. As Hattie (2009) emphasises, the more challenging the goal, the more important teacher feedback becomes, and both teachers and curriculum planners will have to factor in additional time for higher feedback requirements.

To conclude, I would like to offer some general guiding questions, which can further contribute to the dissemination of pedagogical knowledge derived from motivational research. It may be useful for practitioners working in different learning environments, who are concerned that their students do not engage as fully in language learning as they should. The visual representation (see Figure 2) shows a question cycle that taps into five aspects of learning and motivation.

1. Do students generally feel happy with the language learning experience, in particular with the progress they are making?
2. If this is not the case: Can students imagine themselves to be proficient in the target language? What are students' long-term language learning goals, and which aspect of the language, e.g. speaking, listening, reading or writing skills, are they most interested in improving?
3. How much deliberate language practice is there within the framework of the curriculum to support students in their particular language-learning goal?

Figure 2. Question cycle

4. Do proximal goals in language tasks provide students with an appropriate level of challenge and take students' linguistic knowledge and their intellectual capacities into account?

5. Does teacher feedback provide students with indicators of progress towards their learning goal? Is it focused, informational and shows how to improve future performance? Does it take students' self-efficacy beliefs into account? Do students have the opportunity to give feedback and articulate their learning needs?

While the figure and the questions above have no claim to completeness, they may help practitioners to systematically explore and identify potential motivational trouble zones and thereby improve students' learning experience. Referring back to Hattie, the question cycle may help teachers to make student motivation more visible.

References

Anderson, R., Manoogian, S.T., & Reznick, J.S. (1976). The undermining and enhancing of intrinsic motivation in preschool children. *Journal of Personality and Social Psychology*, 34, 915–922. DOI: 10.1037/0022-3514.34.5.915

Arnold, J., Puchta, H., & Rinvolucri, M. (2007). *Imagine that! mental imagery in the EFL classroom*. Cambridge: Cambridge University Press.

Bandura, A. (1997). *Self-efficacy: The exercise of control*. New York, NY: W.H. Freeman.

Bandura, A., & Cervone, D. (1986). Differential engagement of self-reactive influences in cognitive motivation. *Organizational Behavior and Human Decision Processes*, 38, 92–113. DOI: 10.1016/0749-5978(86)90028-2

Beauchamp, M.R., Bray, S.R., & Albinson, J.G. (2002). Pre-competition imagery, self-efficacy and performance in collegiate golfers. *Journal of Sports Sciences*, 20, 697–705. DOI: 10.1080/026404102320219400

Becker, L.J. (1978). Joint effect of feedback and goal setting on performance: A field study of residential energy conservation. *Journal of Applied Psychology*, 63, 428–433. DOI: 10.1037/0021-9010.63.4.428

Bitchener, J. (2008). Evidence in support of written corrective feedback. *Journal of Second Language Writing*, 17, 102–118. DOI: 10.1016/j.jslw.2007.11.004

Bitchener, J., & Knoch, U. (2008). The value of written corrective feedback for migrant and international students. *Language Teaching Research*, 12, 409–431. DOI: 10.1177/1362168808089924

Bitchener, J., & Knoch, U. (2010a). The contribution of written corrective feedback to language development: a ten month investigation. *Applied Linguistics*, 31, 193–214. DOI: 10.1093/applin/amp016

Bitchener, J., & Knoch, U. (2010b). Raising the linguistic accuracy level of advanced L2 writers with written corrective feedback. *Journal of Second Language Writing*, 19, 207–217. DOI: 10.1016/j.jslw.2010.10.002

Boggiano, A.K., Main, D.S., & Katz, P.A. (1988). Children's preference for challenge: The role of perceived competence and control. *Journal of Personality and Social Psychology*, 54, 134–141. DOI: 10.1037/0022-3514.54.1.134

Britner, S.L., & Pajares, F. (2006). Sources of science self-efficacy beliefs of middle school students. *Journal of Research in Science Teaching*, 43, 485–499. DOI: 10.1002/tea.20131

Burns, M.K. (2002). Comprehensive system of assessment to intervention using curriculum-based assessment. *Intervention in School and Clinic*, 38, 8–13. DOI: 10.1177/10534512020380010201

Busse, V. (2013a). An exploration of motivation and self-beliefs of first year students of German. *System*, 41, 379–398. DOI: 10.1016/j.system.2013.03.007

Busse, V. (2013b). How do first-year students of German perceive feedback practices at university? A motivational analysis. *Journal of Second Language Writing*, 22, 406–424. DOI: 10.1016/j.jslw.2013.09.005

Busse, V., & Walter, C. (2013). Foreign language learning motivation in higher education: A longitudinal study of motivational changes and their causes. *The Modern Language Journal*, 97, 435–456. DOI: 10.1111/j.1540-4781.2013.12004.x

Busse, V., & Williams, M. (2010). Why German? Motivation of students studying German at English universities. *Language Learning Journal*, 38, 67–85. DOI: 10.1080/09571730903545244

Byrnes, H. (Ed.). (2008). Perspectives. *The Modern Language Journal*, 92, 284–312. DOI: 10.1111/j.1540-4781.2007.00719_1.x

Byrnes, H., Maxim, H.H., & Norris, J.M. (2010). Main text. *The Modern Language Journal*, 94, 1–202. DOI: 10.1111/j.1540-4781.2010.01136.x

Csikszentmihalyi, M., & Nakamura, J. (1989). The dynamics of intrinsic motivation: A study of adolesents. In C. Ames & R. Ames (Eds.), *Research on motivation in education* (Vol. 3, pp. 44–71). San Diego, CA: Academic Press.

Cumming, J. (2008). Investigating the relationship between exercise imagery, leisure-time exercise behavior, and self-efficacy. *Journal of Applied Sport Psychology*, 20, 184–198. DOI: 10.1080/10413200701810570

Czsikszentmihalyi, M., Rathunde, K., & Whalen, S. (1993). *Talented teenagers*. Cambridge: Cambridge University Press.

Dafouz Milne, E., & Núñez Perucha, B. (2010). Metadiscursive devices in university lectures: A contrastive analysis of L1 and L2 teacher performance. In C. Dalton-Puffer, T. Nikula & U. Smit (Eds.), *Language use and language learning in CLIL classrooms* (pp. 213–231). Amsterdam: John Benjamins. DOI: 10.1075/aals.7.11daf

Danner, F.W., & Lonky, E. (1981). A cognitive-developmental approach to the effects of rewards on intrinsic motivation. *Child Development*, 52, 1043–1052. DOI: 10.2307/1129110

Deci, E.L. (1971). Effects of externally mediated rewards on intrinsic motivation. *Journal of Personality and Social Psychology*, 8, 105–115. DOI: 10.1037/h0030644

Deci, E.L., & Ryan, R.M. (1985). *Intrinsic motivation and self-determination in human behaviour*. New York, NY: Plenum. DOI: 10.1007/978-1-4899-2271-7

Doiz, A., Lasagabaster, D., & Sierra, J.M. (2013a). Future challenges for English-medium instruction at the tertiary level. In A. Doiz, D. Lasagabaster & J.M. Sierra (Eds.), *English-medium instruction at universities* (pp. 213–222). Bristol: Multilingual Matters.

Doiz, A., Lasagabaster, D., & Sierra, J.M. (2013b). *English-medium instruction at universities: Global challenges*. Bristol: Multilingual Matters.

Dörnyei, Z. (1994). Motivation and motivating in the foreign language classroom. *Modern Language Journal*, 78, 273–284. DOI: 10.1111/j.1540-4781.1994.tb02042.x

Dörnyei, Z. (2005). *The psychology of the language learner: Individual differences in second language acquisition*. Mahwah, NJ: Lawrence Erlbaum Associates.

Dörnyei, Z. (2008). New ways of motivating foreign language learners: Generating visions. *Links*, 38, 3–4.

Dörnyei, Z. (2009). The L2 motivational self system. In Z. Dörnyei & E. Ushioda (Eds.), *Motivation, language identity and the L2 self* (pp. 9–42). Bristol: Multilingual Matters.

Dörnyei, Z., & Csizér, K. (1998). Ten commandments for motivating language learners: Results of an empirical study. *Language Teaching Research*, 2, 203–229. DOI: 10.1177/136216889800200303

Dörnyei, Z., & Kubanyiova, M. (2014). *Motivation and vision for language learners and teachers*. Cambridge: Cambridge University Press.

Dörnyei, Z., & Ushioda, E. (2011). *Teaching and researching motivation*, 2nd edn. Harlow: Longman.

Duijnhouwer, H., Prins, F.J., & Stokking, K.M. (2010). Progress feedback effects on students' writing mastery goal, self-efficacy beliefs, and performance. *Educational Research and Evaluation*, 16, 53–74. DOI: 10.1080/13803611003711393

Dunkel, C.S., & Anthis, K.S. (2001). The role of possible selves in identity formation: A short-term longitudinal study. *Journal of Adolescence*, 24, 765–776. DOI: 10.1006/jado.2001.0433

Ellis, R., Sheen, Y., Murakami, M., & Takashima, H. (2008). The effects of focused and unfocused written corrective feedback in an English as a foreign language context. *System*, 36, 353–371. DOI: 10.1016/j.system.2008.02.001

Erez, M. (1977). Feedback: A necessary condition for the goal setting-performance relationship. *Journal of Applied Psychology*, 62, 624–627. DOI: 10.1037/0021-9010.62.5.624

Fisher, C.D. (1978). The effects of personal control, competence, and extrinsic reward systems on intrinsic motivation. *Organizational Behavior and Human Performance*, 21, 273–288. DOI: 10.1016/0030-5073(78)90054-5

Gardner, R.C. (1985). *Social psychology and second language learning: The role of attitudes and motivation.* London: E. Arnold.

Gardner, R.C., & Lambert, W.E. (1972). *Attitudes and motivation in second language learning.* Rowley, MA: Newbury House.

Gickling, E.E. (1984). *Operationalizing academic learning time for low achieving and handicapped mainstreamed students.* In Paper presented at *the Annual Meeting of the Northern Rocky Mountain Educational Research Association.* Jackson Hole, WY.

Hadfield, J., & Dörnyei, Z. (2013). *Motivating learning.* Harlow: Longman.

Harter, S. (1974). Pleasure derived by children from cognitive challenge and mastery. *Child Development*, 45, 661–669. DOI: 10.2307/1127832

Hattie, J.A. (2009). *Visible learning: a synthesis of over 800 meta-analyses relating to achievement.* New York, NY: Routledge.

Hattie, J.A. (2012). *Visible learning for teachers: Maximizing impact on learning.* New York, NY: Routledge.

Hattie, J.A., & Timperley, H. (2007). The power of feedback. *Review of Educational Research*, 77, 81–112. DOI: 10.3102/003465430298487

Hellekjaer, G.O. (2010). Language matters: assessing lecture comprehension in Norwegian English-medium higher education. In C. Dalton-Puffer, T. Nikula & U. Smit (Eds.), *Language use and language learning in CLIL classrooms* (pp. 233–258). Amsterdam: John Benjamins. DOI: 10.1075/aals.7.12ole

Higgins, E.T. (1987). Self-discrepancy: a theory relating self and affect. *Psychological Review*, 94, 319–340. DOI: 10.1037/0033-295X.94.3.319

Hirsh, D., & Nation, P. (1992). What vocabulary size is needed to read unsimplified texts for pleasure? *Reading in a Foreign Language*, 8, 698–696.

Hunt, J.M. (1966). The epigenesis of intrinsic motivation and early cognitive learning. In R.N. Haber (Ed.), *Current research in motivation.* New York, NY: Holt, Rinehart & Winston.

Hunt, J.M. (1975). Implications of sequestional order and hierarchy in early psychological development. In B.Z. Friedlander, G.M. Sterritt & G.E. Kirk (Eds.), *Exceptional infant* (Vol. 3). New York, NY: Brunner/Mazel.

Hyland, K., & Hyland, F. (2006). Feedback on second language students' writing. *Language Teaching*, 39, 83–101. DOI: 10.1017/S0261444806003399

Kaplan, R.B., Grabe, W., Swain, M., & Tucker, G.R. (2002). *The Oxford handbook of applied linguistics.* Oxford: Oxford University Press.

Kluger, A.N., & DeNisi, A. (1996). The effects of feedback interventions on performance: A historical review, a meta-analysis, and a preliminary feedback intervention theory. *Psychological Bulletin*, 119(2), 254–284. DOI: 10.1037/0033-2909.119.2.254

Koestner, R., Ryan, R.M., Bernieri, F., & Holt, K. (1984). Setting limits on children's behavior: the differential effects of controlling vs. informational styles on intrinsic motivation and creativity. *Journal of Personality*, 52, 233–248. DOI: 10.1111/j.1467-6494.1984.tb00879.x

Kormos, J. (2012). The role of individual differences in L2 writing. *Journal of Second Language Writing*, 21, 390–403. DOI: 10.1016/j.jslw.2012.09.003

Lantolf, J., & Pavlenko, A. (2001). (S)econd (L)anguage (A)ctivity theory: Understanding second language learners as people. In M. Breen (Ed.), *Learner contributions to language learning* (pp. 172–182). London: Longman.

Latham, G.P., & Locke, E.A. (2006). Enhancing the benefits and overcoming the pitfalls of goal setting. *Organizational Dynamics*, 35, 332–340. DOI: 10.1016/j.orgdyn.2006.08.008

Latham, G.P., & Locke, E.A. (2007). New developments in and directions for goal-setting research. *European Psychologist*, 12, 290–300. DOI: 10.1027/1016-9040.12.4.290

Lee, I. (2008). Student reactions to teacher feedback in two Hong Kong secondary classrooms. *Journal of Second Language Writing*, 17, 144–164. DOI: 10.1016/j.jslw.2007.12.001

Locke, E.A. (1996). Motivation through conscious goal-setting. *Applied & Preventive Psychology*, 5, 117–124. DOI: 10.1016/S0962-1849(96)80005-9

Locke, E.A., & Latham, G.P. (1990). *A theory of goal setting & task performance*. Englewood Cliffs, NJ: Prentice Hall.

Locke, E.A., & Latham, G.P. (2002). Building a practically useful theory of goal setting and task motivation. A 35-year odyssey. *American Psychologist*, 57, 705–717. DOI: 10.1037/0003-066X.57.9.705

Magid, M., & Chan, L. (2011). Motivating English learners by helping them visualise their Ideal L2 Self: lessons from two motivational programmes. *Innovation in Language Learning and Teaching*, 1–13.

Markus, H., & Nurius, P. (1986). Possible selves. *American Psychologist*, 41, 954–969. DOI: 10.1037/0003-066X.41.9.954

Martin, A.J. (2006). Personal bests (PBs): a proposed multidimensional model and empirical analysis. *British Journal of Educational Psychology*, 76, 803–825. DOI: 10.1348/000709905X55389

Matsui, T., Matsui, K., & Ohnishi, R. (1990). Mechanisms underlying math self-efficacy learning of college students. *Journal of Vocational Behavior*, 37, 225–238. DOI: 10.1016/0001-8791(90)90042-Z

MLA Ad Hoc Committee on Foreign Languages. (2007). *Foreign languages and higher education: new structures for a changed world*. New York: Modern Language Association of America. Available at <http://www.mla.org/flreport> (Last retrieved on 30 January 2014).

Munroe-Chandler, K., Hall, C., & G., F. (2008). Playing with confidence: The relationship between imagery use and self-confidence and self-efficacy in youth soccer players. *Journal of Sports Sciences*, 26, 1539–1546. DOI: 10.1080/02640410802315419

Noels, K.A. (2001). New orientations in language learning motivation: towards a model of intrinsic, extrinsic and integrative orientations and motivation. In Z. Dörnyei & R. Schmidt (Eds.), *Motivation and second language acquisition* (pp. 43–68). Honolulu, HI: University of Hawai'i.

Pajares, F., & Johnson, M.J. (1996). Self-efficacy beliefs and the writing performance of entering high school students. *Psychology in the Schools*, 33, 163–175. DOI: 10.1002/(SICI)1520-6807(199604)33:2<163::AID-PITS10>3.0.CO;2-C

Reeve, J., & Jang, H. (2006). What teachers say and do to support students' autonomy during a learning activity. *Journal of educational psychology*, 98, 209–218. DOI: 10.1037/0022-0663.98.1.209

Reeve, J., Jang, H., Carrell, D., Jeon, S., & Barch, J. (2004). Enhancing students' engagement by increasing teachers' autonomy support. *Motivation and Emotion*, 28, 147–169. DOI: 10.1023/B:MOEM.0000032312.95499.6f

Rogers, C. (1951). *Client-centred therapy*. Boston, MA: Houghton-Mifflin.

Rogers, C., & Dymond, R. (1954). *Psychotherapy and personality change*. Chicago, IL: University of Chicago Press.

Ryan, R.M. (1982). Control and information in the intrapersonal sphere: An extension of cognitive evaluation theory. *Journal of Personality and Social Psychology*, 43, 450–461. DOI: 10.1037/0022-3514.43.3.450

Schunk, D.H. (1991). Self-efficacy and academic motivation. *Educational Psychologist*, 26, 207–231. DOI: 10.1080/00461520.1991.9653133

Schunk, D.H. (2003). Self-efficacy for reading and writing: Influence of modeling, goal setting, and self-evaluation. *Reading and Writing Quarterly*, 19, 159–172. DOI: 10.1080/10573560308219

Schunk, D.H., & Swartz, C. (1993). Goals and progress feedback: effects on self-efficacy and writing achievement. *Contemporary Educational Psychology*, 18, 337–354. DOI: 10.1006/ceps.1993.1024

Shapira, Z. (1976). Expectancy determinants of intrinsically motivated behavior. *Journal of Personality and Social Psychology*, 43, 1235–1244. DOI: 10.1037/0022-3514.34.6.1235

Sheen, Y. (2007). The effect of focused written corrective feedback and language aptitude on ESL learners' acquisition of articles. *TESOL Quarterly*, 41, 255–283.

Sheen, Y. (2011). *Corrective feedback, individual differences and second language learning*. New York, NY: Springer.

Sheen, Y., Wright, D., & Moldawa, A. (2009). Differential effects of focused and unfocused written correction on the accurate use of grammatical forms by adult ESL learners. *System*, 37, 556–569. DOI: 10.1016/j.system.2009.09.002

Shohamy, E. (2013). A critical perspective on the use of English as a medium of instruction at universities. In A. Doiz, D. Lasagabaster & J.M. Sierra (Eds.), *English-medium instruction at universities*. Bristol: Multilingual Matters.

Swain, M. (2000). The output hypothesis and beyond: mediating acquisition through collaborative dialogue. In J.P. Lantolf (Ed.), *Sociocultural theory and second language learning* (pp. 97–114). Oxford: OUP.

Taylor, F., Busse, V., Gagova, L., Marsden, E., & Roosken, B. (2012). Identity in foreign language learning and teaching: Why listening to our students' and teachers' voices really matters. In *British Council ELT Research Papers*. Retrieved April 04, 2013 at <http://www.teachingenglish.org.uk/publications/identity-foreign-language-learning-teaching-why-listening-our-students%E2%80%99-teachers%E2%80%99>

Tremblay, P.F., & Gardner, R.C. (1995). Expanding the motivational construct in language learning. *Modern Language Journal*, 79, 505–520. DOI: 10.1111/j.1540-4781.1995.tb05451.x

Waterman, A.S. (1982). Identity development from adolescence to adulthood: An extension of theory and a review of research. *Developmental Psychology*, 18, 341–358. DOI: 10.1037/0012-1649.18.3.341

Wesch, N.N., Milne, M.I., Burke, S.M., & Hall, C.R. (2006). Self-efficacy and imagery use in older adult exercisers. *European Journal of Sport Science*, 6, 197–203. DOI: 10.1080/17461390601012512

Williams, M., & Burden, R.L. (1997). *Psychology for language teachers: A social constructivist approach*. Cambridge: Cambridge University Press.

Epilogue

CHAPTER 9

Motivation

Making connections between theory and practice

Aintzane Doiz, David Lasagabaster and Juan Manuel Sierra

> Love doesn't grow at a steady rate, but advances in surges, jolts, wild leaps, and this was one of those.　(McEwan 2013:233)

This final chapter serves as a bridge between the theoretical contributions in Part I and those focused on empirical data in Part II in an attempt to provide a more integrated perspective of motivation and foreign language learning. Despite the undoubtedly high level of sophistication reached by motivation research, the results obtained are, more often than not, difficult to turn into clear-cut and practical recommendations for the L2 teacher (Dörnyei 2001). Ushioda (2011) shares this perspective and affirms that motivation theory has been lagging behind classroom practice. In this book, cutting-edge motivation theories are accompanied by classroom strategies, enabling teachers and researchers to link these two worlds that sometimes seem to run parallel rather than interconnecting. An "education-friendly" approach (as called for by Crookes & Smith 1991) provides the reader with the best of both worlds. The ever increasing workload of teachers leaves little time for searching through the currently abundant literature on motivation, let alone for converting theories into practical strategies for the classroom. This book is intended to help teachers make some of those connections.

The theoretical backgrounds embraced in the chapters that make up the first part of this collection are generalizable to most (if not all) L2 learning contexts, namely the Directed Motivational Current (Dörnyei, Muir and Ibrahim, Chapter 1), the interaction between motivation and metacognition to sustain motivation (Ushioda, Chapter 2), the inclusive approach to investigating classroom practices by teachers and learners to boost motivation (Coyle, Chapter 3), and the principles for motivating language teachers through vision (Kubanyiova, Chapter 4). However, the more practical and data-based chapters in the second part cannot be applied to other settings without some previous adaptation and consideration of the idiosincracy of the context concerned, because as Dörnyei (2001:103) puts it:

> For these reasons, the most educational researchers can do at present is to raise teachers' 'motivational awareness' by providing them with a menu of potentially useful insights and suggestions from which they can select according to their actual priorities and concerns, and the characteristics and composition of their students.

In the following pages we will connect the theoretical and practical issues dealt with by the contributors, taking the dimensions of the Directed Motivational Current (DMC) as a basis. In their characterization of the DMC, Dörnyei, Muir and Ibrahim (Chapter 1) call it a finite highly intense burst of motivational energy that will help students to accomplish long-term goals – not unlike McEwan's quotation above in relation to what keeps love alive. The DMC draws from the currently leading motivation theories to create a novel concept whose five dimensions (goal/vision orientedness; salient/facilitative structure; ownership and perceived behavioural control; perception of progress; and positive emotional loading) help us integrate the two sections of this book. At the end of each dimension a number of questions are posed in order to enhance teachers' awareness of motivational strategies and help them develop suitable pedagogical strategies.

The first dimension revolves around the *goal/vision orientedness*, which leads the individual to the achievement of a specific abstract cognitive goal supported by a powerful, personalized vision. Ushioda (Chapter 2) highlights the importance of personal goals and observes how motivational theories and research over the past fifty years have been structured around desired or imagined self-representations following Dörnyei's (2005, 2009) L2 Ideal Self theoretical framework. Busse (Chapter 8) also highlights the importance of setting short-term goals and this involves designing activities that students find challenging, while avoiding minimum effort on the part of the students. An illustrative case is that provided by Henry (Chapter 5), who concludes that students in Sweden find English classes in school unchallenging because teachers do not bring students' interests into the activities, in contrast with the personally meaningful tasks they carry out in English outside school. Henry (2013) stresses the importance of classroom practices as an interface to establish relationships between the classroom environment and the outside world. Lorenzo (Chapter 7) states that CLIL (Content and Language Integrated Learning) is an approach that has a triggering effect of goal-oriented behavior, as opposed to mainstream foreign language classes. Similarly, Doiz, Lasagabaster and Sierra (Chapter 6) observe that CLIL can be a meaningful approach which prevents student boredom and lack of commitment typical of many traditional foreign language class activities, in which students often feel that classrooms activities are not authentic but rather distant from reality (Henry, 2013). Concerning this first dimension, relevant questions to be asked could be:

- Do activities, tasks, projects and courses include clear goals?
- Are the goals of language tasks challenging considering students' cognitive and linguistic stages?
- Do activities suit students' preferences?

As for vision, Kubanyiova (Chapter 4) highlights that not only do learners need "to construct their Ideal L2 Self, that is, to *create their vision*" (emphasis on the original: Dörnyei 2009: 33), but also teachers' vision, an area little explored so far (Dörnyei 2005). In a recently published work Dörnyei and Kubanyiova (2014: 3) address this issue and affirm that teachers' vision is the transformational drive that brings about change and improvement: "The good news about this vision is that it is highly contagious: it has the potential to infect students and generate an attractive vision for language learning in them." Kubanyiova (Chapter 4) tackles the principles that motivate teachers through inspiring vision, namely who teachers are as a result of past experiences and current practice, which values and philosophies guide their ideal language teacher self, and the construction of this ideal image. Language teacher education should pay attention to how language teachers can be helped to generate vivid images of their future selves. If both students and teachers face challenging goals and are motivated through vision, the DMC is more likely to arise and to become a burst of motivational energy. Thus, teachers should ask themselves questions such as:

- Do activities, tasks, projects and courses include the learner's personalized vision?
- If you were allowed to highlight only three of your strengths, what would these be?
- What are the philosophical, ethical and value dimensions that lead your teaching?
- What are you and your students doing in your ideal language classroom?

The second dimension has to do with providing a *salient and facilitative structure*. This facilitative structure provides a framework for the process of motivation and also plays an active role in sustaining the DMC's current. As regards language learning, some pedagogical approaches such as Task-Based Language Teaching (Bygate, Norris & Van den Branden 2009; Ellis 2003; Nunan 2004), project work (Fried-Booth 2002) or cooperative learning (Slavin 1995) incorporate this type of salient and facilitative structure which helps to boost and maintain the learner's motivation through a guided and flexible framework which allows the effective guidance of work during the different phases of classroom implementation, taking into account the increasing complexity of classroom tasks. This guided and flexible structure provides 'meaningful subgoals and useful subroutines' as Dörnyei, Muir and Ibrahim (Chapter 1) propose. Careful planning of the structure of many classroom tasks and projects articulates the different programs around diverse tasks, and whole projects, activities and tasks develop through different stages and steps which provide the necessary scaffolding (Leaver & Willis 2004; Sierra 2011). Concurrent with DMC theory, this structuring permits adding regular feedback points which hopefully will intensify the motivational flow.

Within the CLIL approach, subgoals and subroutines become useful and meaningful because students are learning content through a foreign language (Coyle, Hood & Marsh 2010). Lorenzo (Chapter 7) provides examples of activities and material development that help to achieve the double objective of learning both language and content by means of a salient and facilitative structure that sustains students' motivation. For example, he exemplifies the use of role-play as an integrated task applied to teaching science content in which in order to deal with the demanding content the learners need proper scaffolding. The data gathered by Doiz, Lasagabaster and Sierra (Chapter 6) confirms that students are highly motivated by structured group work as opposed to some traditional book activities and individual work. Accordingly, teachers could ask themselves questions such as:

- Why do I choose these particular materials?
- What sort of activities am I using and why?
- Are they meaningful to the students?
- Do the activities, tasks and projects incorporate a well-defined structure that provides the suitable scaffolding for motivation to be sustained?

The third dimension relates to *participant ownership and perceived behavioural control*. Students should become active agents and see themselves as owners of the learning process, for motivation and autonomy are closely intertwined (see Murray, Gao & Lamb 2011). As van Lier (2007: 48) puts it: "[…] ultimately motivation and autonomy are but two sides of the same coin of agency." This author elaborates on this respect and asserts that, while learning an L2, the learner strives to forge a new identity that is true to the self and whose core is voice, which implies agency: "Although imitation and mimicry are essential elements in trying out the L2 voice, the learner must be allowed to appropriate the new sounds and meanings and make them his or her own" (van Lier 2007: 47). This process strengthens the learner's motivation and autonomy. A crucial issue is that they should see themselves as capable of fulfilling the different tasks and activities carried out in the classroom. Coyle (Chapter 3) claims that ownership is supported through co-constructed dialogic reflection, while raising awareness of learner strategies and developing self-regulation so that learners overcome the least motivating aspects of their language learning. If discussions involve teachers and learners, the latter are given the opportunity to articulate their own ways of knowing how they learn and under which conditions. In this vein, the *LOCIT* process helps teachers and learners to identify learning moments and to see themselves as owners of the learning process. Ushioda (Chapter 2) delves into this dialogic process and envisages the teacher's role as a mediator between motivation and metacognition to sustain students' engagement. To underpin their motivation, the development of metacognitive know-how and students' sense of personal agency and control (that is, learner autonomy) is essential and should be carried out through problem-focused dialogue with learners. This dialogue will help to foster students' perceived ability to use appropriate metacognitive strategies to cope with difficulties in their learning process, to carry out tasks successfully and to achieve their goals because they feel confident (Mills, Pajares & Herron 2007). Henry (Chapter 5) also underscores the paramount role of self-efficacy beliefs. Thus, teachers should ask themselves questions such as:

– How can I make my students more autonomous?
– How can I make my students more self-efficient?
– How do I challenge my students to make the right questions about language learning?
– How do I avoid questions whose answers are obvious to my students?

Clear perception of progress represents the fourth dimension and is closely connected to the concept of tangible feedback. Busse (Chapter 8) focuses on the importance of combining challenging goals and the provision of optimal feedback as a means to foster motivation, because the more challenging the goals are, the more effective they are and the more important teachers' feedback becomes (Hattie 2009). In Busse's data students were dissatisfied with the feedback they received which negatively affected their motivation. This author argues that feedback needs to be informative, positive and non-judgemental, as otherwise it may become detrimental to students' self-efficacy beliefs (Mills, Pajares & Herron 2007) and ideal L2 selves (Dörnyei 2005, 2009). In addition, the students should take an active role in the feedback process, as a result of which their agency is promoted. In any case, as Henry (Chapter 5) remarks the presence of actual progress is not as important as their perception that progress is taking place. Questions worthy of deliberation here include:

– Is the feedback I am providing my students informative?
– Does my feedback help improve students' language development?

- Do my students play an active role in the feedback process? Are they aware of and happy with their progress?

The fifth and final dimension is *positive emotional loading*, that is, the excitement provoked by goal attainment even when the language activities are not particularly appealing. As Henry (Chapter 5) shows, the Swedish context represents a good example of the opposite, because students believe that goal attainment is not ensured at school. Swedish students feel that they attain their goals concerning English proficiency better through out-of-school encounters rather than in the school setting, resulting in a negative emotional loading that has a detrimental impact on their motivation at school. The materials (Lorenzo's Chapter 7) and the activities that students enjoy most (Doiz, Lasagabaster and Sierra's Chapter 6) could help teachers to create the classroom conditions that would allow DMC to emerge and boost the short-term motivational bursts that will facilitate the achievement of long-term goals. By choosing alluring teaching materials that combine both language and content and by choosing activities that students find more enjoyable and productive, *DMC drives* will be achieved more easily. As for this final dimension, teachers might ask themselves:

- How can I make my students aware of the important role to be played by school when it comes to attaining their goals?
- What can I do to bridge the gap between motivating activities outside the classroom and less motivating class activities?

We hope that the concepts outlined and issues raised will encourage teachers to reflect upon their own teaching. In addition, consideration of the questions posed concerning each of these five DMC dimensions will hopefully help teachers to enhance their motivational awareness and to spark their students' motivation. Finally, we hope the theoretical and practical ideas presented here will encourage researchers to make space in their motivation research agendas to explore these new avenues.

Acknowledgements

We would like to thank Zoltan Dörnyei for his comments and suggestions on an earlier version of this chapter. Any inconsistencies remain our responsibility. We would like to acknowledge the funding by the Spanish Ministry of Economy and Competitiveness FFI2012-34214 and the Basque Department of Education, Research and Universities IT311-10 (UFI11/06 UPV/EHU).

References

Bygate, M., Norris, J.M., & Van den Branden, K. (2009). *Task-based language teaching: A reader.* Amsterdam: John Benjamins.

Coyle, D., Hood, P., & Marsh, D. (2010). *CLIL: Content and language integrated learning.* Cambridge: Cambridge University Press.

Crookes, G., & Smith, R.W. (1991). Motivation: Reopening the research agenda. *Language Learning,* 41, 469–512. DOI: 10.1111/j.1467-1770.1991.tb00690.x

Dörnyei, Z. (2001). *Teaching and researching motivation.* London: Longman.

Dörnyei, Z. (2005). *The psychology of the language learner: Individual differences in second language acquisition.* Mahwah, NJ: Lawrence Erlbaum.

Dörnyei, Z. (2009). The L2 motivational self system. In Z. Dörnyei & E. Ushioda (Eds.), *Motivation, language identity and the L2 self* (pp. 9–42). Bristol: Multilingual Matters.

Dörnyei, Z., & Kubanyiova, M. (2014). *Motivating learners, motivating teachers: Building vision in the language classroom.* Cambridge: Cambridge University Press.

Ellis, R. (2003). *Task-based language learning and teaching.* Oxford: Oxford University Press.

Fried-Booth, D.L. (2002). *Project work.* Oxford: Oxford University Press.

Hattie, J.A. (2009). *Visible learning: A synthesis of over 800 meta-analyses relating to achievement.* New York: Routledge.

Henry, A. (2013). Digital games and ELT: Bridging the authenticity gap. In E. Ushioda (Ed.), *International perspectives on motivation: Language learning and professional challenges* (pp. 133–155). Houndmills: Palgrave MacMillan.

Leaver, B., & Willis, J. (Eds.) (2004). *Task-based instruction in foreign language education: Practices and programs.* Washington, DC: Georgetown University Press.

McEwan, I. (2013). *Sweet tooth.* London: Random House.

Mills, N., Pajares, F., & Herron, C. (2007). Self-efficacy of college intermediate French students: Relation to achievement and motivation. *Language Learning,* 57, 417–422. DOI: 10.1111/ j.1467-9922.2007.00421.x

Murray, G., Gao, X., & Lamb, T. (2011). *Identity, motivation and autonomy in language learning.* Bristol/Buffalo/Toronto: Multilingual Matters.

Nunan, D. (2004). *Task-based language teaching.* Cambridge: Cambridge University Press. DOI: 10.1017/CBO9780511667336

Slavin, R.E. (1995). *Cooperative learning: Theory, research and practice* (2nd ed.). Boston, MA: Allyn & Bacon.

Sierra, J.M. (2011). CLIL and Project Work. Contributions from the classroom. In Y. Ruiz de Zarobe, J.M. Sierra & F. Gallardo del Puerto (Eds.), *Content and foreign language Integrated learning* (pp. 211–239). Bern: Peter Lang.

Ushioda, E. (2011). Motivating learners to speak as themselves. In G. Murray, X. Gao & T. Lamb (Eds.), *Identity, motivation and autonomy in language learning* (pp. 11–24). Bristol: Multilingual Matters.

van Lier, L. (2007). Action-based teaching, autonomy and identity. *Innovation in Language Learning and Teaching,* 1, 46–65. DOI: 10.2167/illt42.0

Name index

Subject index